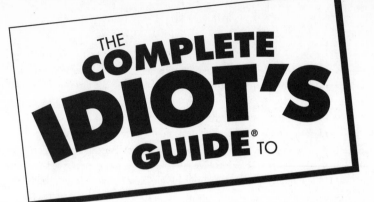

THE COMPLETE IDIOT'S GUIDE TO

Beating Stress

by Arlene Matthews Uhl

ALPHA

A member of Penguin Group (USA) Inc.

ALPHA BOOKS

Published by the Penguin Group

Penguin Group (USA) Inc., 375 Hudson Street, New York, New York 10014, U.S.A.

Penguin Group (Canada), 10 Alcorn Avenue, Toronto, Ontario, Canada M4V 3B2 (a division of Pearson Penguin Canada Inc.)

Penguin Books Ltd, 80 Strand, London WC2R 0RL, England

Penguin Ireland, 25 St Stephen's Green, Dublin 2, Ireland (a division of Penguin Books Ltd)

Penguin Group (Australia), 250 Camberwell Road, Camberwell, Victoria 3124, Australia (a division of Pearson Australia Group Pty Ltd)

Penguin Books India Pvt Ltd, 11 Community Centre, Panchsheel Park, New Delhi—110 017, India

Penguin Group (NZ), cnr Airborne and Rosedale Roads, Albany, Auckland 1310, New Zealand (a division of Pearson New Zealand Ltd)

Penguin Books (South Africa) (Pty) Ltd, 24 Sturdee Avenue, Rosebank, Johannesburg 2196, South Africa

Penguin Books Ltd, Registered Offices: 80 Strand, London WC2R 0RL, England

International Standard Book Number: 1-59257-556-0
Library of Congress Catalog Card Number: 2006927530

08 07 06   8 7 6 5 4 3 2 1

Interpretation of the printing code: The rightmost number of the first series of numbers is the year of the book's printing; the rightmost number of the second series of numbers is the number of the book's printing. For example, a printing code of 06-1 shows that the first printing occurred in 2006.

Printed in the United States of America

Note: This publication contains the opinions and ideas of its author. It is intended to provide helpful and informative material on the subject matter covered. It is sold with the understanding that the author and publisher are not engaged in rendering professional services in the book. If the reader requires personal assistance or advice, a competent professional should be consulted.

The author and publisher specifically disclaim any responsibility for any liability, loss, or risk, personal or otherwise, which is incurred as a consequence, directly or indirectly, of the use and application of any of the contents of this book.

Most Alpha books are available at special quantity discounts for bulk purchases for sales promotions, premiums, fundraising, or educational use. Special books, or book excerpts, can also be created to fit specific needs.

For details, write: Special Markets, Alpha Books, 375 Hudson Street, New York, NY 10014.

Publisher: *Marie Butler-Knight*
Editorial Director: *Mike Sanders*
Managing Editor: *Billy Fields*
Senior Acquisitions Editor: *Paul Dinas*
Development Editor: *Jennifer Moore*
Senior Production Editor: *Janette Lynn*
Copy Editor: *Molly Schaller*

Cartoonist: *Chris Eliopoulos*
Cover Designer: *Bill Thomas*
Book Designers: *Trina Wurst/Kurt Owens*
Indexer: *Brad Herriman*
Layout: *Becky Harmon*
Proofreader: *John Etchison*

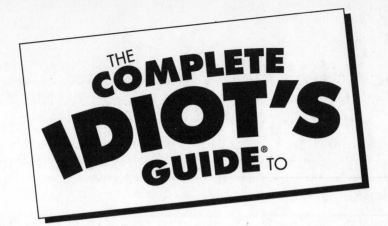

Beating Stress

Contents at a Glance

Contents

Introduction

Do you want to feel less frazzled and more focused? It might seem like a goal beyond your control, but it's not. You can enjoy the physical, mental, and emotional well-being that comes from an inner sense of calm in the face of life's pressures. And no, you will not have to seal yourself up in a cave far from civilization to do so.

Maybe you've come to believe that the state of tension in which so many busy, active people exist is just par for the course—the price of being alive and aware in hectic times. Perhaps it never occurred to you that there was anything you could do about it. Well, there is. Hence *The Complete Idiot's Guide to Beating Stress*—a step-by-step guide for smart people who happen also to be stressed people.

The *Complete Idiot's Guide to Beating Stress* is not a magic bullet that will remove stressful situations from your world. It's better! It's a compilation of tools and strategies that will enable you to remain calm no matter what comes your way.

Life's ups and downs are inevitable, but how you interpret them and react to them is more of a choice than you might have realized. As you make your way through these pages, you will learn how to make calming choices more and more frequently. Soon, the new choices will empower new habits and a new way of existing in the world, of relating to others, and of caring for yourself.

How This Book Is Organized

This book is divided into six parts.

Part 1, "Twenty-First-Century Stress," offers an overview of what stress is and what beneficial purposes it serves. It also examines maladaptive responses to stress—which most of us exhibit—and explains how the times we live in contribute to stress-related problems.

Part 2, "The Stress-Free Mind Makeover," offers strategies for beating stress that center on attitude adjustments and mind training. It looks at the role of optimism, humor, and altruism in countering the stress response, and offers the latest information on how mediation, visualization, and personal spirituality can help.

Part 3, "Restoration Through Love and Work," looks at the stress-beating advantages of maintaining healthy relationships with family and friends. It also tells how to cope with work so that it offers more satisfaction and less stress.

Part 4, "Bodywork," offers information on relieving stress through aerobic exercise, yoga, t'ai chi, and all manner of playful endeavors—from tennis to gardening to, yes, sex.

Part 5, "Anti-Stress Self-Care," looks at how eating smart, sleeping well, and getting away from it all—whether to a home-based retreat space or a stress-beating spa—can protect us from the negative impacts of stress.

Part 6, "The Stress-Beating Workbook," offers step-by-step tools for putting what you've learned into practice in your daily life, and beating stress on a permanent basis.

Stress-Beating Sidebars

Sidebars have been placed throughout this book to make it even more accessible and to make it easy to begin calming down right from the start. Within them are all kinds of useful tips and bits of knowledge. There are four types of sidebars:

Stress Less

These soothing tips help minimize the impact of potentially stressful situations.

def•i•ni•tion

Look here for an elaboration of terms used in the text.

Too Tense

Warning: these sidebars highlight behaviors that are likely to jeopardize your equanimity or even put you at risk for stress-related illness.

It Works for Me

Here you'll find anecdotes and advice from men and women who are learning to better cope with the stressors in their lives.

Acknowledgments

Thanks to Paul Dinas for his stress-busting editorial guidance. Likewise to Janette Lynn, Jennifer Moore, and Molly Schaller for their careful attention to this manuscript. Right before beginning this book, I was able to spend a little time in the company of—and even exchange a few words with—his Holiness the Dalai Lama. I wish to acknowledge him for being an inspiration to me and to millions who seek a calmer, kinder way.

Special Thanks to the Technical Reviewer

The Complete Idiot's Guide to Beating Stress was reviewed by experts who double-checked the accuracy of what you'll learn here, to help ensure that this book gives you everything you need to know about managing stress. Special thanks are extended to Michael Broder and Arlene Goldman.

Trademarks

All terms mentioned in this book that are known to be or are suspected of being trademarks or service marks have been appropriately capitalized. Alpha Books and Penguin Group (USA) Inc. cannot attest to the accuracy of this information. Use of a term in this book should not be regarded as affecting the validity of any trademark or service mark.

Part 1

Twenty-First-Century Stress

Stress has always been a part of human life, because it helps us deal with danger. But today the effects of stress can be among the most dangerous threats to our physical, emotional, and mental well-being. This part of the book offers an overview of negative—and positive—impacts of stress, looks at how we respond to it as a species and as unique individuals, and explains why attempts to beat stress must involve both body and mind.

What's New About Stress?

In This Chapter

- ◆ Why the stress response evolved
- ◆ How brain and body respond to stressors
- ◆ Special circumstances of modern stress
- ◆ The costs of stress-related ailments
- ◆ New hope for lessening stress

It seems we're always hearing about the effects of stress—how it can harm us physically, mentally, and emotionally. On a personal level, we are always complaining about it. "I'm so stressed out," we say, or, "I'm under a lot of stress."

Yet for something we hear and talk so much about, most of us don't know all that much about how stress operates. Has stress always been such a strong component in human life? What, exactly, is stress for? And is it taking more of a toll on us than it ever took on people in the past?

Before we can begin to protect ourselves against too much stress, we need to become better acquainted with it.

The Natural History of Stress

Life is filled with perils. It always has been. If our species was going to make a fair go of survival, we needed a mechanism to help alert us to danger and react to it in ways that would up our odds of self-preservation.

Nature cleverly arranged that we, like many other species, be equipped with an internal alarm system that went off whenever we encountered a threat. Each threat that comes along is, as far as our alarm system is concerned, a *stressor*—that is, it is a cause of alertness and reaction. That alertness and subsequent reaction—*"What's that and what can I do about it right now?"*—is technically known as the *stress response*, even though we tend to simply call it "stress."

It's not splitting hairs to note that stressors and the stress response are two different things. In fact, it's critical to understand the distinction between the two if you're going to follow the strategies for dealing with stress outlined in this book. Stressors are everywhere, and always will be. But, despite our innate biology, we do have some degree of control over how we interpret stressful situations and how we react to them.

def•i•ni•tion

A **stressor** is any stimulus or situation that we perceive as endangering us.

The stress response, which we commonly call *stress,* is the brain and body's alarmed and alert response to a threatening situation.

But let's not get ahead of ourselves. First, it's important to know more about this thing we call stress. To do that, imagine yourself for a moment not in the modern world, but back in the primeval jungle, being chased by a bloodthirsty predator—let's make it a man-eating tiger.

In this sudden acutely stressful (*Yikes, a tiger!*) situation, you would become highly aroused. Your breathing and heart rate would accelerate, your blood pressure would rise, your pupils would dilate (*the better to see you with, tiger*), and you would sweat profusely.

But arousal alone wouldn't help you deal with the threat of being a jungle cat's lunch. Thankfully, the human brain evolved to coordinate a slew of simultaneous reactions in the nervous system, the muscles, and the endocrine system (the system that secretes hormones). Together these reactions—many of which are automatic and reflexive—give us the extra strength we need to protect ourselves.

So just how would you protect yourself from a man-eating tiger? You could fight him off or run for it. If you're anything like me, you'd choose the latter, but to your brain it's all the same. For your brain has just initiated the best-known manifestation of the stress response: *fight-or-flight*.

As we'll see in the course of this book, fight-or-flight is not the only possible response to stress. We can also, for example, engage in nurturing behavior and form protective alliances to help counter perceived dangers. This is known as the *tend-and-befriend* response (much more on this in Part 3 of this book).

def•i•ni•tion

The **fight-or-flight** response is a sequence of internal reactions that prepare an organism to do battle with or seek escape from a stimulus that it considers a threat. The term was coined by physiologist Walter Cannon.

The **tend-and-befriend** response is reacting to threats by caring for one's family and forming social alliances. The term was coined by psychologist Shelley Taylor.

But the fact that so many aspects of fight or flight are innate—that is, pre-wired into the brain—is why stress can be so debilitating. While the fight-or-flight pattern is ideally suited to acute emergencies, it unfortunately does not serve us as well when we are under ongoing, chronic stress.

You've Got GAS (General Adaptation Syndrome)

Today, we take it as a given that people who go on for a long time "under stress" are candidates for illness. But this discovery was quite a revelation, and like many significant discoveries it happened more or less by accident.

It occurred when endocrinologist Hans Selye (pronounced *SELL-ya*) was injecting rats to test the effect of a newly isolated hormone. Some rats were injected with only saline solution, but *all* the rats developed shrunken immune tissues, ulcers, and enlarged adrenal glands (glands that secrete stress hormones).

Selye realized that the stress of receiving any injection at all, regardless of what was in it, was harming the rats. He then noticed that other stressors, such as extreme changes in temperature, provoked the same symptoms. In the face of a broad range of stressors, the body manifests a strikingly similar response.

Too Tense

Our response to stress can be more dangerous than the initial stressor itself. A response that evolved to be adaptive can become maladaptive.

Because all stressors provoke an attempt at adaptation—that is, adjustment to the situation—Selye called the bodily response to stress the General Adaptation Syndrome (GAS).

The General Adaptation Syndrome unfolds in three stages:

1. **Alarm.** In this initial stage, the presence of a stressor (falling tree, typhoon, angry elephant, or what have you) is noted, and the body's warning system goes into effect, mobilizing its resources. The hypothalamus (a part of the brain controlling involuntary reactions) sets off a reaction in the hormonal system, especially the adrenal glands. Steroid hormones flood the bloodstream. Simultaneously, the hypothalamus sends messages to internal organs. The heart accelerates, the liver releases sugar into the bloodstream, the bronchial tubes dilate—all part of a state of readiness.

2. **Resistance.** In this second stage of GAS, initial arousal subsides and the outward symptoms of the alarm reaction recede. The adrenal glands, which earlier swelled, now return to normal size, and decrease their output of emergency steroids. However, at a more subtle level, the hormonal struggle against the stressor goes on.

3. **Exhaustion.** In this final phase of the General Adaptation Syndrome, if the stressor is not removed, the alarm reaction reappears. Alas, by this time, we are not dealing from a full deck. Our system is exhausted and depleted.

Originally, it was believed that illness resulted in the exhaustion stage when organisms basically ran out of steam and had no defenses left. But it's now thought that prolonged time spent in the first two stages is responsible for serious systemic damage, because when GAS is in progress, many other health-maintaining bodily processes are shut down.

Why would the earlier stages of GAS be prolonged? The answer is: the human condition. Unlike other species that are subject to the stress response, humans can initiate that response simply by *thinking* about something. We do not have to be in the presence of an immediate threat to feel stressed. All we have to do is *anticipate* a *possible* stressor. Sure, we might not have to deal with an angry elephant now, but *what if one should happen along?* Sure, our job might be secure today, but *what about that new guy they hired?*

We will always have to deal with the bugaboos of our own minds in addition to in-the-moment dangers that come our way. So, as you can see, it's not always easy being human. To make matters even more complicated, many believe that with regard to stress and its consequences, it's harder now than ever before.

New Stressors with a Twist

For as long as we have had the ability to think, we have had the dubious ability to initiate the stress response all on our own. And even before we discovered what kind of toll stress was taking, that toll was being exacted. Yet many people say that life today is more stressful than ever before. In a way, that's so. But before getting into what is, in fact, unique about contemporary stressors, let's put things in perspective.

We would be doing a great disservice to those who came before us to imagine life in the past as an idyllic time where everyone felt calm, centered, and collected. It's a good bet that it was extremely stressful to be, say, a pilgrim in a new land or, for that matter, a native *among* pilgrims in a new land. A serf during the Dark Ages, a factory worker during the Industrial Revolution, a hunter in the African savannah—they all had their share of stress. You can count on it.

That said, there are some particular factors that contribute to the wide spread of twenty-first-century stress-related problems. Because they're the icing on the cake of intrinsic human stress, we should certainly be aware of them. The more awareness we have about them, the better able we will be to address them and bring them under some control.

Stress Less

Stress might be endemic in our time, but it's not exclusive to it. Sometimes it helps to remember that stress is a part of the human condition and that part of being human means learning to deal with it.

Faster, Faster

After World War I, a wristwatch became a popular—almost indispensable—item. Suddenly, everyone was acutely aware of what time it was, how fast time was going, and how long it took to do anything. In ensuing years a wave of "efficiency experts" came along to tell us how to shave minutes off tasks and so save time. But "saving time" is not exactly what we did. We only found more and more tasks to fill our time with, in the belief that no moment should be wasted.

Technological developments from the personal computer to the Internet to e-mail (now handily accessible via Blackberry) to the omnipresent cell phone then added another wrinkle. Everyone was instantly accessible all of the time. Suddenly, everyone expected every task to be completed instantly, and the number of tasks proliferated—until working at what once would have been considered a manic pace became the norm.

As the last century segued into the new millennium, "so much to do, so little time" became the prevalent attitude not only at work, but also in our so-called leisure hours. Relaxation was often a matter of watching jump-cut TV dramas or music videos, and fast forwarding through shows we'd captured on the VCR or TiVo. Even our more intellectual pursuits were sped up. If we strolled through a museum, we spent less time than ever before glancing at each painting (an estimated five seconds per piece of artwork). If we watched a classic old movie, we impatiently tapped our fingers thinking, *Wow, things sure moved slowly back then.*

If you're waiting for things to slow down any time soon, don't. We are raising a generation that has never spent time dialing a telephone and that is largely unfamiliar with any type of oven except the instantly gratifying microwave. The world they shape will get faster and faster still.

As you have probably noticed, being in a rush all the time is stressful. Perennial "hurry up" messages cause the brain and body to flip the emergency response mode on and never quite flip it off. We are left with no downtime in which to process our experience, reflect on events, and objectively evaluate their consequences.

If we are going to control our stress levels, one of the things we need to do is restore downtime to our experience. Without at least occasionally stopping to savor the most rewarding parts of life and to ponder the more challenging ones from a calm, still perspective, we stand a slim chance of getting off the stress merry-go-round.

Media Frenzy

Another factor contributing to the intense nature of twenty-first-century stress is our continual exposure to media—particularly to an overabundance of news. If you feel stressed out by the news, you are far from alone. Yet somehow many of us seem unable to prevent ourselves from tuning in to an extreme degree.

The further back we go in human history, the longer news took to travel from place to place, and the less news we had of distant people and lands altogether. The printing press obviously changed all that, as did every subsequent development in transportation and telecommunication.

When television came along, it proliferated like a population of rabbits. In 1950, there were 100,000 television sets in North American homes; one year later there were more than a million. Today, it's not unusual for a home to have three or more television sets, each with cable access to perhaps over a hundred channels. News is the subject of many of those channels, and on several of them it runs 24 hours a day.

What's more, after the traumatic events of September 11, 2001, live newscasts were paired with perennial text crawls across the bottom of the screen—so that viewers could stay abreast of every story all the time.

Needless to say, the news that is reported to us is not good news, but rather disturbing images and sound bytes alluding to disaster (natural and man-made), upheaval, crime, scandal, war, and the like. Compounding the problem is that when actual breaking news is scarce, most broadcasts fill in with scare stories about things that possibly might threaten our health, safety, finances, relationships, waistline, hairline, or very existence in the future. This variety of story tends to treat with equal alarm a potentially lethal flu outbreak and the bogus claims of a wrinkle cream that overpromises smooth skin.

Are humans meant to be able to process so much trauma—not to mention so much overblown anticipation of potential trauma— at once? The human brain, remember, is programmed to slip into alarm mode when danger looms. Danger looms for someone, somewhere at every moment. Exposing ourselves to such input without respite and without perspective cannot be anything other than a source of chronic stress.

> **Too Tense** _____
>
> The most stressful time to overexpose yourself to television news is during quarterly ratings "sweeps" periods in February, May, July, and November. Stress-inducing "what if..." stories about potential dangers tend to proliferate. Find an engaging, relaxing activity to substitute for TV viewing.

Achievement and Acquisition Stress

Human societies, from the primitive tribes to complex civilizations, have always had hierarchies. In the harsh ancestral environment, who was "on top" was based on raw strength and survival skills. In later times what counted was one's class—a social strata one was born into based on the relative wealth and social status of one's forebears. Today we say ours is a classless society—in that anyone can, at least theoretically— achieve wealth and power. Ideally, this presents limitless opportunity, but it also presents significant stress in the form of achievement anxiety.

How we measure status today has mostly to do with acquisition. We don't have to be a Rockefeller or a Vanderbilt to be respected, but we do believe we have to acquire things with cachet. And so we strive, endlessly it seems, to purchase certain cars and clothes, and buy homes in certain neighborhoods. We strive to send our children to brand-name colleges, with whose sweatshirts and bumper stickers we can augment our wardrobes and adorn our automobiles.

Striving itself need not create agitation. In fact, as you'll see later in this book, you can actually feel close to euphoric when you're fully engaged in a challenging process that truly engages you. What is stressful, however, is that feeling that one is striving only to obtain "stuff" and that no matter what, one never quite has enough of it.

Stress Less

Think back over the past year, recalling the major purchases you made. Did any of them make you feel any more peaceful or joyful? If so, for how long? Think about whether excessive attention to acquiring things is easing stress or creating it for you.

Here, by the way, the media also plays a role. Advertising, is now virtually everywhere—including on your computer screen, at the movies, and *in* the movies due to extensive product placement in films. Ads stoke our continual cravings and fuel our feelings that we are not doing well if we are not continually getting more.

Too Many Choices

Somewhat related to achievement and acquisition stress is the modern phenomenon of too much choice. It seems that every decision we make affords us an overwhelming array of options.

We evolved living in extended family tribes and, later, in small villages of one or two hundred inhabitants. Although out-of-the-ordinary events certainly occurred from time to time, day-to-day life was fairly predictable and did not require continual critical decision-making. Today, we can't go anywhere or do anything without having to decide something.

Have you bought orange juice lately? Did you get it with or without pulp? Did you buy the kind made from concentrate? (And if so, is it as nutritious?) Did you go for the added calcium? (And if not, why not—aren't you worried about bone health?) How about toothpaste? Did you buy tartar-control, breath-freshening, or tooth-whitening?

Sadly, things get even more complicated. Have you tried to pick a health-care plan lately? Have you attempted to sort through the service options offered by your cable company? Have you chosen an Internet service provider?

Trying to do the right thing, whatever that might be, we find ourselves in a constant state of stress. Remember, much human stress is rooted in anticipation. We are continually imagining the possible negative consequences of not picking the options we passed up.

It Works for Me

"Thoreau said, 'Simplify, simplify.' I read that in high school. It took me half a lifetime to figure out what he was talking about. Finally, I noticed how stressed out I felt every time a smaller cell phone or a new iPod came out. I couldn't decide if I needed to upgrade. Then I realized what I was doing to myself. I've stopped paying attention to what was 'the latest' thing. I have better things to do."

—Sean, 46

Disconnection from Nature

For most of human existence, we lived in intimate connection with nature. We spent a good part of our waking hours outdoors: we farmed the land, we hunted or lived among domesticated animals, and we arranged our lives so as to sleep when it was dark and wake at dawn. We were, of course, highly sensitive to changes in the natural environment. Our lives altered dramatically if a season brought a climate that was unusually rainy or hot, or if there was a drought or an early frost.

This inextricable intertwinement with nature's fluctuations was, to some degree, a cause of stress. After all, we never knew how what was coming would alter our lives. But arguably there is even more stress in feeling utterly disconnected from the natural world.

Today we are, much of the time, oblivious to nature and its cycles. It literally takes a disaster of epic proportions—a Class Five hurricane or a tsunami—to get our attention. We don't need to heed when it gets dark or light; all we need to do is flip a switch. The outdoor temperature needn't concern us, for we have central heating and air conditioning. If a crop fails somewhere in the world because of frost or drought, we just import the same commodity from somewhere else.

With regard to the outdoors, we are largely ignorant of the signs nature sends us. We literally don't know which way the wind is blowing. Most of us could not find our way around by following the sun. And even if we wanted to navigate by the stars, we would find them blotted out by light pollution.

On some level, most of us sense something is amiss, and we do what we can to reconnect with the natural world. Witness how we long to reconnect with the outdoors on our vacations. Think about how many of us feel our life would be incomplete without pets. These are good, restorative tendencies, and more will be said about making the most of such stress-relieving opportunities later in this book. Still, the fundamental symbiotic relationship between humankind and the earth is sorely wanting, and this is a draining deprivation.

Nature, if observed and respected, offers limits and boundaries that would slow our frenetic rhythms. It offers moments of awe in which to contemplate. It tempers our constant achievement and acquisition with humility. Without nature to balance and regulate our existence, life can seem like an artificial, never-ending treadmill.

Disconnection from People

In addition to our loss of nature, many of us have also lost a meaningful connection to family and friends. People used to spend their lives in one location, interdependent with the same group of people. Now we move from place to place, severing ties as we go.

Many of us have completely lost touch with the people we grew up with. Many of us have lost touch with our extended families. Some of us have little or no intergenerational contact.

The tend-and-befriend response to stress—a far superior protective long-term strategy than fight-or-flight—is impossible to implement when we are socially isolated. As we'll see going forward, establishing meaningful social connections is a powerful inoculation against the effects of perennial negative stress.

The Costs of Modern Stress

Not all the costs of stress in our world are quantifiable. It's impossible to say with precision how much being under stress mutes the rewards of daily living, depletes our ability to love ourselves and others, or distracts us from finding our most meaningful purposes. But more and more, it is becoming possible to quantify how stress harms our mental and physical health. It's been estimated that …

- ◆ 75 to 90 percent of visits to family doctors are stress related.

- ◆ At least 20 percent of the total number of health-care claims are stress related.

- ◆ 60 to 80 percent of worksite accidents are the result of stress.

- ◆ Stress is becoming the biggest reason for worker disability claims.

- ◆ Costs associated with stress might reduce U.S. industry profits by 10 percent.

- ◆ Stress, according to the U.S. Centers for Disease Control, helps account for half the deaths to Americans under 65.

Numerous surveys confirm that adult Americans perceive they are under much more stress than a decade or two ago. According to *Prevention* magazine, almost 75 percent feel they have "great stress" one day a week with one out of three indicating they feel this way more than twice a week. And self-reported stress levels have escalated not only in adults but also in children, teenagers, college students, and the elderly.

Ironically, these statistics might cause anyone reading them a great sense of—you guessed it—stress. But, take heart, not all the new news about stress is bad.

A Mind-Body Approach

The encouraging news, in a nutshell, is this: although our systems can be damaged by stress, we have within us the power to recover—and to protect ourselves from further negative effects of stress. That power comes from the conscious choices we make about how we live our lives each day.

Moreover, science, medicine, and psychology all agree that we can begin to heal ourselves through myriad approaches—physical, mental, emotional, social, and spiritual. Any and all of these approaches will benefit the totality of our well-being, because mind and body are really one interwoven whole. This *mind-body connection* means that what happens to us on the physical plane resonates psychologically; what affects our mind-set impacts our physiology.

def•i•ni•tion

The mind-body connection refers to the inseparable connection between the human mind and body and the complex interactions that take place among thoughts, feelings, behaviors, and physical health.

We succumb to the negative effects of stress not because of any one thing, but because of many interconnected variables. So we can begin to beat stress by altering any number of variables in our lives. Among many simple starting points, you can …

- ◆ Stop working for a few minutes and take a walk outside.

- ◆ Call a missed friend or family member you haven't seen in a while.

- ◆ Turn off the television and get back to an old hobby.

- ◆ Decide not to buy an item you don't really need.

- ◆ Tell a funny story—or listen to one.

- ◆ Look on the bright side for a change.

- ◆ Meditate or center yourself with prayer.

- ◆ Do something nice for someone.

- ◆ Get a good workout.

- Take a yoga or t'ai chi class.

- Plan a week of healthy meals.

- Cut back on alcohol, caffeine, and junk foods.

- Get a good night's sleep.

- Take a thoughtfully planned, peaceful vacation.

- Find a quiet space in your house and simply sit and enjoy it.

- Slow down for a minute and breathe—just breathe.

Although some of these actions might seem small, the point is that each and every one can mark a beginning. Each one can set off a chain of circular causality, meaning they can set in motion other changes, and still others. The rewards you gain, even if incremental at first, can strengthen your resolve to heal yourself further.

We used to think that biology was destiny. Now we now know that the mind-body system is far more malleable than was ever imagined. By creating new experiences and cultivating new attitudes, we can actually rewire what nature has pre-wired. We need not be passive casualties of stress, but active participants in shaping a new, more healthy and vibrant reality.

The Least You Need to Know

- Because life can be perilous, nature equipped us with an internal alarm response—but that response itself can be dangerous when it stays switched on for long periods of time.

- Humans are subject to the stress-related ailments because we can trigger the stress response by imagining what *might* happen.

- Uniquely modern stressors include fast-paced living, media saturation, an over-abundance of choices, achievement anxiety, and disconnections from nature and social contact.

- The costs of stress are high, not only in term of quantifiable dollars, but in terms of our quality of life.

- The good news is that modern science and psychology have adopted a mind-body view of stress—and we can begin stress recovery via a wide range of approaches.

Sources of Stress

In This Chapter

- ◆ How we respond to disaster and its aftermath
- ◆ Why life transitions are stressful
- ◆ The stress toll of daily frustrations
- ◆ Dealing with reoccurring stress cycles

If modern circumstances are the icing on the cake of stress, what are the main ingredients in the cake itself? Uncommonly disastrous events are stressful, but then again so are parts of life that that are generally viewed as quite common—some perhaps quite positive developments.

Day-to-day aggravations, although minor irritants in life's grand scheme, can often seem like the most stressful things of all. And when they group together in predictable yearly cycles, they can be especially draining.

Combined, all these elements make up a canvas of stress that can be the background of our existence—but only if we let it be.

No Calm During Calamity

The stress response initially evolved to protect us when we were in mortal danger. Intense episodes of mortal danger still impact humankind today. No matter how sophisticated we think our society and technology have become, the very foundations of our daily lives can be torn apart by, among other things, hurricanes, earthquakes, tsunamis, fires, floods, and the ravages of war and terrorism.

It should come as no surprise that stress in the extreme accompanies such devastating events. Calamities of such an extreme nature can threaten us with death or severe bodily harm. In one fell swoop they can rob us of our homes, our livelihoods, and a lifetime's worth of treasured possessions.

Catastrophe does not discriminate—it can impact an entire population at once: prosperous and poor, young and old, healthy and infirm. Because so many people have, unfortunately, been impacted by tragic ordeals, psychologists have had a large population of subjects to study. Contemporary research has often taken the form of interviewing disaster survivors every few weeks for the course of a full year after the initial event unfolds. The resulting surveys reveal the following multiple-stage pattern:

1. **Shock and confusion.** This first phase occurs at the time of the calamity's occurrence and immediately afterward. In it, victims are unable to fully comprehend what has happened. This sense of psychic numbness can last moments, minutes, or—for some—days.

2. **Mobilization.** In this phase, victims take automatic action—doing what needs to be done to save themselves and others in the immediate moment. Emergency stress hormones are coursing through the bloodstream, in some cases helping people perform feats of strength and speed that would be impossible under ordinary circumstances. Later, victims will likely be unable to recall precisely what they did or in what order events unfolded. Memories become a blur.

3. **Communal effort.** At this phase, although many individuals have a distinct sense of weariness, survivors work together to resolve ongoing problems and collaborate about plans for future recovery.

4. **Letdown.** In the fourth phase, exhaustion sets in. Survivors feel depleted of energy. During letdown, survivors can experience additional stress at the added day-to-day frustrations that linger in a disaster's aftermath (e.g., lack of electricity or difficulty in communicating with the outside world). Community feeling dissipates and people focus on their own troubles, and stress can rise even more as survivors sense that the support and concern of others is diminished.

5. **Recovery.** The final phase of disaster can go on for years. During this time, in addition to mourning their losses, survivors of large-scale disasters face many logistical problems as they go about the many tasks involved in rebuilding homes, businesses, and lives. Inevitable delays and setbacks can create a situation of chronic stress.

Also contributing to ongoing stress during this period is something that everyone in every situation—disastrous or routine—finds stressful: people must give up the familiar and adapt to change.

> **Stress Less**
>
> In the aftermath of a disaster, survivors' stress is lessened if they have opportunities to tell their stories. Anything that can be done to help a disaster victim make sense of his or her experiences and ventilate some pent-up tensions is helpful.

> **Too Tense**
>
> In some situations, mass panic and disorder can set in after disaster. Contributing to such situations are lack of information (people don't know what will happen next) and lack of effective leadership.
>
> Leaders who emerge during crises are under as much stress as everyone else but have strong coping skills that are reflected in their emotions, thoughts, and behaviors. They help dissipate the stress of others by being role models, by being organized, and by disseminating useful information.

Life Transitions

Change is inevitable. All of life is, in fact, a process of continual change. The seasons come and go, the moon waxes and wanes, and—for those of you who are as yet somewhat unobservant of nature—home mortgage rates and economic markets rise and fall. Our bodies change, too, shedding cells and regenerating, growing and then growing older. Yet change in our everyday lives is perceived as a potent stressor. Why?

The truth is that by and large we feel less tense and anxious in familiar circumstances than we do in unfamiliar ones. Even when familiar circumstances are far from ideal, and even when we wish that they *would* change and take action to *make* them change, the change itself is a kind of "alert" to our system that something is not quite "normal" about our world. Our stress response is, to varying degrees, ignited.

def•i•ni•tion

Life change units (LCUs) are used on the Social Readjustment Rating Scale to indicate the degree of stress associated with different kinds of change. The idea is that by tallying one's LCUs over the last year, one can measure one's current stress level and (perhaps) one's risk for stress-related problems.

Two researchers, Thomas Holmes and Richard Rahe, wanted to learn to *what* degree certain life events engendered stress. They had a large number of people rate different common life events and then ranked them in terms of *life change units* (*LCUs*). They then devised the Social Readjustment Rating Scale (SRRS), which assigned an LCU value to events such as death of a spouse (100), divorce (73), marriage (50), retirement (45), pregnancy (40), change in responsibilities at work (29), change in residence (20), and so on. Total LCUs—measured over the course of the past year—equaled total a person's stress load.

The Social Readjustment Rating Scale became widely used. You couldn't open a psychology textbook or, for a long while, a popular magazine without seeing a copy. But the scale met with some criticism.

Holmes and Rahe had noted that there was a correlation between a high LCU score and the occurrence of heart attacks, diabetes, multiple sclerosis, pregnancy complications, cognitive dysfunction, and on and on. But a high degree of life change does not guarantee ill health any more than a low degree of change guarantees good health. What is much more likely is that we are affected by how we interpret our life events and how we, as individuals, react to them.

It would be foolhardy to think we could eliminate change from our lives. Even if we could do so, who would really want to? What kind of life would that be?

But it's well worth bearing in mind that virtually all life transitions bring with them the *potential* for negative stress. This way, when they come along, we can do all the things we need to do—with body, mind, and spirit—to protect ourselves. Transitions needn't make you ill, but they are more likely to do so if you are unaware of their power to upset your emotional apple cart.

With that in mind, let's look at a few extremely common life transitions that many people do in fact find stressful.

The Start of Marriage

How can getting married—something that most people consider a happy event—be stressful? Let us count the ways. Marriage means embarking on a new way of life, and leaving behind the habits of single existence. Suddenly everything we do involves taking someone else's feelings and preferences into account. Our autonomy is no longer a given. We must negotiate and compromise.

Getting married also involves learning whether one's premarital expectations about the relationship come to pass. We all marry carrying a bouquet of hopes, dreams, and fantasies—some shared with our spouse, some kept to ourselves—about how our partnership will work. But there are always some surprises, even in the most harmonious pairing. When our real-life marriages fall short of our images, the fantasy-reality gap can be a stressor.

Marriage also involves a great many other related changes in our lives. We now have an altered relationship to our family and friends, who can no longer claim our first allegiance. We are living in new surroundings, and saving—or spending—our money according to new priorities. We're now planning for the future much more seriously, and such anticipation can spark worries as well as joys.

Finally, let's not overlook the wedding itself. As anyone who has ever planned one knows, weddings can be both emotionally and financially stressful. The pressure to stage a fairy-tale event is continually fueled by a wedding industry that stokes anxiety even as it promotes bliss.

But relax—there's no need to cross marriage off your list of life goals in order to reduce your stress. On the contrary: over the long haul, a strong marriage can be a potent defense against life's stressors. Happily married people enjoy the significant benefits of ongoing emotional support. They have someone to look out for their well-being, someone to talk to, someone to nag them to take good care of themselves. But no matter how well things work out, the *transition* to marriage can be a highly stressful period.

It Works for Me

"Before I got married I was lucky enough to have a good friend talk to me about how it was perfectly normal to be anxious. Just knowing that what I was feeling was par for the course helped me calm down. People romanticize weddings and marriage, and of course it can be wonderful, but it is good to acknowledge how many things will be changing and what that does to you."

—Elisa, 26

The End of Marriage

Even more so than the beginning of marriage, the end of marriage can be a major stressor—and not only for the partner who initiates it. Whether or not divorce is one's choice, it inevitably involves an emotional upheaval, with feelings of abandonment, guilt, and so on. It also involves disruption of long-ingrained day-to-day habits, and leads to secondary stress-filled events such as a change of residence and a change in financial circumstances. If children are involved, the stress factor can rise exponentially, as parents worry about the effects of their separation on their family and sort through the complex logistics of sharing parenting duties with an ex-spouse.

New Parenthood

Anyone who's experienced the joy of bringing home a new baby also understands that such a profoundly life-altering experience is pretty much synonymous with stress. To accommodate this new—and utterly helpless and dependent—family member, every aspect of day-to-day habits has to be reconfigured.

Babies are by nature endlessly demanding. They require constant care on both a physical and emotional level. This level of attention is not optional for parents, as they know their infant's very existence and healthy development depends upon it. That awesome level of responsibility, coupled with social pressures to be a superior parent who raises an exceptional child, can certainly turn up the pressure.

On top of all these inherently stressful dynamics, add the cherry on the stress sundae: sleep deprivation. As we'll see in Chapter 18, a good night's sleep is a powerful buffer against stress. But try getting an uninterrupted eight hours with a new baby in the house!

Too Tense

The new parent who never allows time for self-care will be highly vulnerable to the negative effects of stress. Allow extended family members or paid caregivers to relieve you from time to time. You'll feel better—and that's better for your baby, too.

On an ongoing basis, parenting can continue to be stressful, but it's also very rewarding. The comforts of a loving family far outweigh the ill effects of the time we spend worrying about them. Don't cross having children off your to-do list in an attempt to stay stress-free, but do be prepared to take care of yourself the best you can even as you care for a new little one.

The Loss of a Parent

Once again, we look at the impact of mourning on stress, and find that it can be weighty. Specifically, losing a parent can foster feelings not only of sorrow but also of abandonment. One can feel like an orphan at any age. With a parent gone, we have the sense that we have lost an ever-present protector and a source of unconditional love.

Losing a parent as an adult is also likely to give rise to anxiety-provoking thoughts about one's own mortality. How much time do I have left? What kind of legacy will I leave behind? Will I have time to accomplish all I hope to? These kinds of questions can cause us to rethink our priorities, and so they can ultimately be very constructive, but that largely depends on our attitude.

Retirement and Aging

Attitude, in general, has a great deal to do with how we handle the inevitable transitions of our later years. We all age, and aging wears on our bodies. But it is how we view aging that can make a difference in how it impacts our minds—and that perspective in turn can affect our overall health and well-being.

Take the issue of retirement. By and large, people look forward to it. But when the time arrives, some find themselves at a loss as to what to do with their time. Retirees, it turns out, spend an extraordinary amount of time watching television, which would seem to indicate that they simply don't know what to do with themselves or don't feel confident that they can continue to be useful. But for some, retirement can be perceived as a whole new beginning, an opportunity to be useful in new and challenging ways: to volunteer, to learn new skills, to explore creative outlets, perhaps even to start a whole new career.

Our society adds social stress to the aging process by—quite irrationally—stigmatizing aging. As a result, many of us will spend an inordinate amount of time trying to "stay young." Because there is no such thing as a fountain of youth, embarking on an endless, unsuccessful quest for one is by definition stressful.

On the other hand, resolving to age gracefully by exercising, eating well, keeping the mind active, and cultivating social and spiritual support can serve to ease us into our senior years with a sense of integrity and peace.

Financial Transitions

Each transition mentioned here, and a great many more, has a significant financial component. Changes in living circumstances and new responsibilities require funding, and we often worry about how far our resources will stretch. Lack of resources threatens our survival today as surely as any man-eating predator did back in the primeval jungle, albeit not as immediately. So it is natural that money, or anticipation of the lack thereof, is a stressor.

But although money is a stressor on a practical level, it can—if we let it—be an even greater one on an emotional level. Our propensity to judge ourselves by the size of our paycheck or bank accounts or stock portfolios adds fuel to the fire of self-imposed stress. If our very sense of self-worth is tied up in money, we put an inordinate amount of pressure on ourselves to keep getting more and more of it, perhaps working to excess at the expense of other activities that could keep us balanced.

> **Stress Less**
>
> Many activities that involve living in the moment can lessen stress. Yet sound finances always require an element of planning for the future. This seemingly stressful paradox can be lessened by budgeting some money for pleasurable pastimes and allocating some for savings.

Financial health is important, make no mistake. It is well known that poverty is a profoundly debilitating stressor. But for those with enough resources to live a middle-class economic existence, it is the attitude toward money—what it can and cannot do, and what we will and will not do to obtain it—that ultimately has the greatest impact on overall quality of life.

Day-In, Day-Out Hassles

Disasters and life's transitions—all large matters indeed—are stressful business. Yet often it seems that it's the little things that "put us over the edge." Who among us hasn't felt our body go rigid and our brains practically sizzle with irritation and resentment when …

- ◆ We can't find a parking space?

- ◆ We find a parking space—and *someone else takes it*?

- ◆ We get in a supermarket express line behind someone with more than the allowed number of items?

- ◆ We get in a supermarket line behind someone who wants to cash a check—*without any I.D?*

- We miss the train/bus/plane?

- We get on the train/bus/plane and *it just sits there?*

- We're put on hold?

- We're put on hold—*and then get disconnected?*

- Our Internet server is down?

- Our Internet server is *s ... l ... o ... w?*

- Someone's car alarm is incessantly beeping?

- Someone's car alarm is incessantly beeping—*and it turns out to be ours?*

Such a list could go on and on. And on. But you get the idea. Every time we are blocked from achieving a goal, even a minor one, we feel frustrated. Taken one at a time, each frustration might be tolerable, but they tend to pile up. The cumulative effect of daily hassles tends to wear down our resistance and resilience.

In a study of people keeping "hassle diaries," those who reported a large number of irritations over the course of a year did, in fact, also report a much higher incidence of ailments. But here is a critically important point: what is one person's infuriating, stress-spiking hassle could be someone else's minor blip—an event she doesn't pay much attention to at all, or just chalks up as "one of those things."

We can't eradicate from our lives events that cause a certain amount of discomfort or inconvenience. But we can work on our reactions to them. The bottom line: the more we interpret hassles as an affront to our well-being, the more they will be. The more we can shrug them off using coping skills like optimism and humor (see Chapters 6 and 7 for more on this), the more we can keep stress at bay.

Yearly Stress Cycles

In addition to stress being induced by disasters, transitions, and daily hassles, many people report experiencing particular times each year when they feel especially on edge. Those times might vary according to an individual's personal circumstances, but some are quite common.

Winter Woes

If you have ever had the sense that you are more prone to feeling stressed in winter-time, you are not alone. Six percent of Americans suffer from what is known as

def•i•ni•tion

Seasonal Affective Disorder
(SAD) is a mood disorder associated with depressive episodes
and related to seasonal variations of light. SAD was first noted
in the mid nineteenth-century, but
was not officially named until the
early 1980s.

Seasonal Affective Disorder (*SAD*) and another 10 percent to 20 percent might experience mild SAD symptoms.

Although SAD is primarily categorized as a form of cyclic depression, one of its symptoms is a low threshold for frustration. During SAD episodes it is more difficult to deal with daily hassles, and goodness knows daily hassles abound in winter for those who live in northern climes: there are icy roads to be navigated, snow to be shoveled, and five layers of clothing to don when it's time to walk the dog.

SAD is believed to be related to changes in levels of the light-sensitive hormone melatonin, which affects body temperature and sleep patterns. Those who notice depression and stress vulnerability for two winters running might want to explore light therapy. In light therapy, you sit a few feet from a special lamp that's ten to twenty times brighter than are ordinary indoor lights for 30 or more minutes each day, usually in the morning.

Of course it's also possible that your higher winter stress levels are linked to a milder form of "winter blues." Most people for whom this is the case can ease their symptoms with increased physical activity and increased amounts of light in the home and work environment.

Finally, don't forget that attitude can be an important factor in mitigating stress. Consider taking an optimist's view of winter: it's inevitably followed by spring.

Tax Tension

Have you taken all your legal deductions? Remembered all your income? Do you need to pay the alternative minimum tax? Have you done anything dumb enough to merit an audit—or might you just get audited randomly? If such questions cause your brow to perspire and your teeth to clench, you might be one of the 40 percent of Americans who say that tax time is the most stressful time of year.

Even if your taxes are reasonably straightforward, and even if you generally get a tidy refund check, the run-up to tax time is fraught with so much cultural angst and media hype that one almost feels left out if one is not in a panic by April 15.

Even though computer programs for doing taxes are widely available, many people feel less stressed if they get help in the form of a human touch. A tax professional knows what they're doing and can offer a bit of emotional support in the bargain. Perhaps most important, they can advise you as to how to organize your records throughout the year so that you don't feel overwhelmed as the deadline approaches. This is a situation where our own procrastination can seriously up the stress ante.

Not-So-Happy Holidays

Forty-nine percent of Americans, says *Time* magazine, contend that the holiday season is their most stressful time of year. Whether you celebrate Christmas, Chanukah, or Kwanza, the pressure is on to socialize, entertain, decorate, find the perfect gift for everyone, and act nice to people who you might spend the rest of the year assiduously trying to avoid.

The joy of the holiday season can be offset by all of these time-consuming and emotionally taxing chores. The result can be an attempt to deflect one's accumulating stress by overeating, over-drinking, and overspending. Such strategies invariably make things worse, because when the holidays are done, overindulgers will be left with the ongoing stressors of being in poor physical and financial shape.

Simplification is key to de-stressing the holiday season. You'll find that most people would be more than willing to tone down the festivities to a more reasonable level if you only broach the subject. Consider setting spending limits for gifts, and making holiday get-togethers potluck affairs. If you put up a Christmas tree, investigate the new pre-decorated right-out-of-the-box kind. The most important thing is to place the emphasis on spending time with those you love most—one of the best antidotes to stress available to us.

Work-Related Cycles

No matter how busy we are at work all year long, many occupations—if not most— have their busiest seasons. Accountants have the run-up to IRS filing, teachers have the start of school, salespeople have deadlines to make their yearly quotas, and retailers have Black Friday (the first shopping day after Thanksgiving). The list, of course, goes on.

Every year, the cycles repeat—and yet every year many of those who are affected respond with physical complaints and signs of mental and emotional overload. Short of changing professions, there is nothing to do to prevent a busy season from coming on. Nor, in many cases, would we want to, for such periods might contribute greatly to our income.

What we can do, however, is spend the months beforehand making sure that our mind and body are in the soundest possible shape. Eating right, getting enough rest and exercise, and tending to our social and spiritual needs ahead of time gives us a stress-beating bank account of sorts to draw on when times get tough. Think of it as preventive stress management.

The Least You Need to Know

- ◆ Disastrous events are stressful, but so are common life transitions and day-to-day frustrations.

- ◆ Our systems are wired to mobilize during catastrophes, and that's useful, but chronic stress can accrue in their aftermath.

- ◆ Life transitions (such as marriage, new parenthood, and retirement) are stressful because they involve change; but how we interpret and respond to each transition is an important factor.

- ◆ Day-to-day hassles can be stressful if we let them be; but one person's hassle can be another person's "no big deal."

- ◆ Recurring yearly stress cycles are not uncommon, but because they are predictable, we can to some extent minimize their impact by taking good care of ourselves beforehand.

The Downside of Stress

In This Chapter

- ◆ When fight-or-flight fails us
- ◆ Stress and heart health
- ◆ Other stress-related illnesses
- ◆ How stress threatens immunity
- ◆ How stress affects memory
- ◆ The impact of stress on aging

Several years ago I went to see a doctor about a mild but annoying skin condition. In the course of our consultation, I asked her if she thought the condition might be stress related. She laughed and asked, "What isn't?"

Good question. And the answer, in terms of our health, is not much.

By now, most of us have come to understand in a general way that stress is somehow "not good for us." Doctors have been saying this for some 50 years. But just how stress exacts its toll on health is less well understood. That is the focus of this chapter. The more we know about the "how" and "why" of such matters, the more we will understand why tackling our response to stress will be so beneficial.

Flight or Fight ... or Else What?

If we've established one principle so far, it's that our biological stress response is right on the money when it comes to attending to immediate emergencies. If I'm being chased by a rabid dog, or accidentally set my kitchen on fire, or notice a tornado heading my way, I'll be very grateful that I am programmed to take swift action in order to save my hide. If I need to defend myself or a loved one in a threatening situation, I'll be very glad I have some extra adrenaline to repel an assailant.

But let's be realistic. In most of life's stressful situations, we have the option neither to run away nor to punch someone in the nose. Sure, it's tempting to think of running away the next time we have to face an overdrawn checking account, a crashed computer, or a prickly note home from our kid's teacher. Maybe we could just pack a bag and rack up some frequent flyer miles.

> **Too Tense**
>
> Be grateful for your pre-programmed responses, even while learning to manage them in nonemergency situations. Those with the *inability* to activate the stress response—such as people with Addison's disease or Shy-Drager syndrome—are at serious risk because they are unable to respond effectively to serious physical challenges.

But where would we go? How long could we defer the problem? We know that avoiding our troubles tends to only make them worse. Most of the time, flight just isn't an option.

What about a fight? If pressed, we could each could probably come up with a list of people whom we've at one time or another fantasized about bopping on the head: an abusive boss, an annoying co-worker, a thoughtless neighbor, a cheating lover, that person next to us on the train who simply will not stop hollering into his cell phone. But for the most part, no matter how hostile we rightly feel in the moment, we control such impulses, and that's good. We are civilized folk who understand that violence doesn't solve things and only breeds more violence. Besides, we don't want to get sued. So physical aggression, for the most part, is out.

Now, what about the fact that much of our stress doesn't revolve around events or feelings of the moment at all, but around anticipation of what might occur down the road? Worries about jobs that might be outsourced, relationships that might falter, and bills that might be unpayable can last for months, perhaps years. Here, too, the fight-or-flight strategy has nothing to offer us.

When fleeing or fighting are simply not viable choices, we are left with a dilemma. Our brain and body—troopers that they are—are still trying to protect us *as if* we were in immediate jeopardy. We are physically tense and awash in stress hormones. But, ironically, this "survival strategy" mode now promotes the opposite of safety and well-being. Unable to flee or to attack an enemy, we now begin to do the equivalent of attacking ourselves.

Stress Is a Heartbreaker

One of the most widely known and commonly discussed negative health effects of chronic stress is the effect it has on our hearts. That's understandable. Cardiovascular disease is the premier killer in the United States and, for that matter, in the entire developed world. What's more, the Mayo Clinic has identified psychological stress as the strongest indicator of future cardiac events. As leading stress researcher Robert Sapolsky unequivocally puts it, "Never is the maladaptiveness of the stress response during psychological stress clearer than in the case of the cardiovascular system." What it all adds up to is this: stress can literally be a heartbreaker.

When we are in immediate danger, our cardiovascular system is dramatically activated. Have you ever, for example, narrowly avoided a car crash? While you were busy swerving to avoid a collision, lots of other things were going on inside you. You know that thumping feeling you experienced in your chest? That was because your *sympathetic nervous system* was turned up and your *parasympathetic nervous system* was turned down. The result shifted your heart into overdrive, causing it to beat more rapidly.

def•i•ni•tion

The **sympathetic nervous system** is the half of the autonomic nervous system that is switched on during emergencies, or what we think of as emergencies. It helps us be aroused, active, mobile, and vigilant.

The **parasympathetic nervous system** is the other half of the autonomic nervous system (*para* meaning *alongside*). It plays an opposing role, promoting calm and initiating activities that contribute to our body's maintenance, growth, and development.

At this point your heart also beats with more force. For this, your blood pressure needs to rise. That's done by the sympathetic nervous system causing the veins that return blood to your heart to constrict. As these veins get more rigid the blood moves through them with more power, literally slamming into the heart walls. The walls distend and then snap back.

The body is reacting to a threat in a very aggressive manner. In addition to accelerating heart rate and increasing blood pressure it is also sending more blood to the muscles, while decreasing blood flow to your digestive tract, skin, and kidneys.

But for now, forget the near car crash that has caused this reaction. Imagine instead that your cardiovascular system does its emergency preparedness drill to some extent every time you get an e-mail from your demanding supervisor or every time your spouse forgets to pick up her socks. In effect, that's what's going on during chronic stress.

Chronic stress can promote hypertension (chronically elevated blood pressure), and that's dangerous. All that powered-up blood slamming into your heart results in over-developing one of its four quadrants. This lopsided heart—called left ventricular hypertrophy—is the single greatest predictor of heart problems.

Too Tense

Even if you eat healthfully and watch your diet for cholesterol, stress can put you at risk for clogged arteries. In a study where 55 men were subjected to stress by immersion in cold water, their cholesterol level rose immediately.

On top of that, high blood pressure damages blood vessels, which contributes to atherosclerosis (clogged arteries). When blood vessels are damaged, odds are increased that circulating fat, cholesterol, and other kinds of injurious plaque will adhere to the injured sites. Clogged coronary arteries lead to heart attack; clogged brain arteries lead to stroke.

All in all, what chronic stress can do to your cardiac health is not a pretty picture. The damage results not only from turning the stress response on too often but also from neglecting to turn it off.

Stress and Other Ailments

In addition to contributing to heart disease, chronic stress can contribute to a whole host of other ailments. To go into detail about each and every one would take a book all its own—or, more likely, several volumes. But even a brief look at the vast array of conditions potentially created or aggravated by stress is eye opening.

Diabetes

When we become anxious, stressed, or fearful, the hormones that rev up cause the body to release extra sugar (glucose) into the bloodstream. That's so we'll have the energy needed to deal with the situation. The mobilization of glucose involved in an ongoing stress response can accelerate the development of diabetes and cause major diabetic complications.

Irritable Bowel Syndrome (IBS)

Among the most common of stress-sensitive disorders, IBS is characterized by pain after eating, bloating, and diarrhea or constipation. Studies show that chronic stress increases the risk of IBS appearing, and worsens symptoms in existing cases. Stress increases contractions in the colon in an attempt to rid the body of excess baggage so that fight-or-flight can take place.

It Works for Me
"In a strange way I was relieved when my doctor suggested my gastrointestinal problems were stress-related. At least I felt that to some extent they were in my control. That's when I decided I had to learn to deal better with the stress in my life." —Jon, 37

Ulcers

Ulcers are holes in the walls of an organ, such as the stomach. Of late there has been much attention paid to the discovery that a certain kind of bacteria—*helicobacter pylori*—contributes to 85 to 100 percent of ulcers. However, this bacterium cannot be the whole story, because only 10 percent of people infected with it get ulcers.

Study after study shows that ulceration is more likely to occur in people faced with serious life stressors. When stress causes people to drink and smoke, it contributes in yet another way to ulcer development.

Psoriasis

Psoriasis is a chronic skin condition that occurs when skin cells reproduce faster than normal, and pile up on the surface. The connection that doctors have long recognized between stress and psoriasis has also been proven in clinical studies. It's been found that psoriasis sufferers have a greater number of nerves in their skin that release substances called neuropeptides (chemical messengers that help transmit nerve impulses). The neuropeptides found in psoriasis lesions are similar to neuropeptides in the brain that are altered by stress. Researchers believe that these stress-altered neuropeptides help trigger or aggravate psoriasis.

The Common Cold

Perhaps you are lucky enough not to have any of the foregoing conditions—and, if that is the case, hopefully you never will. But there is one stress-related condition nearly all of us have had: the common cold.

We have probably all had the experience of contracting a cold just as we were coming up to a major stressful event, like a week of final exams or a work-related conference at which we would be center stage. "Drat," we think, "there couldn't be a worse time." Nevertheless, there it is.

But wait a minute. We all know that colds are the result of being exposed to a virus, don't we? What could stress have to do with them?

According to controlled studies, stress can weaken our resistance to the rhinovirus (the type that causes colds). When subjects were divided into groups of the highly stressed and the not-so-stressed, those who reported high stress were about three times more likely to succumb to a cold when a solution containing the rhinovirus was sprayed directly into their noses. Stressors that lasted over a month provided the greatest risk.

The bottom line: if common colds are really common for you, learning to manage your stress response might ultimately save you the cost of lots and lots of Kleenex.

Stress and Immunity

As noted earlier, the list of medical conditions that stress, at least in part, can cause or worsen, is extensive. But now let's shift our focus a bit. Given all the illnesses we might contract, isn't it amazing how many we don't? Our bodies have an amazing ability to ward off illness because of our immune system. When we do fall ill, it could be because our immune system has fallen down in the job. Just how might stress contribute to that?

Let's say your town has just been hit by a massive blizzard. Emergency road crews get up before dawn to start plowing the roads and sprinkling sand or salt. Power crews attend to downed lines. Ambulances venture out to carry those who need to get to the hospital. Everywhere you look, you see and hear emergency vehicles blinking and bleeping.

At the same time, normal services are suspended. The schools mark up a "snow day." The supermarket shelves are nearly bare as delivery trucks fail to get through with supplies. The local bank branch is closed because employees can't get in, and even the ATM is out of cash. If you had scheduled a routine doctor's visit, a haircut, or a meeting with your financial planner, you'd no doubt postpone it. It would be too hard to get there; and besides, you're too busy shoveling the driveway.

The point is that business as usual takes a backseat when emergencies arise. All resources are diverted from routine to exceptional activities. Desperate times, as they say, call for desperate measures.

For most of us, the immune system—like our towns on calm, sunny spring days—functions well on a routine basis. It has a serious job to do: defending the body against dangerous invaders such as viruses, parasites, harmful bacteria, and fungi. This defense system consists of different types of *white blood cells*. White blood cells produce both the antibodies and the chemical messengers necessary to sort out our healthy cells from the bad guys and target the bad guys for destruction. This might sound like a western shoot-out, but as far as our immune system is concerned, this is workaday stuff, all routine.

def•i•ni•tion

White blood cells is the collective term for lymphocytes and monocytes (*cyte* means "cell"). Lymphocytes themselves are divided into T and B cells, both of which attack infectious agents in different ways.

Your body's health maintenance routines, alas, are interrupted when urgent business looms. It makes sense when you think about it. After all, you wouldn't stop to floss if your bathroom ceiling were caving in! In much the same way, our body opts to tend to short-term threats over matters that impact health in the long haul.

The stress response suppresses the formation of the type of white blood cell known as lymphocytes and slows their release into the bloodstream. It inhibits the production of antibodies and disrupts the usual communication via chemical messengers that takes place among white blood cells. As a result, our cells are less efficient when it comes to battling infection. With our defenses disrupted, we are more vulnerable to harmful agents in our bodies. And when we are more vulnerable, we can more easily get sick.

Just how much stress we have to be under, and for how long, to decrease immunity substantially is currently a matter of intense study. But odds are scientists will not come up with a one-size-fits-all formula. In this situation, as in most things, individuals are likely to vary depending on innate characteristics and also in the way they handle chronic stress. Still, evidence is overwhelming that when the body employs a short-term strategy over a long period of time, the upshot could result in our contracting anything from the sniffles to serious diseases.

Stress Less

Chronic stressors have the potential to suppress immunity, but our disposition can enhance immunity. People who rate in the upper reaches of happiness on psychological tests develop about 50 percent more antibodies than average in response to flu vaccines.

Stress and Accelerated Aging

One thing many of us seem to believe intuitively is that stress can age people prematurely. Our hunches with regard to this stem from simply looking at people we know who have undergone long periods of chronic stress. Are those more wrinkles we see? More gray hairs? What if we look at pictures of the U.S. presidents at the beginnings and ends of their four-year terms? Don't they seem to be aging more quickly than normal?

When we evaluate how we look and feel after prolonged periods of emotional strain, we have a similar intuition. Aren't we looking older than we might have expected to? Aren't we feeling less energetic? Aren't our joints a little creakier? Our minds a little foggier?

As it turns out, our perceptions about stress speeding up the aging process seem to be correct. Scientists have recently identified a link between long-term psychological stress and the phenomenon of healthy people growing older before their time. According to a study involving mothers caring for chronically ill children—a highly stressful situation—chronic stress appears to hasten physical deterioration and abbreviate life span.

The researchers came to this conclusion by examining something called *telomeres*, which are caps at the end of our chromosomes (molecules that carry genes). Each time a cell divides, telomeres get shorter. In the aging process, the telomeres ultimately get so short that cells can no longer divide, and so die. The researchers also measured levels of an enzyme called telomerase, which helps rebuild telomeres to stave off this process.

def•i•ni•tion

Cortisol is a hormone produced in the adrenal glands. It primes the body for activity in the face of stress by increasing the blood sugar.

The chronically stressed subjects had shorter telomeres and less telomerase than their same-aged counterparts. The longer they had been caring for an ill child, the more this was the case. Although it's not clear exactly how stress affects telomeres and telo-merase levels, a prevalent theory is that chronically elevated levels of stress hormones such as *cortisol* are involved.

In addition, the women caring for ill children had higher levels of something called *oxidative stress*—a process in which "free radicals" in the body damage DNA, including telomeres. Free radicals are oxygen molecules with missing electrons, and they cause cellular damage by taking electrons from molecules in healthy cells.

So, are we all doomed to sag and have our energy flag ahead of schedule if we experience a lot of stress? Will a stressful life be a shorter life? It hardly seems fair, does it?

But once again, a key factor appears to be people's perception of how much stress they are under. The researchers found that the greater a woman's perception of her negative stress, the worse she scored. Compared to women with the lowest levels of perceived stress, women with the highest perceived stress had telomeres equivalent to someone 10 years older. The findings emphasize the importance of attitude and of effectively coping with life stress.

Too Tense

Stress can also contribute to osteoporosis, a condition in which our bones become more brittle as we age. Stress hormones interfere with the trafficking of the calcium necessary to keep bones strong.

Stress and Memory

To lessen your stress, how about if we kick this section off with some good news: mild to moderate short-term stressors, such as performing in a friendly competition, actually improve memory. The stimulation of stress increases glucose delivery to the brain, which in turn makes more energy available to neurons involved in forming and retrieving recollections.

From an adaptive perspective, this is perfectly logical. It's handy, when confronting a stressor, to remember how you got into the situation you're in, and how the heck you're going to get out of it.

However, most of us have had the experience of being under high pressure and having our memory utterly fail us. When the stakes are high, we've sometimes drawn a blank on a piece of knowledge we could have sworn we knew "like the back of our hand." Ever forget where your registration is when a policeman pulls your car over, or forget your Social Security number when filling out forms at the emergency room? What about moving into a new house? If you're anything like me, you've spent weeks misplacing everything from your wallet to your watch again and again.

That's because under what we perceive as severe stress, or under stress that goes on for long periods of time, memory suffers. Both the formation and the retrieval of memories are disrupted.

In such situations, excessively high amounts of circulating stress hormones impair what's known as explicit memory—conscious awareness of facts and events. The hippocampus neurons no longer function as well, and connections between them—necessary for the act of recalling information—are disrupted. In cases of severe anxiety disorders, such as post-traumatic stress disorder, which can occur after being exposed to a traumatic stressor, the hippocampus has even been known to shrink.

Stress Less _____

Keep your mind sharp *and* reduce stress by playing challenging word games, such as Scrabble, Sudoku, or doing the daily crossword puzzle. The short-term stimulation improves cognition; the mental focus calms you.

The reasons that a little stress can perk up the memory, but a great deal can damage it, are complex, but they all have to do with the way our brains have thus far evolved chemically and physiologically. Perhaps one day we'll evolve to the point where our minds are clearer during periods of high stress. But although this would certainly be a useful development, don't count on Mother Nature pulling this rabbit out of her hat anytime soon. In the meantime, it's up to us to take the initiative to respond to our stressors in ways that help us keep a clear head.

The Least You Need to Know

- In most of life's stressful situations, fleeing or fighting are not practical options—when our brain and body still gear up for such strategies, the response itself can do us harm.

- One of the most widely documented negative health effects of chronic stress is the effect it has on our cardiovascular systems.

- Chronic stress can contribute to a whole host of ailments, from the common cold to serious conditions like diabetes.

- The stress response weakens immunity because when we are under its influence, our body mobilizes for emergencies and disrupts long-term maintenance and upkeep activities.

- Prolonged periods of stress can accelerate the aging process by prematurely damaging cells.

- Mild to moderate stress enhances memory; severe or prolonged stress interferes with recollection.

Chapter 4

The Upside of Stress

In This Chapter

- The good kind of stress
- How good stress helps us
- Changing "bad" stress to "good" stress
- Addictions to pleasurable stress
- Finding a life balance

If anything you've read in this book up until now has caused you to wish that you could completely eliminate stress from your life, think again. Under certain circumstances stress is not only useful, but also pleasurable.

The fact that it's not possible to have a stress-free life is actually good news. That's because such a life, even if plausible, would not be desirable.

I Stress, Eustress (*Eu* as in *Euphoric*)

Hans Selye, one of the revered grandfathers of stress research, coined a new term in 1980. The term was *eustress*, with the Greek prefix *eu* signifying "good."

Good stress? What was Selye taking about? After all, this was the scientist who discovered that prolonged periods of exposure to the stress response was damaging to organisms.

What Selye was getting at was that a modest level of stress—as opposed to prolonged, intense stress—is absolutely necessary in order for us to feel satisfied, engaged, and capable in all the critical areas of life, including work, love, and play. When our level of eustress is optimal, life is immeasurably enriched.

Imagine yourself in these scenarios:

- You're in the midst of a tennis game with a worthy opponent whom you'd love to beat. The advantage keeps shifting back and forth. You're psyched to win; you're playing hard. You're so totally involved in the game you don't know, or care, who's watching you or what time it is. Though you sense how hard you're perspiring, and how much you're exerting yourself, you feel like you could go on playing this game forever.

- You're on a white water rafting trip. You're about to run through a set of rapids you've never attempted before. Your heart beats quickly as you round the bend and see the rushing waters, but you're smiling with the thrill of anticipation. As you enter the rapids, you can feel your skin tingling and hear yourself shouting with excitement.

- You're visiting a country where the customs, dress, and language are very different from your own. You're not quite sure what to expect, but you're delighted by this opportunity to explore a culture so foreign to you. You're invigorated by the experience of interacting with the natives of this exotic land. When you feel you've made a connection, you're elated. You feel brave and adventurous—you're proud of yourself for moving off the beaten path.

Depending on your personal preferences, feel free to envision a chess match or a video game match in lieu of a tennis match, or riding a roller coaster instead of white water rafting, or a trip to any unusual locale you wish. But you get the idea. Eustress—pleasurable stress—can occur in any situation in which you are challenged and caught up in the spell of the moment.

*Eu*stress—as opposed to *dis*tress, or negative stress—tends to occur in situations of known limited duration, and when the person encountering the situation feels, to some extent, that things are more or less in control even though some element of risk is at hand. Eustress always involves stressors, i.e., events that create a state of alert in brain and body. But those stressors are perceived as—to use a nonscientific term—fun.

Eustress Enhances Performance

Eustress is not harmful, but rather helpful. One area in which is it especially so is in enhancing performance. Ask anyone who is successful in athletics, theatrics, or any business endeavor that involves being "on" before a group, and they will tell you a secret. Before they perform they feel "a little nervous" and while they perform they feel "a little jazzed."

Think about what the stress response does in its early stages. The sympathetic nervous system sharpens the memory. It dilates the pupils, enabling more acute vision. It adds energy to the bloodstream in the form of glucose. It increases blood flow to the muscles. To use another nonscientific term, it makes us feel "up."

"Up" is just the way we want to feel, of course, when it's necessary to perform at our best. In fact, performers in all arenas would worry if they *didn't* experience a little stress before their moment in the limelight. It's part of what gives them an edge.

It Works for Me

"As someone who has entered many ice skating competitions, I can honestly say I get nervous if I don't get nervous. Those butterflies in my stomach, tingly goose bumps on my skin, and a bit of dryness in my mouth beforehand tell me I'm at the level I need to be emotionally.

"If I don't feel these sensations, it might be because I am mentally overconfident. Maybe I don't 'fear' the other competitors so much. In the end, that hurts me. I do better when I sense I have to fight for the win. And I enjoy the competition more, regardless of what happens."

—Kristin, 19

The arousal involved in any kind stress has an optimal level. You can picture it as an upside down "U." At the top of the curve, with just enough stimulation, you'll be at your peak performance level.

Even watching a performance, we can generally see who is at the ideal arousal mode. Those with too much stress can falter; those with too little will put on a lackluster display. Eustress is the "mama bear" of stress responses. It provides just the right amount of stimulation, which helps performers achieve their personal best.

Eustress Gives Life Bounce

We don't have to be professional performers of any sort to reap the rewards of eustress. We can experience eustress when we're getting ready for a first date with someone we find really attractive. We feel it on the job, when we are working in a team in which things are clicking as we come up with an innovative plan. We feel it when we're working on any kind of intellectual problem that we feel is just beyond our immediate grasp, but still within reach. We feel it when we are tackling a physical task that we enjoy and at which we are proficient.

If we go too long without eustress in our lives, things take on a "blah" quality. Our mood can sink, our motivation can diminish. On some level, even if we've never heard of eustress before, we know we need it. We look for an activity that will add some "zip" to our humdrum existence. To shake things up, we try something new and deliberately alter the status quo.

The brain and body always respond with some degree of alertness and readiness—the kick-off of the stress response—when we leave our comfort zone. But periodically *choosing* to leave that comfort zone is a good thing, as it promotes growth and resilience.

Converting Distress into Eustress

There is a critical difference between the consequences of eustress and distress. Remember that in chronic distress—the kind that has the potential to threaten our health—the sympathetic nervous system keeps on cranking out stress hormones and sapping energy from long-term bodily maintenance projects. When this system is in the "on" position, the complementary parasympathetic nervous system remains in the "off" mode. We're unable to recover completely from the strain of our continuing arousal. With eustress, on the other hand, we recover, regain our balance, and move on.

So, are there any ways in which we can convert distress to eustress? It isn't always possible, but some people are very good at employing strategies that are effective in doing so.

Compartmentalizing

First, remember that eustress events tend to be events of limited duration. We enjoy a roller-coaster ride or a spirited tennis match, but we also know that they're going to end in the not-too-distant future. Often, the problem with chronic distress is that an end is not in sight. To convert distress to eustress, we can try thinking of the stressor as temporary.

Facing a seemingly endless series of knotty problems at work, for example, can be perennially stressful. Let's say that if you solve problem A with manufacturing, that means you next have to solve problem B with logistics, problem C with sales, and so on. Focusing on this entire string of complex events at once paralyzes you with anxiety; but on the other hand, you can choose to focus on the most immediate task at hand, psyching yourself up so that you can perform at your peak. For now, problem B and the rest can wait.

Think of it this way: a baseball outfielder trying to intercept a hard-hit ball will be invigorated if he focuses on the catch he needs to make in the moment. If he stops to ponder what might happen in the next inning, in the next game, or for the rest of the season, he'll not only be more likely to miss the ball, but to make himself sick with worry and become an ineffectual player altogether.

Taken in bite-size pieces, stressful problems that loom large can seem like invigorating challenges. When the immediate challenge is behind us, we are rewarded with a sense of relief and relaxation. Instead of draining our energy resources, we can continually replenish them.

It Works for Me

"I write technical manuals for a living. They are long and detailed. People have often asked me how I can possibly keep all that information in my head at once. If I tried to, I'd explode. I tackle my assignments page by page, chapter by chapter. I'm utterly consumed with each section as I write it. Then I pat myself on the back and take a break before moving on."

—Sean, 30

Reframing the Stress Sensation

Another way of converting distress to eustress is to learn to interpret the specific physical sensations that accompany the start of the stress response as helpful—as a jolt of energy instead of a jolt of fear.

I once knew a singer who was terrified that the jitters she felt before her solos would literally render her mute. The fact that she might be

Too Tense

Eustress and distress create the same arousing physical pattern. Labeling the revved up sensation as "fear" can hinder us. Try thinking of it as an energizing jolt of joy juice.

silenced by stress was itself so stressful she could barely sleep the night before a show. A singing coach delivered her from this debilitating distress cycle by suggesting she think of her "panic" as "electricity" that would power her vocal chords. With some practice, she was able to reframe her flushed face and sweaty palms as signs that her "switch" was being turned on. She learned to enjoy her singing as never before, and all who saw her enjoyed it as well.

Can Stress Be Addictive?

Of course, just about anything can be taken to extremes, which leads us to a question: Do some of us create too much stress in our lives precisely because of the euphoric rewards it might offer?

Just about anything can be addictive to certain people, and stress is no exception. For reasons that have to do with individual neurochemistry as well as personality, some people enjoy to a magnified extent the "rush" that facing a stressor can provide.

def•i•ni•tion

Endorphins are pain-desensitizing substances in the brain that attach to the same receptors as the drug morphine.

Dopamine is a chemical compound involved in the formation of adrenaline. It plays a role in the sensation of pleasure when it is released into a section of the brain that, when stimulated, creates positive sensations.

Part of what happens during the stress response is that brain chemicals called *endorphins* are released. These chemicals serve to dull our perception of pain, and so they come in handy if we are about to try to wrestle a hungry hyena or a rabid Doberman. But, being morphine-like substances, endorphins can also make us feel exhilarated. Increased glucose and oxygen delivery to the brain can add to the sensation of transient ecstasy, as does the release of another brain chemical called *dopamine* along our neural pleasure pathways.

For reasons that are somewhat analogous to innate pleasure "thermostats" being faultily set, some people come to rely on a continual stream of stressors to give them the uplifted feeling they crave. Such people have been called "adrenaline junkies" as a shorthand way of indicating that they are addicted to a variety of natural chemicals involved in the stress response.

So-called adrenaline junkies can be prone to engage in excessive behaviors. While eustress, for most of us, involves situations of only limited risk (we're really not very likely to fall off a roller coaster), people addicted to stress take pleasure in activities that are exceptionally risky. They live life on the edge in any number of ways, continually raising the stakes as their systems become habituated to the level of chemicals that used to stimulate them in the past.

Adrenaline junkies can be physical daredevils, taking ill-advised risks with their physical health. This could include anything and everything from pushing themselves too hard when fatigued to driving too fast to abusing certain substances. But they might just as easily be emotional daredevils, weaving in and out of a string of high-drama dysfunctional relationships. Sometimes they are even financial daredevils, perhaps gambling compulsively or repeatedly investing in high-risk get-rich-quick schemes.

In each case, even if odds are overwhelmingly stacked against them, adrenaline junkies take their chances. Then, win or lose, they will gravitate toward the next risk-laden endeavor for the sheer sake of thrill it provides. If the activities they engage in don't end up harming them, their extreme level of continual stress hormone stimulation could well do so.

> **Too Tense**
>
> Not all adrenaline junkies appear to be endangering themselves. Some are workaholics whose excess is rewarded with worldly success. But continually upping the stress ante in any situation will eventually take a toll on well-being.

A Spectrum of Sensation Seeking

The majority of us are not reckless stress-addicted risk takers. Nor—at the other extreme—are most of us likely to hide from all of life's challenges. Most of us seek a certain level of eustress sensation that is considered within the realm of normal. Nevertheless, we fall in different places on a spectrum that ranges from low to high.

The following table offers examples of the preferences of those who feel most comfortable with a low level of potentially stressful sensation and those who enjoy novel, moderately risky stimuli.

To see where you fall on the scale, simply circle the choices that appeal to you.

Low Sensation Seekers	High Sensation Seekers
Prefer to stay put	Prefer changes of scene
Prefer familiar friends	Prefer meeting new people
Avoid activities with any physical risk	Seek activities with some physical risk
Dislike scary movies	Enjoy scary movies

continues

(continued)

Low Sensation Seekers	High Sensation Seekers
Prefer predictable people	Prefer eccentric or unpredictable people
Prefer low-key company	Prefer gregarious company
Enjoy only temperate weather	Enjoy weather extremes (snow, cold, heat)
Dislike trying new foods	Like trying new foods
Dislike spicy foods	Enjoy spicy foods
Enjoy solitude	Dislike solitude
Rarely feel bored	Often feel bored
Dislike unconventional art, music, and literature	Seek out unconventional art, music, and literature
Dislike getting messy or dirty	Don't mind getting messy or dirty
Would dislike being given a surprise party	Would enjoy being given a surprise party
Dislike being the center of attention	Enjoy being the center of attention

If you've circled 8 or more answers in the left column, you are on the low end of the sensation-seeking scale.

If you've circled 8 or more than answers in the right column, you are on the high end of the sensation-seeking scale.

The more you've circled answers in either column, the more pronounced are your preferences for low or high stimulation.

There are no "right" or "wrong" choices to make here. What's important is to know where you fall—because that will help you determine what, for you, might comprise distress or eustress.

Low sensation seekers would be *dis*tressed if subjected to many of the experiences that high sensation seekers prefer. High sensation seekers would feel extremely deprived and unhappy if their experiences were limited to those that low sensation seekers would choose.

> ### It Works for Me
>
> "My brother enjoys taking long hikes in the mountains without knowing exactly where he's going. He says it's invigorating to have to find his way, and that he likes not knowing what he'll come across. I find that so stressful that I never used to go along with him. Now I look at a map ahead of time and keep the information to myself. We're both happy during our hikes, both at our own comfort level."
>
> —Joe, 35

Life Without Eustress ... Boring!

Even if we are generally low sensation seekers, we would unquestionably rate our lives as intolerable if nothing ever gave our mind-body system an exciting jumpstart. Life without any eustress whatsoever would be, in a word, b...o...r...r...ing. And, ironically, boredom itself is a source of distress.

In monotonous situations, we are unengaged, unchallenged, and understimulated at every level. Ultimately our reaction will be restlessness, irritability, and a desire to fight or flee the circumstances. Boredom also produces physical tension, such as joint and muscle aches and stiffness.

When boredom looms, take the opportunity to deliberately plan some event in your life that is apt to put you in a eustress state.

- ◆ Seek out an activity that offers some degree of challenge, while allowing you to use your skills. Identify what you're good at and also would enjoy getting better at. Put yourself in a situation where you'll be sure to use an ability you already have cultivated and are likely to develop a bit further. Each incremental advance will offer an opportunity to savor a sense of reward.

- ◆ Take a calculated risk. Try your hand at an undertaking where the outcome is not 100 percent certain, but evaluate the downside beforehand and see whether you could tolerate a negative outcome. For example, imagine you want to try out a somewhat complicated new recipe when dinner guests are coming over. Worst case: you'll all order pizza. If you can stand that outcome, break out your Cuisinart and go for it. If not, take a different sort of chance—but do something. Taking on some amount of risk on a regular basis not only livens up your life but builds up your resilience to distress should a crisis occur.

♦ Have realistic expectations. Although we need to change, grow, and develop, we also need to be practical—else we truly will disrupt our prospects for a balanced life and set ourselves up for failure and disappointment. We need to keep our responsibilities and obligations to ourselves and others in mind even while planning to go out on a bit of limb.

> **Too Tense**
>
> Although we live in a society where social and legal trends encourage minimizing risk, it's not possible to live a risk-free or stress-free life. Try to be philosophical about risk. There are no guarantees—and that's okay.

Finally, keep in mind that many of life's opportunities offer both some eustress and a bit of distress simultaneously. But the more we can focus on the rewards of stress, the less its potential to harm us will come into play. Life's a mixed bag, but what's the alternative? As Hans Selye put it, "Complete freedom from stress is … death."

The Least You Need to Know

♦ Positive stress, known as eustress, is a vital part of living—offering stimulation, positive challenge, and opportunities to grow.

♦ An optimal level of the arousal that accompanies stress can enhance performance and provide a competitive edge.

♦ To help convert distress to eustress, try tackling problems one step at a time and reframing your "jitters" as energizing electricity.

♦ Some people are addicted to highly stressful sensations, but most of us fall within a normal range of low to high sensation seeking that offers sufficient opportunity to experience eustress.

♦ Life without *eu*stress is boring and *dis*tressful. Liven things up by taking some calculated risks.

Chapter 5

Stress Styles

In This Chapter

- Discover your stress style
- Risks of highly reactive Type A behavior
- Benefits of relaxed Type B behaviors
- Inborn versus learned stress style
- Converting your style

This book has emphasized, and will continue to emphasize, the importance of how we *choose* to perceive and react to stressful situations. But it does not always feel as if we have a choice in how we respond to negative events.

It's true that our long-term habits with regard to stress are deeply engrained. This chapter will help you examine what your usual response style is, how you developed that style, and what you can do to begin to alter it.

What's Your Stress Style?

Some of life's stressors are unavoidable. We all have bad days when no amount of pre-planning—nor money, nor connections, nor even dumb luck—can protect us from being on the receiving end of a hot potato. As the saying goes, stuff happens.

When things go wrong, or even when we suspect they *might* go wrong, we each respond in our own way. Some of us become angry or aggressive. We might rail against our ill fortune, or look for someone in the immediate vicinity to blame. Some of us are more apt to take things in stride. We make the best of circumstances wherever we can. And if we can't make lemonade out of lemons, well, we'll calmly deal with life's sour parts.

What's your stress style? You probably already have a hunch. But here's a quiz to help you learn more.

Imagine yourself in the following circumstances and select which of the two reactions you'd be most likely to have:

1. You're stuck in a traffic jam that looks as if it might last for hours. You …

    A. Repeatedly blare your horn and consider wedging your vehicle onto the shoulder of the road so you can pass some other cars.

    B. Pop an audio book into your CD player and get ready to hear a good story.

2. You've spent two hours writing up an important report and then accidentally delete it from your computer. You …

    A. Slam your fist into your desk.

    B. Try to retrieve it and, if you can't, start over.

3. The automated teller machine at your bank swallows your ATM card. You …

    A. Go inside and start yelling at the first employee you see.

    B. Go inside and ask who can help you.

4. Your new puppy has an accident on the rug. You …

    A. Yell at him and tell your family it was a dumb idea to get a puppy.

    B. Look for the carpet cleaner.

5. Your teenager slams a door while you're talking. You …

    A. Slam a door right back at her.

    B. Ask her not to slam doors and continue what you're saying.

6. Your boss says you may not take the vacation week you asked for. You …

    A. Storm into his office and threaten to quit.

    B. Ask his reasons and see if you can change his decision.

7. You're on a committee that needs to elect a chairman. You ...

   A. Automatically try to obtain the position because you want to be in control.

   B. Consider the position only if you feel you have ample expertise and enough time to devote to it.

8. You're in the midst of a disagreement in a meeting. You ...

   A. Talk more and more loudly as the debate goes on.

   B. Continue to speak in your normal tone of voice even if others' voices are being raised.

9. You are given a challenging task to accomplish, with a deadline a few weeks away. You ...

   A. Start in on it immediately.

   B. Let it sit for a while, believing you'll get some creative inspiration by doing so.

10. You notice a grocery store checkout clerk ringing up items very slowly. You ...

    A. Roll your eyes, tap your feet, and look around for another checkout line.

    B. Take a weekly newsmagazine off the counter rack and flip through it.

11. You open an upsetting piece of mail at night, then learn you can't reach its sender until morning. You ...

    A. Stay up and stew most of the night.

    B. Find a relaxing activity that helps you get to sleep.

12. You look at your watch ...

    A. Frequently.

    B. Infrequently.

13. You engage in numerous tasks at once ...

    A. Frequently.

    B. Infrequently.

14. You work, walk, eat, and do most everything else quickly ...

    A. Frequently.

    B. Infrequently.

15. If you lose in any kind of competition, you are upset and feel it's unfair …

    A. Frequently.

    B. Infrequently.

If you circled between 11 and 15 "A" answers, your habitual reaction to stress is high.

If you circled between 8 and 10 "A" answers, your habitual reaction to stress is moderately high.

If you circled between 11 and 15 "B" answers, your habitual reaction to stress is low.

If you circled between 8 and 10 "B" answers, your habitual reaction to stress is moderately low.

Those with moderately high to high habitual stress reactions correlate with a spectrum of behavior known as Type A.

Those with moderately low to low habitual stress reactions correlate with a spectrum of behavior known as Type B.

Pure Type As and Type Bs are comparatively rare. Most of us fall somewhere between the two extremes. But whatever your tendencies are, it is helpful to be aware of them.

Read on to learn more about what research has shown about "As" and "Bs".

Type A: Aggressive, Ambitious, and Aggravated

Part of the inspiration behind one of the seminal studies of stress styles and their consequences reputedly occurred in the 1970s when two San Francisco cardiologists, Meyer Friedman and Ray Rosenman, noticed that the upholstery on the chairs in their waiting room was becoming frayed at the edges. Were their patients—people with heart conditions—literally "sitting on the edge of their seats"? Did these people tend to share certain high-stress personality traits?

The two doctors undertook a nine-year study of 3,000 healthy men between the ages of 35 and 59. At the start of the study, each man was interviewed for 15 minutes about his lifestyle habits. While these subjects were being interviewed, the researchers also observed how they presented themselves and how they behaved. Those who were the most verbally aggressive, easily angered, impatient, time-conscious, hard-driving, and ambitious were given the label Type A. Those who were more soft-spoken, self-effacing, and low-key were labeled Type B.

By the time the study was over, 257 of the men had suffered heart attacks, and nearly 70 percent of them had been classified as Type A. On the other hand, none of the men who were identified as extreme, full-fledged Type Bs had had heart attacks.

Subsequent studies have shown that Type A individuals are at risk not only for heart attacks, but also for other forms of cardiovascular problems, including stroke, as well as a number of other illnesses that have been associated to some degree with negative stress—including colds, headaches, and stomach disorders.

In neutral situations, Type As and Type Bs can appear to be much the same, but things can change rapidly as the stakes rise. Tell a group of Type As they're about to be tested on a difficult task and given electric shocks for incorrect answers, for example, and their pulse rate and blood pressure rise much more rapidly than do those of Type Bs.

Ongoing research into Type A behavior shows some other fairly consistent behavioral patterns.

Type As:

- Try to accomplish too many things in too short a span of time.

- Are irritated by trivial things.

- Are impatient with others who do not function as they do.

- Are easily angered when they feel their goals are thwarted by other people.

- Prefer to work alone or be in charge so they can have total control.

- Resent ever being told what to do, or being given suggestions.

- Work even faster than usual when deadlines and pressure are involved.

- Are "combat-ready," reacting with aggression when they feel threatened.

- Are cynical and mistrustful about other people's motives.

Type A behavior can itself be a self-fulfilling prophecy. The ways in which Type As act can create distressing circumstances. For example, they can sometimes bring on conflict by exhibiting abrasiveness and by finding targets at which to aim their free-floating hostility.

Too Tense

A Duke University study followed law students for 25 years. Those who tended to be hostile and cynical were far more likely than easy-going classmates to die by middle age.

Type As can also increase their susceptibility to physical ailments by smoking cigarettes and drinking a large number of caffeinated drinks, both of which they might do to keep going even when they are fatigued. They might also get a lot less sleep, because they are busy burning the candle at both ends so that they can accomplish more.

Type B: Is Laid-Back "B" Better?

In contrast to Type As, Type Bs are decidedly more relaxed. They are willing to let events unfold before jumping in and deciding to "do something."

Type Bs are more open to advice and feedback from others—less likely to "jump down the throat" of those with whom they might disagree or who might criticize them. They are perceived as more gentle, and are more apt to be trusting and accepting of others.

You might be wondering about now, however, whether Type Bs are cut out for success in our modern world. After all, people who are compulsively ambitious, perfection-driven, speedy, and self-promoting—all Type A traits—do appear to have an advantage in arenas such as the workplace, academics, and sports. But Type As are far less adept at tasks that require patience, such as people management, and at any endeavor that requires attention to detail than are Type Bs.

Stress Less _____

Contrary to what your instincts might tell you, more CEOs are Type Bs than Type As. Perhaps this is because many Type As don't stick around long enough to make it to the very top!

Besides, Type A gains can be short-term. Over the long haul, their behaviors can be unhealthy and self-defeating.

So, knowing what you now know about Type A behavior, you might conclude that Type B behavior is preferable. But beware, if you're going to try to change your stress style, it won't work to just "pretend" to be a B. Recent studies show that people who feel angry and hostile but simply suppress their emotions as opposed to working with altering their underlying attitudes are, like Type As, predisposed to heart attacks.

The key to revamping Type A behavior is not wishful thinking but stress management strategies. These can be remarkably—and demonstrably—effective. Those who have already had one heart attack, for example, have a far reduced risk of having another when they undertake stress management training in conjunction with medical follow-up as compared to those who receive medical follow-up alone.

If you believe you are a Type A, don't despair. Here's a piece of good news for you: your motivated personality can actually work to your advantage. The trick is applying it to developing new, healthy habits with regard to handling stress.

It Works for Me

"My doctor told me that for the sake of my health, I needed to learn to calm down and relax. When I told this to my friends they laughed and said, 'Who, *you*?' But I've always been up for a challenge and I decided to make this mine. I learned all I could about things I could do to help me relax. I vowed to be more aware of the good things in my life and to be more tolerant of others. So far, so good. My friends are amazed at the changes they notice in me, and I am in much better health."

—Ed, 50

Is Your Style in Your Control?

It can be tempting—all too tempting—to throw up our hands and say, "Oh well. I am who I am. There's nothing I can do about it." Maybe we'll add, "I was just born this way." To some extent, that could actually be so, but that's hardly the whole story.

It's never too late to change your stress style. Although some aspects of your stress style might be inborn, many *are* within your realm of deliberate influence.

What Part Are You Born With?

Parents with new babies are often heard to describe their infants in one of two ways: easy or difficult. What parents are seeing evidence of is the baby's inborn *temperament*, his or her characteristic emotional responses.

So-called easy babies adapt to changes in their schedule and environment with relative ease. Their intensity of crying is low. For the most part, their general mood is one of contentment.

def•i•ni•tion

Temperament is the biological basis of personality, consisting of inborn character traits such as the degree of sensitivity to stimuli and intensity of reaction.

So-called difficult babies, on the other hand, fuss when their schedule or environment changes. They cry loudly. Their general mood is somewhat cranky.

Where does this inborn temperament come from? To some extent, it is based on genetic traits that determine factors such as the nature of chemical receptors in the brain. To some extent, it can be impacted by the in-utero environment and the hormones to which the developing baby was exposed.

Is temperament predictive? Do those highly reactive babies become highly reactive adults? To some extent, research says yes. But this is hardly the whole ball game. Some parents tell stories of how their baby's disposition never changed; some will say just the opposite.

The adult personality that develops over ensuing years is a complex multilayered overlay of abilities, preferences, and—very significantly—acquired habits. When it comes to how we grow up to respond to stress, social learning plays a large role.

What Part Is Learned?

Humans are born mimics, naturally imitating the people around us as we grow. We learn by observation, and we do this so efficiently that we are capable of mastering the intricacies of dance steps without moving a muscle—simply by watching other people engage in the steps.

Humans' extraordinary ability to imitate actions comes, at least in part, from recently discovered specialized brain cells known as *mirror neurons*. These brain cells become active when we watch another person perform a task or take any sort of action. They help us understand not only the action itself, but also the intention behind that action.

Mirror neurons have only recently been discovered, and are probably only one mechanism by which we engage in social imitative learning. But developmental psychologists have long known that as we grow we absorb and recreate not only the actions of those around us but also their attitudes. We "read" what those close to us are thinking and feeling via subtle clues such as facial expressions. We then use these people as role models—templates on which to pattern our own behaviors.

def•i•ni•tion

Mirror neurons are specialized neurons that fire when we observe the behaviors of others. They are one reason human beings are so good at social imitation. Mirror neurons were first discovered by researchers who were looking for brain cells involved in physical movement in primates.

What this all boils down to is that if you grew up around people who were highly reactive to stress, you observed a lot of their habits and are, perhaps unwittingly, recreating them. Your own stress style was, at the very least, influenced by that of your parents and perhaps by that of others to whom you looked for clues as to how to live life.

If you came from a social environment in which those to whom you looked for guidance were high-strung, you are likely to be on the high-strung end of the A-to-B stress spectrum yourself. If your role models' tempers were on a short fuse, you're more likely to flare up than someone who was raised by placidly patient types.

There's no point in blaming anyone for your stress style, however. That won't solve a thing, and your resentment itself would be a source of tension. Instead, consider the upside of your profound imitative abilities. Now that you know they exist, you can begin deliberately to model yourself after people whose more low-key stress style would be beneficial for you to adopt.

Type C: Becoming an A-to-B Convert

If you have gotten this far in this book, there's a pretty good chance you are looking to overhaul your stress style—at least to some degree. That is certainly possible. No matter what genetic patterns you might have been born with, or what social patterns you observed and absorbed, you can convert your style.

The first step is to reframe the way you think about your style. Instead of thinking of yourself as a Type A *person*, think of yourself as a person who has Type A *behaviors*. Don't concern yourself with changing who you are; concern yourself with changing how you *think* about things and what you *do*.

- Learn to focus. Make a conscious effort to spend at least a small part of each day doing only one thing at a time.

- Maintain perspective. Notice what small irritants tend to set off a big stress reaction and ask yourself which is likely to harm you more: the minor annoyance or your major upset.

- Be tolerant. Try to view people with different approaches to life than yours—who perhaps do things more slowly and methodically—as role models you can learn something from.

- Trust someone else to take charge. Once in a while, relinquish your need to take control of events. Give someone else a chance to rise to the occasion—he or she might surprise you.

- Stay open to feedback and suggestions. You might learn something constructive when you are actually listening without being defensive.

- Slow down. In the long run, you'll gain a much greater quantity of time by living longer and a greater quality of time by living more healthfully.

Stress Less

Time is not the enemy. Make it your ally by imagining yourself 10 years into the future. If something is irritating you now, ask yourself if it will make any difference then. If the answer is no, try to let it go.

♦ Refuel with good energy sources. Caffeine, tobacco, and other stimulants are short-term fixes that ultimately backfire. Sound nutrition, sleep, and exercise offer long-term stamina.

The rest of this book will offer numerous concrete suggestions for putting these strategies into effect. Keep an open mind and take it one step at a time. Soon, your stress style conversion should be underway.

The Least You Need to Know

♦ Some of us react intensely to stressors; some are more apt to take them in stride.

♦ The stress style known as Type A is typified by aggression, ambition, and impatience.

♦ The stress style known as Type B is typified by an easy-going, patient, and relaxed demeanor.

♦ Some aspects of our stress style are due to inborn temperament; others are learned—and can be unlearned.

♦ A stress style *can* be changed by creating new habits of thoughts and behavior.

Part 2

The Stress-Free Mind Makeover

One person's stress-filled event might be another's invigorating challenge, and yet another's source of knee-slapping guffaws. Attitude can make all the difference. This part of the book discusses how to cultivate a stress-beating attitude with optimism, laughter, and altruism. It also looks at the profound effects that meditation, visualization, and personal spirituality can have on reducing stress and on rebounding from times of strain.

6

The Optimist's Edge

In This Chapter

- ◆ The anti-stress advantages of optimism
- ◆ Explaining things like an optimist
- ◆ Focusing on the good
- ◆ Bouncing back after stress
- ◆ Meeting stressful challenges with optimism
- ◆ Learning to be more optimistic

Imagine you visit a fortune-teller who predicts with grave certainty that for you, "stressful times lie just around the corner." What would your reaction be?

You might start to feel anxious and anticipate all the ways in which you could possibly fail to rise to the coming occasion. You might recall all the times in your life that stressful events occurred, dwelling on those where the situation did not turn out so well. You might feel hopeless about the future. Right then and there, even though nothing has happened yet except a prediction, your body would likely kick into its stress-ready emergency alert mode.

On the other hand, you might say, "Oh, well that's okay. I often do well under pressure." You might even add, "And if things don't work out, there's always an opportunity to try something new." Your mind would stay calm, though alert. Your bodily state would remain balanced.

If you think your response would be more like the second scenario than the first, then that makes you an optimist. If you're not an optimist now, this chapter will help you learn to better understand how optimistic people handle stress—and how you can learn to adopt a more positive outlook as part of your stress-beating repertoire.

The Stress-Beating Rewards of Optimism

For a long time, the field of psychology focused almost exclusively on "maladaptive responses" to life's challenges. But what about people who adapted well because of their upbeat outlook? What about people who generally exhibited traits like confidence and hopefulness about the future?

For a long time such people—optimists—were not particularly looked upon as role models to emulate. Actually, they weren't looked upon much at all. They were doing fine, so psychology pretty much ignored them.

Naturally, it's important to investigate the emotions that make life difficult—but psychologists are beginning to realize that emotions that make life less difficult are equally worthy of attention. Today *positive psychology* focuses on such people and their skills so that we might all learn from them. One of the things we might learn best is how to cope with stress.

def•i•ni•tion

Positive psychology is the scientific study of characteristics and attitudes that lead to optimal human functioning—especially in the face of stressful challenges.

Optimists are natural stress-beaters. Remember that part of the human condition is our ability to anticipate what *might* happen. That anticipation, in and of itself, can trigger the stress response. If our expectations are poor, our very thoughts become stressors.

Positive expectations, on the other hand, can work wonders. As evidence, think about the placebo effect. In virtually every study of a potentially healing drug, a certain number of subjects are given an inert sugar pill, a placebo, in lieu of the actual medication. A significant number—usually around a third—of those subjects get better, quite possibly because they anticipated that they would. That shows the amazing power of expectations to shape reality.

Those with an optimistic attitude expect things to work out. They perceive the world as a less threatening, more benevolent place than do pessimists. When optimists experience pressure they don't become immobilized. Rather, they are more easily able to make decisions because they are not made vulnerable by the stress response.

Optimists also enjoy less stressful relationships with others. They are more cooperative and more playful. They are also more willing to give other people the "benefit of the doubt." (If you interview for a job, you'd be lucky to interview with an optimist, because they tend to rate job applicants much higher than their pessimistic counterparts.) Their good opinion of others has a self-sustaining impact. Treat someone well and they respond in kind. The level of tension in social interactions takes a nosedive as goodwill prevails.

Not surprisingly, optimists also seem to enjoy many health benefits. Hopelessness exacerbates the impact of stressful situations by weakening the body's immune system. But an optimistic attitude has the opposite effect. It actually allows the immune system to function more smoothly and efficiently. Optimism is, in effect, preventive medicine. Optimists avoid the toxic biochemical reactions that stress can trigger. For example, optimistic moods lower levels of the hormone cortisol, which depresses immune function.

Study after study shows that optimists outlive pessimists and live with fewer stress-related illnesses. Optimism appears to reduce the risk or limit the severity of cardiovascular disease, pulmonary disease, hypertension, diabetes, and colds and upper-respiratory infections.

Stress Less

It's not just their rosy outlook that enhances optimists' well-being. Faced with stressful challenges, optimists take care to care for themselves. They don't drink to excess, smoke, or overeat. Instead, they make proactive choices that enable them to deal with life and to stick around for many years to come. They want to be here for all the good times they foresee ahead.

An Optimistic Spin

What exactly makes an optimist an optimist? One key, according to the positive psychology expert Dr. Martin Seligman, is the way in which they explain their circumstances to themselves. It lies in the "spin" they put on things.

- Optimists see negative events as temporary; pessimists view them as permanent.

- Optimists see negative events as limited in scope; pessimists see them as global.

- Optimists have faith that they have the power to improve things; pessimists feel powerless.

To illustrate how the optimistic spin eases stress, let's look at some potential stressors and see how an optimistic person and a pessimistic person might react.

Permanent vs. Temporary

The situation: a campaign to win a new client's business is unsuccessful and the client signs with a competing firm.

In this situation, a pessimist might typically conclude, "I will never get any more new clients. I'm a has-been." An optimist might say, "I was a bit off my game this time," or perhaps, "That client and I were not a good match."

Think what apprehension the pessimist will feel the next time he has to pitch a campaign to a potential client! He's added to the inherent stress of that situation by convincing himself he will never again be successful.

On the other had, the optimist is likely to be all fired up with enthusiasm and confidence, determined to prove that last time's loss was a fluke.

Pessimists and optimists default to different phrases when they explain negative situations to themselves.

The Stressed Pessimist Says ...	The Less-Stressed Optimist Says ...
I'm *always* wrong.	I was mistaken *this time*.
I'll be down *forever*.	I'm in a slight slump *right now*.
I'll *never* succeed.	Things didn't work out *today*.
I'm *constantly* losing.	*Lately*, I've had some setbacks.
I come in second *all the time*.	I don't always win—but it's really the client's loss!

But guess what? When things go right, optimists and pessimists switch scripts. Now optimists foresee that positive events will endure. When they're on a roll they expect things to stay good. What's more, as Seligman wisely notes, they take personal credit for the good things that are happening.

Although pessimists and optimists also default to different phrases when they explain positive situations to themselves, note the flip-flop in attitude in the following table.

The Stressed Pessimist Says ...	The Less-Stressed Optimist Says ...
I got lucky *this time*.	I'm a lucky guy, *as usual*.
I made a good call *for once*.	I was right *again*.
My competitor had a *bad day*.	My competitor *can't* hold a candle to me.

Is this strictly logical? Hey, don't be a nitpicker. It's emotionally logical, in that the strategy seems to have a good outcome. Optimists lessen the lingering stress of negative events by minimizing their perception of their duration. In the aftermath of positive events, they work harder to fulfill their rosy prophecies—their resulting burst of energy is a eustress state.

It Works for Me

"I'm an architect with my own business. Typically, I have a lot of projects at one time, and then there is a bit of a lull. In those lulls, I used to tell myself I would never work again. I could not enjoy the free time because I was so stressed about 'eternal unemployment and poverty'. Now I've learned to tell myself, 'I'm on a break.' I enjoy my time off, reminding myself that I'll be extremely busy again soon enough."

—Allison, 42

Global vs. Limited Scope

The situation: A romantic interest cools off the relationship.

Here, the pessimist is likely to say, "No one wants to date me" or "I'm ugly and undesirable." The optimist says, "This person is not for me" or, " or "Next time I'll date someone with better sense."

The explanatory style of the pessimist dooms him to dredge up excessive social stress the next time desirable date material comes along. After all, he's set himself up to find *all* romance intimidating and has defined himself as inadequate.

As for the optimist, one failed relationship is seen as an anomaly. She can meet, greet, and flirt with the next candidate with an unflappable attitude.

Once again, the pessimist and the optimist explain things to themselves differently when things go awry.

The Stressed Pessimist Says ...	The Less-Stressed Optimist Says ...
Everyone rejects me.	We weren't a good fit.
I'm dumpable.	If they hadn't dumped me, I'd have dumped them.
I can't go through this again.	Next!

Now, how will an optimist explain the situation when a romantic interest is in hot pursuit? You guessed it—they will explain this circumstance as simply the much-deserved status quo. The pessimist, on the other hand, will see it a rare event.

When things are on the right track, get ready for the hat-switch again.

The Stressed Pessimist Says ...	The Less-Stressed Optimist Says ...
This person seems to like me.	I'm a desirable partner.
It's nice feeling wanted for a change	I'm hot!
Can this last?	Hmmm ... I might not want to stay off the market too long.

By viewing their desirability as "more of the same," optimists de-stress the romance-in-progress. Pessimists, however, are likely to be so stressed about losing the relationship that they will hang on too tightly. Their very clinginess can have the effect of a cold shower on a budding romance.

Power vs. Powerlessness

Now let's look at another potentially stressful situation: After the holidays, you get on the scale and see you have gained seven pounds.

If you're a pessimist, you'll assume there's nothing you can do about it. Those pounds just somehow got there, and there they are going to stay. You'd better have your pants let out!

The optimist, however, becomes immediately proactive. "Unwanted weight? That means I consumed too many calories. It's time to eat less and exercise more. In fact, I plan to have this weight gone in six weeks."

Note that the optimist takes responsibility for getting himself into a situation and likewise for getting himself out. Note also that the optimist sets a realistic goal—losing seven pounds in six weeks—for turning things around.

Differing perspectives on control are critical when it comes to what separates optimists from pessimists. Pessimists have what is known as an *external locus of control.* They believe that outside forces control their fate. Obviously to some extent, we're all at the mercy of outside forces. But because pessimists think in terms of permanence and universality, they believe that external forces reign over all aspects of their lives and that they are without influence in their own destiny.

Optimists, conversely, have an *internal locus of control.* They believe that, to a significant extent, they can exert influence over the outcome of most situations. Sure "stuff happens," but they have resolute faith in their ability to tip the scales in some way by the way they react emotionally and by the behavior they exhibit.

Too Tense

It's great to exercise control, but don't set goals that are impossible to reach. Being optimistic isn't about trying to be superhuman. If you set unreachable goals, you only create more stress.

def•i•ni•tion

An **external locus of control** refers to an underlying belief that the outcome of events is out of one's hands, and is characteristic of a pessimistic outlook.

An **internal locus of control** refers to an underlying belief that one can impact the outcome of events. It is characteristic of an optimistic outlook.

Talking the Talk

Now that you know how optimists spin things, consider: how many times a day do you say something pessimistic—perhaps even under your breath, or "just as a joke"?

If your negative predictions have become second nature, bring new awareness to them by keeping a log. Write down any negative predictions you make. Include the times you predict that negative events will go on and on without improvement. Include the times you use one negative aspect of a situation to "prove" to yourself that everything in your world has gone bad. Include any instances in which you "give up" and say there is nothing you can do.

At the end of each day, review your statements to see how you can soften them. For example, is there an "always" you can change to "sometimes"? Is there a universally self-denigrating comment you can alter to one that simply says you did one thing that was, perhaps, less than perfect? Is there an "I give up" you can revise to an "I'll try one more time"?

Put your negative comments under Spinning Down. Write your revised comments under Spinning Up.

Spinning Down, Spinning Up

Spinning Down	Spinning Up

Don't worry if making revisions seems unnatural at first. All new behaviors feel strange, but you'll get the hang of it. Meanwhile, even a little improvement goes a long way.

Focus on Positive Elements

Another trait indicative of optimism is the ability to focus on a positive element in any given circumstance. In fact, the thing we most often associate with optimists is this proverbial ability to see a glass as "half full" rather than "half empty." This might sound a little corny, but research backs up the stress-reducing benefits of this tendency. Studies prove that focusing on positive stimuli reduces tension.

In one such University of Michigan study, researchers created a stressful situation for participants by telling them they would have to give a speech shortly. (For many people the prospect of public speaking is extremely stressful.) The research team monitored participants' cardiovascular reactions, and noted patterns indicative of the stress response. Then some of the participants were shown a video that included scenes of a frolicking puppy and of waves breaking gently against a coastline. The researchers found that those who focused on the dog and the ocean quickly returned to their normal level of cardiovascular function. Despite the looming stressor of the speech, honing in on positive stimuli eased stress.

Reading this study, I was actually reminded of a parable I heard years ago. It is one that always helps me personally when I am caught in a tough situation:

A man was being chased by a tiger. With nowhere to go, he jumped off a cliff, where he hung on to a vine. Then the man noticed another hungry tiger waiting for him down below. The vine itself was beginning to break, so what did he do? He plucked a strawberry from the vine and ate it, enjoying its sweetness.

Now, whenever I'm in a stressful situation with what seems like an uncertain outcome, I remind myself to "look for the strawberry." I am instantly calmer when I find something of value to turn my attention to.

Too Tense

Don't try to make your mind "a blank" in a stressful situation. Focusing on the good is different than seeking mere distraction. In a study that compared subjects' response to positive images to the response to neutral ones—like a benign video of a computer screen saver—the neutral ones did not induce the calming heart rate that the positive images did.

Making the Most of a Situation

Now imagine this situation: fifteen minutes before an airline flight is scheduled to board, an announcement is made informing passengers that the flight will be delayed for an indefinite period of time until high wind conditions clear at the destination airport. What would a pessimist focus on? What would an optimist focus on? And which one do you think would be more stressed?

The pessimist would likely begin to sigh and pace, look at her watch repeatedly, and barrage airline personnel with a bunch of unanswerable questions, such as "When is it exactly that this wind is going to die down?" She might make a series of frantic phone calls explaining to anyone who will listen the extent of her inconvenience and the depths of her misery. Might she do something constructive with the time? Not on a bet. She's simply too tense to concentrate. She's in a fight-or-flight action mode, even though there is nowhere she can go, and no one to fight with—unless she wants to get carted off by airport security.

Unlike this fidgety sad sack, the optimist—although equally inconvenienced and quite possibly less than thrilled about it initially—would very likely limit her stress by accepting the part of the situation over which she has no control (the weather) but then focusing on something good that could come out of the situation. Having unexpected "found time" on her hands, and knowing that what she does with it is in her control, she might take the opportunity to read a good book she's been wanting to get to, or browse the airport stores and find a small gift or card for a loved one. Maybe she'll just take a nice nap (which, as you'll see in Chapter 18, can be a stress reliever of its own). Whatever she does, she will relish the "silver lining" aspect of it. If her plane had not been delayed, she'll remind herself, she would not have had this chance.

Withholding Catastrophe Status

One thing optimists won't do is create catastrophes. They won't whip themselves up into a frenzy and turn a flight delay—or a missed connection, or a traffic jam, or a long line at the bank—into an apocalyptic event. They'll use their focus on the positive to keep things in perspective.

As we saw in Chapter 2, life is bound to provide a share of catastrophes all on its own. Catastrophes are exceedingly stressful. So why look for more of them?

There is little need for us to grant relatively minor events disaster status. Doing so revs up the stress response to a seriously unhealthy degree. If you over-react to everything, your body will know only one mode of reaction: severe. Your autonomic nervous system can't tell the difference between a tsunami and an overflowing toilet, but your thoughts can.

On the Rebound

Another important characteristic of optimists is their resilience. Being an optimist does not offer any insurance against the occurrence of stressful events—some are simply inevitable—but it does correlate with the ability to recover from them relatively quickly.

def•i•ni•tion

The **undo effect** refers to the power of positive emotions to counterbalance the impact of stressful negative emotions, as well as providing an added boost beyond the initial emotional starting point.

Because optimists have a mind-set that does not perceive the future as threatening, they can see that what's done is done. Moreover, they are eager to put their difficulties behind them. They not only rebound from setbacks of crisis faster than pessimists, but also bounce back to a higher level of positive energy than where they were before.

This kind of "bounce back plus" phenomenon is known as the *undo effect* of the optimistic outlook. Studies show that after experiencing a loss, optimists—over the course of the following few months—begin to actively count their personal blessings, and focus more on ties to friends and loved ones.

> **Stress Less** _____
>
> To bounce back from stress, actively recall a time in your life when you went through a bad patch and came out the other side. Make a list of the good things that came out of that period: the lessons you learned, the inner strengths you discovered, the ways in which you allowed yourself to be flexible, the strategies you used to solve problems, the love and support you got from those close to you. Remind yourself that every negative event contains the seeds of new, positive events.

Meeting Challenge Head-On

Some people think that optimists feel less stress simply because they are in denial. They say that optimists' "rose colored glasses" blind them to reality. (Hence the derogatory term *cock-eyed optimist*.) But the truth is that genuine optimists are pretty clear-sighted and practical.

Faced with a visit to traffic court or a tax audit or a job layoff, an optimist won't jump up and down and shout, "Hooray, a stressor!" Nor will he ignore the matter at hand and pretend that everything is fine. What he will do is meet his stressful challenges head-on. Optimists will …

- Mobilize their inner resources, understanding that now is the time to summon up extra energy and to draw upon their accrued life wisdom.

- Leverage their good relationships and seek the guidance of trusted others, staying open to ideas of those who can offer specialized knowledge and experience, or solid emotional support.

- Imagine numerous alternative outcomes to the situation at hand—coming up with a Plan A, Plan B, Plan C, and so forth.

- Remain flexible and creative, reasoning that if one plan does not work, another just might.

There are also a number of things optimists won't do. Or at least not very often. For one thing, they won't react impulsively. An optimistic attitude buys time. Because optimists see the future as less threatening than pessimists, they are willing to let that future unfold a bit before rushing into an approach that might be less than opportune. For another thing, they won't whine. Complaining, they've learned, not only doesn't solve anything—it serves to waste energy and to dampen their spirits.

Given the fact that unfortunate things do happen in this world, it's tempting to think that pessimists are more often "right" than are optimists. But pessimists get no benefit from being right, even when they are. Even when they are correct in their predictions that things will turn out badly, they still feel worse! It turns out that saying "I told you so" does nothing to alleviate stress.

Is optimism realism? It's all a matter of perspective. And perspective is what optimism is all about.

It Works for Me

"I am a successful money manager and I describe myself as an optimist. But as my clients know, my positive attitude does not translate into risky behavior—just the opposite. I don't advise my clients to buy stocks when the market is shaky—but I do remind them that market corrections happen, that money can be made during them with a careful strategy, and that we've all been through bear markets and survived."

—Eric, 37

Becoming More Optimistic

As with the Type A or B styles discussed in Chapter 5, optimism might be, in part, the result of inborn traits. Neurologically, optimism correlates with increased activity in a brain region known as the *left prefrontal cortex*. Babies with relatively low activity in their left prefrontal cortex tend to cry when their mothers leave the room; those with more activity remain calm. By viewing brain scans, researchers can correctly predict which infants will cry.

So here's a key question: Can we learn to be optimistic even if that is not our natural default mode? In a word: Yes.

def•i•ni•tion

The prefrontal cortex is a brain region that appears to play a critical role in modulating emotions. **Left prefrontal cortex (LPFC)** activation appears to be associated with a cluster of positive attributes, including reduced levels of the stress hormone cortisol.

There is evidence that programs that teach the skills inherent in optimism are very effective. So are therapies such as cognitive-behavioral therapy that train clients to alter their explanatory style and eliminate negative behavior patterns. But even without going through formal training or therapy, there are things that all of us can do on our own to tilt our attitudes in the direction of optimism.

Give Yourself Permission

Even though pessimism might not benefit you in terms of coping with stress, the scripts that accompany it are familiar. We do like to hang on to the familiar—ironically, we imagine that doing so will prevent stress even when it will do the opposite.

Instead of clinging to past ways, remind yourself of the many stress-beating benefits of optimism. Added up, they have more to offer than mere familiarity.

Now, resolve to break out of any assigned pessimistic role. Our friends, family members, and co-workers get used to viewing us in a certain way. If you've always been a naysaying pessimist—the type who predicts negative events will go on forever—others close to you might unwittingly be counting on you to present that point of view. When you begin to change, even a little, they might try to nudge you back into your former niche. Be aware of this natural tendency and stay alert so as not to accommodate this dynamic.

If you need role models to help you reinvent yourself, seek out other optimists and spread optimism yourself. Upbeat outlooks—like many attitudes and behaviors—are contagious. When optimism has "carriers" it is bound to spread.

Stress Less

Bring your newfound optimism to work and see the difference it makes. Research shows that optimism can decrease workplace stress and make a significant difference in a team's ability to reach its goals and accomplish its mission. Leaders who use positive outlooks enhance chances of success by offering inspiration, vision, and a compelling direction. Former Secretary of State Colin Powell has called perpetual optimism "a force multiplier."

Forgive, Forget, Move On

If someone has wronged you, resist the temptation to nurse a grudge or figure out how to "get them" back. Optimists have better uses for their time than ill will and revenge, both of which increase stress.

If something bad occurred in the past, acknowledge that reality. Be alert to the life lessons you received. Ask "What have I learned from the past that can help me now?" Ask "What can I learn from this situation that will help me in the future?" Then move on. For optimists, every start is a fresh start, a less stressful prospect than if you bring along all your burdensome baggage.

Control Yourself

In every situation, no matter how stressful and overwhelming, look for some element over which can exert influence. There is always something, because even though you might not be able to control events, you can control your reaction to events.

Avoid passive optimism. An "everything-will-be-all-right" attitude is not enough to counter stress in the long run. Stay well informed. If risk and danger lurk ahead, don't bury your head in the sand. Knowledge is power, and a sense of empowerment fuels a calm, focused attitude.

Be dynamic and proactive as you cope with pressure. Be alert to possibilities and act on promising opportunities. That way you can, in effect, make your own luck.

Onward, with Optimism

Stress-beating optimism, as you can see, is anything but a narrow concept. It is a skill set that can counter stress by mobilizing self-awareness, confidence, creativity, adaptability, resiliency, and initiative.

Finally, optimism, like pessimism, or any *-ism*, is not made up of a fixed point, but a spectrum. Even a resolute pessimist can become a little less pessimistic, which is moving toward the direction of optimism. No one can flip a switch and move from one mode to another overnight, but if you learn to be a little more optimistic, additional optimism will follow, and your stress will lessen accordingly.

The Least You Need to Know

- Optimism offers many stress-beating rewards, including better decision-making skills, more satisfying relationships, and lessened vulnerability to illness.

- Optimists lessen stress by viewing negative events as temporary and limited in scope—and by taking ownership of aspects of events that they can control.

- Optimists make a choice to find and focus on positive aspects of situations that are stressful or generally negative.

- Resilience is a trait of optimists—after stressful events they bounce back relatively quickly, sometimes with a more positive attitude than ever.

- Optimists do not pretend problems don't exist; they meet challenges head-on—summoning their strengths for the occasion.

- An optimistic attitude, although probably inborn to some degree, can be enhanced by actively working on altering one's perspective.

Chapter 7

Stress-Busting Laughter

In This Chapter

- Why we're programmed for laughter
- How laughter eases social stress
- How laughter counters emotional stress
- The connection between laughter and well-being
- Putting more laughs in your life

We know that stress is an adaptive response—one that evolved to benefit our species. But there is another adaptive response that can help battle the deleterious effects of stress. You might not have thought of laughter in this light before, but get ready to learn a lot about how laughing can ease tension in many stressful situations.

The Evolution of Laughter

Imagine you're an alien who has just dropped in from another solar system. You are observing two earth inhabitants—known as humans—speaking to one another. All of a sudden they throw back their heads, open their mouths wide, and make a series of hooting, whooping sounds. As the sounds grow louder, they bend over and slap their knees. Their eyes begin to tear. Finally, they pant, sigh, and resume their regular conversation.

What's with these strange beings and this odd behavior? Does it signify that they're insane?

You couldn't be expected to know this, being an alien and all, but in fact laughing is anything but pathological; it's just the opposite. Laughter can have a lot to do with staying sane, happy, healthy, and—above all—calm.

Although some primates exhibit grins and what are known as *play faces*, full-fledged laughter—also known as *social play vocalization*—probably evolved as our early ancestors clambered down from the treetops in search of new viable environments in which to dwell.

def•i•ni•tion

The primate facial expression known as a **play face** is a relaxed, open-mouthed display. Accompanied by panting noises, it signals a primate's availability for friendly social interaction.

Social play vocalization refers to the uniquely human *ha-ha* sound that we instinctively use to get and hold a listener's attention and offer incentive to go on interacting.

At this important evolutionary juncture, laughter served several critical purposes:

- It signaled to others that the environment was a safe one.
- It let others know that it was an appropriate time to relax.
- It facilitated social bonding among group members, and enabled such bonding across distances.
- It enhanced the trust and cooperation necessary to take risks as a group.
- It eased any sense of isolation or loneliness.

All in all, laughter relieved social and emotional tension and ameliorated stress. It helped humans deal with life's minor frustrations and major terrors. It still does.

Today, we still laugh just as raucously as our forebears. And laughter still helps us in honing our life management skills. To laugh is to counter anxious feelings with pleasurable ones, and to indicate to ourselves and others that everything is okay.

The Laughter Bond

One kind of stress that laughter is very likely to relieve is social stress—the kind that results from the awkwardness we sometimes feel around others when we're not quite sure what to say or how they will respond to us. Laughter seems well designed for this purpose, for laughter is something we are more likely to do with others than we are to do alone.

Laughter wordlessly greases the wheels of communication. It creates a kind of wordless conversation. In doing all this, it bonds us to one another.

If you have ever seen—or been—a parent eliciting a laugh from a baby, you know what a powerful elixir a baby's joyful giggling can be. If you've ever gone on a date or otherwise looked for a mate, you know how laughter can be a powerful flirtation lubricant.

Laughter. It makes pleasant exchanges more pleasant; it also makes less pleasant ones much more tolerable. If you've ever been at a tense business meeting where the mood is changed by a sudden witty remark that cracks everyone up, you know how laughter can suddenly make everyone more amenable to making progress. If you've ever watched a lawyer make a stoic jury laugh, you might well have the sense that the case has just been decided.

> **It Works for Me**
>
> "When I answer personal dating ads I always look for those women who say they want a guy with a sense if humor. I know that someone who values laughter is someone I can relax and have a good time with. And when I do make my companion laugh, I feel flattered by the response."
>
> —Kevin, 27

Too Tense

There are a few instances when laughter is an inappropriate response. It won't ease stress if it is at someone else's expense, nor if it's inconsistent with other emotions being expressed.

We're far less likely to feel separate from and different than someone else when we share a laugh with them. Laughing at the same time at the same concept says our brains are working on similar wavelengths.

But laughter is far more than a joint intellectual exercise. It's a social safety valve. In his book *Jokes and Their Relation to the Unconscious*, Sigmund Freud describes laughter as the body's way of safely releasing not only anxiety, but aggression, fear, and anger. It's virtually impossible to feel frightened of someone or mad at him when you are laughing simultaneously. Even when the laughter subsides, you have the feeling "Hey, that person's not so bad after all!"

When someone is making us nervous or self-conscious—or if we feel we are making *them* nervous or self-conscious—we often instinctively try to make them laugh in order to disarm them. Sure, we could invoke a fight or a flight, but going for humor is a far less risky strategy. If we succeed, a rush of relief pervades our mind, and our entire body posture relaxes. We no longer feel threatened, nor are we perceived as threatening; on the contrary, we've got the other fellow in the proverbial palm of our hand.

A reciprocal laugh serves as a powerful and pleasurable reward to the person who initiated humor. Now that person will feel encouraged to go on, and chances are that even more laughter and goodwill ensue. Oddly, even if after a while no one is quite sure what's so funny anymore, laughter might continue. Even bystanders who might have even missed out on the initial funny stuff might well join in. This is because laughter can be, quite literally, contagious.

Laughter can spread among people at an astonishing speed. It's hard to be somber when someone near to you is chuckling, cackling, or hooting in the throes of hilarity. In fact, sometimes despite your most sincere intent to remain straight-faced and serious, you find yourself embarking on a laughing jag. This is not only a social high point but a physical rush.

The breath released during a hearty laugh has been clocked at speeds as fast as 170 miles per hour. As it erupts, laughter stimulates the brain—where it releases opiate-like chemicals—the nervous system, the respiratory system, the hormonal system, and the muscular system. What a pleasure it is to experience such sensations in unison with others. Dare I say, it might even rival a simultaneous orgasm.

Stress Less

Because shared laughter is so uplifting, so infectious, and at once so comforting and energizing, it has even been put into use in some religious services. In some Pentecostal revival meetings, ministers deliberately induce gales of contagious laughter in congregants, likening it to "new wine." Such approaches are even spreading to congregations that have traditionally been somewhat reserved. Even Anglican clergy members have been known to hold "laughing revivals" where the focus is on "holy laughter."

Laughter and Emotional Stress

It's one thing for laughter to guard us against social stress. But can it do the same for personal emotional stress? The answer is an unqualified yes. Laughter can help us tolerate the stress of day-to-day hassles with greater equanimity. Moreover, research shows it can actually help us recover from the extreme stress that can accompany life-changing losses.

"I Don't Know Whether to Laugh or Cry"

You know what it's like when you have "one of those days." It seems as if everything you do backfires. You are thwarted at every turn—by circumstances, by other people (how dare they!), and by sheer dumb luck. It seems like every time you take a step forward, you must then take several steps back—and, as you do so, you trip over your own feet.

It's not uncommon to respond to this kind of frustrating dynamic by exclaiming, "I don't know whether to laugh or cry." In fact, we usually do neither. We grind our teeth, clench and unclench our fists, tap-tap-tap our fingers—all the while awash in stress hormones that alert us to take action when in fact we're stuck in the grips of delays, detours, and assorted other infuriating, immobilizing inconveniences.

But suppose we did find amusement in everyday absurdities? You can already guess the answer to what would happen, I'll bet. We would relax! We would have a new cognitive interpretation of events, a new emotional perspective, and a bodily response that feels like we've just had a mini massage.

In every instance of day-to-day frustration, there comes a moment when we can make a choice as to how we react.

Here, for example, are some situations that might sound all too familiar. But try looking at them with a deliberate aim to find the humorous slant:

- The wrong line, the wrong time. You've picked a queue to wait in at the bank (or the grocery store, or the movie theatre …) based on your careful assessment of which line was moving the fastest. But guess what! Your line is going nowhere, while the people in the line beside you are merrily zipping along.

- The long and winding road. As always, you chose as your route home the one that promised the greatest speed and efficiency. Well, wouldn't you know it? Your road home has a new detour due to road construction (or an accident, or a nasty pothole that just caved in …). You have to go miles out of your way—along with a throng of other vehicles—through now-crowded backroads unsuited for hordes of traffic. For good measure, you're trapped behind a truck with an exhaust pipe that never should have passed inspection.

- On hold—and don't hold your breath. You have something to clear up with your credit card company (or insurance carrier, or long distance service provider …), so you dial their toll-free number and respond to the commands of an electronic voice. But no matter how many times you key in your account number and choose what seem like the right selections from the voice mail menu, you cannot get hold of an actual human being who can help you resolve your problem.

How can you possibly find humor in such situations? Imagine this: Your frustrating scenario has, after some length of time, drawn to a close. Now you're at a party telling the story in a way that will elicit laughs from a group of people. You know there is a certain manner in which you can recount your tale of woe that will have everyone in stitches. It will be pretty easy to get them to see the lighter side of your mishaps because, after all, they too have "been there and done that."

Well, don't wait for a party in order to spin your tale. At the very moment when you simply want to *scream*, tell yourself the story instead. See yourself as what you are: an everyman attempting to cope in the modern world, with limited success. Know that your troubles are shared by many, and laugh.

If you're alone—perhaps in your car or at home dialing the phone—there's no need to feel self-conscious. Let it out! If you're in public—perhaps standing in that crowded line—and feel that bursting into laughter might draw attention of the unwelcome sort,

that's understandable. Try making a witty remark about your shared plight to the person ahead of you, behind you, or beside you. Then you can have the added pleasure of making someone else laugh as well. Now, feel your stress level dissipate.

Laughter provides a sense of control over the stress that goes along with facing frustration—control not over the situation itself, but over your mood. It helps you sustain an upbeat frame of mind, and so goes hand in hand with cultivating optimism. A good laugh also boosts your energy level enough so that you can "keep on keeping on," even on the most exasperating days.

Too Tense

It's easier to laugh at potentially stressful hassles if you don't personalize them. Stuck on the subway—or in some such circumstance? Objectify the situation, and add a healthy dose of humor, by imagining it as a scene in a Woody Allen or Adam Sandler movie. You're the director this time—so play out some funny possibilities in your mind.

Laughter After Loss

What about laughter in the wake of a serious loss—for example, the death of a spouse? Obviously, a period of sadness or anger after such a trauma is considered normal. However, some people are more able than others to laugh—at times—in spite of their sorrow.

A researcher at University of California at Berkeley, Dacher Keltner, Ph.D., studied people who had little reason to laugh: people whose spouses had died six months before. He interviewed widows and widowers and noted which ones preserved the ability to laugh just weeks after their loved one's passing. He found that those who had done so displayed more positive emotions and showed less stress two to four years later.

Apparently, humor can mitigate even the sadness of a tragedy. This is not to say that tragedy itself is a laughing matter—rather that negative emotions and positive ones need not be mutually exclusive. Laughter can be a balm in even the most dire circumstances, girding us against the ills of prolonged stress.

Laughing Your Way to Wellness

The more laughs we have in our life, the better able we will be to handle whatever comes our way. In part, that's because laughter seems to boost our defenses against debilitating illnesses, which are themselves quite stressful. Whoever said laughter is the best medicine wasn't joking.

For a long time, anecdotal evidence seemed to indicate that laughter might cure everything from the common cold to allergy symptoms to much more severe illnesses. In 1979, *Saturday Review* editor Norman Cousins, stricken with a life-threatening collagen disease, attributed his cure, in part, to a daily dose of Marx Brothers movies that alleviated stress by keeping him thoroughly entertained. His best-selling book, *Anatomy of An Illness*, was a catalyst for a good deal of scientific investigation in the healing power of humor.

Although it's always somewhat difficult to pinpoint exactly what factors contribute to the healing process, evidence is indeed mounting that suggests laughter can play a significant role.

Turning Down the Stress Hormone Spigot

In order to test the laughter-health connection, Dr. Lee Berk of Loma Linda University in California recruited ten volunteers and drew three samples of their blood before they watched a one-hour comedy video. He then took another sample every ten minutes during the video and three more afterward. Laughter, he found, indeed appeared to turn down the spigot on the stress hormone cortisol in significant measure.

In a follow-up study, two groups of cardiac patients were tracked for a year after a heart attack. One group was asked to watch 30 minutes of comedy a day as a complement to medical therapy; the other group received medical therapy alone. At the end of the year, the humor-watching group had lower stress hormone levels, not to mention lower blood pressure, fewer episodes of arrhythmia (an irregularity in the normal rhythm of the heartbeat), and fewer repeat heart attacks.

Additional studies indicated a general decrease in other stress hormones that constrict blood vessels and suppress immune activity. One of these, dopamine, is involved in the fight-or-flight response and is associated with elevated blood pressure.

At first these findings might seem a bit paradoxical. Being caught in the grips of laughter doesn't exactly feel like it is putting the body into a less revved-up state. Laughing is a very stimulating activity (and a mild form of cardiac exercise). What many researchers now believe is that the physiological response produced by mirthful laughter is the opposite of what is seen in classical stress. Laughter, they say, is a eustress state—a state that produces healthy reactions.

Boost Immunity

More good news: the effects of laughter do more than simply lessen stress hormones. They increase immune-enhancing, disease-fighting substances in the body. After exposure to humor, there is a general increase in activity within the immune system, including the following:

> **Stress Less** _____
>
> Feeling some pain? Expose yourself to something that makes you chuckle, giggle, or guffaw. Laughter triggers the release of endorphins, the body's natural painkillers. Experts believe that laughter, used as an adjunct to conventional medical care, can lessen pain. At the very least, laughter offers a powerful distraction from pain.

- An increase in the antibody IgA (immunoglobulin A), which fights upper respiratory tract infections) and in IgB (the immunoglobulin produced in the greatest quantity in body)

- An increase in the number and activity level of natural killer cells that attack virally infected cells and some types of cancer cells

- An increase in activated T cells (T lymphocytes)

- An increase in gamma interferon, which signals various components of the immune system to "turn on"

- An increase in Complement 3, which helps antibodies to pierce dysfunctional or infected cells

Some additional good news is that positive effects on the immune system are not only present when we engage in laughter. The residual effect of laughter keeps levels of disease-fighting agents heightened the following day. Laughter might be fleeting, yet its effects are anything but.

Relaxing the Muscles

Another aspect of laughter's stress-busting power has to do with its ability to relax tense muscles. The action takes place in two stages. A hearty burst of belly laughter causes the muscles that do *not* participate in the act of laughter to relax. After we finish laughing, those muscles that *were* involved in the laughter begin to relax.

This tension-busting two-fer packs a double punch. Relaxing the muscles helps the body feel better. Beyond that, when the body feels more relaxed, the mind follows suit. Remember, what happens to the body resonates in the mind, and vice versa.

Sharpening the Mind

In addition to relaxing us, laughing can keep our mental agility strong. Although the physical mechanisms that enable laughter reside in the most ancient area of our brain, laughter also involves the cortex, which modulates our emotional responses.

Brain scans conducted while experiment subjects are listening to jokes show activation of the parts of the brain that are involved in reward-related behaviors. The funnier the joke—and the more unpredictable the humor—the more the reward circuitry fires.

Laughter is nothing less than healthy brain exercise. It helps our brains stay limber, and a limber brain is well prepared to deal with unexpected stimuli in creative ways that keep stress at bay.

> ### It Works for Me
>
> "The Bible says—in Proverbs 17:22—'A merry heart doeth good like a medicine.' I try to remember that when I'm feeling like I'm coming down with something. It helps!"
> —Jennifer, 36

Getting on the Laugh Track

Are we all created equal when it comes to our ability to laugh? Like most behaviors, underlying genetic factors influence how much and how long we laugh. Animal researchers can actually determine which rats are more playful and receptive to tickling, and in doing so actually breed for these traits. In our species, it's been noted that those with extroverted temperaments tend to do more laughing than those with introverted temperaments. But innate temperamental differences aside, all of us can actively strive to add more laughter to our lives.

In some settings, people are banding together with the express purpose of laughing more. Some nursing homes help their charges cope with tension with organized "laughter clubs." Some corporations have formalized "laughternoon" breaks, where employees gather to blow off steam and ease workplace stress. If you like, you can even study a technique called laughter yoga. Originated by Indian physician Dr. Madan Kataria, it combines self-induced laughter, yoga exercises, yoga breathing, and stretching. (Even though this kind of laughter is pre-meditated, Kataria says it offers the same rewards as the spontaneous kind.)

Of course, there's a lot to be said for spontaneous laughter. To up your quotient, try the following:

Stress Less

Want to be a laughing pro? Psychologist and motivational speaker Steve Wilson has launched a therapeutic laughter group website (worldlaughter-tour.com), offering training for what he calls Certified Laughter Leaders. These leaders establish clubs in hospitals and other venues to bring people together and get them laughing.

Too Tense

Keep your laughter good-hearted. One type of humor that is not apt to ease stress is sardonic humor—humor that is scornful and contemptuous of others. Sardonic humor is bitter, and in fact takes its name from an herb that, when eaten, allegedly paralyzes one's face in a grimace.

- Be on a laugh lookout. Because our expectations of any situation contribute to its outcome, simply being prepared to laugh and have a good time more or less guarantees that you're more likely to do so than not.

- Hang out with lighthearted people. Because laughter spreads like wildfire, and because funny people are fun, seek out the companionship of those folks you know are also ready, willing, and able to laugh—and to make you laugh. As much as possible, limit prolonged exposure to fussbudgets, grouches, complainers, and curmudgeons. At holiday time—a potential stress-fest—steer clear of Scrooges.

- Socialize in large groups. Studies show that an enlargement in group size facilitates laughter. You're more likely to "catch" some laughter in a big group, just as you're more likely to catch the flu in a big group—but, hey, let's not think about that last part (especially because laughter has such a salutary effect on immunity).

- Reminisce. Get together with old classmates, co-workers, neighbors, or even people you met on a pleasant vacation. Reunions tend to generate lots of laughter. The context of these occasions is such that everyone has a humorous memory—and perhaps even some laugh-inducing photos—to share.

- ◆ Keep funny materials around. Whether *Monty Python*, the *Daily Show*, or *Dumb and Dumber* is your thing, start compiling a video or DVD library that you can always turn to for a surefire belly laugh. Keep humorous written materials (collections of cartoons, Dave Barry essays, copies of *The Onion*) around the house, especially in spots where you can dip into them quickly and conveniently—such as on the coffee table, the bedside table, or in the bathroom. Having laugh-inducing materials readily available can be a powerful stress-beating pick-me-up.

If all else fails, fake it until you make it. Simply starting to laugh, even if there's nothing in particular to laugh at, can bring you to a point where you're laughing for real—perhaps because the idea of laughing about nothing is, well, just so funny.

Your Daily Laugh Log

One good way to make sure you're on the right track is to keep count of how many times you're laughing and make a concerted effort to raise the bar.

To that end, use this chart—or use your own daily pocket calendar—to make a note of each time you laugh out loud:

My Laugh Log

Monday	_____
Tuesday	_____
Wednesday	_____
Thursday	_____
Friday	_____
Saturday	_____
Sunday	_____

How many laughs a day should we ideally have to counter stress? Some who have pondered the topic suggest 20, but there's really no magic number. Suffice it to say that more is better, and that you can't have too many.

The Least You Need to Know

- Laughter evolved, in part, as an adaptive behavior that helps us signal to one another when the environment is a safe one in which to relax.

- Laughter bonds us to one another and dissipates anxiety, anger, and aggression in social settings.

- Daily frustrations, and even serious setbacks and losses, can be eased by our ability to keep laughing.

- Laughter counters the health-threatening aspects of stress by limiting stress hormones, boosting immunity, easing muscle tension, and keeping our minds agile.

- Whether or not you're innately prone to laughter, you can devise a stress-beating strategy to put more laughter in your life.

Chapter 8

Meditation and Visualization

In This Chapter

- ◆ Meditation and the brain
- ◆ Meditation for well-being and stress relief
- ◆ Overcoming objections to meditating
- ◆ How to begin meditating
- ◆ Visualization and guided imagery

Meditation—the practice of stilling the mind and resting one's attention on a sole point of focus, such as the breath or the repetition of one sound or word—has been around for thousands of years. Nearly every culture has devised some form of meditation. For a long time, such contemplative practice was considered the realm of mystics, but in recent decades the public, and Western scientists, have become intrigued with meditation and its benefits—especially that of stress reduction.

To many of us, meditation might seem like a mysterious practice, or else a deceptively simple one that turns out to be much harder to get a handle on than we'd imagined. But, as this chapter will show, meditation—and its resulting sense of calm—is something that almost anyone can integrate into his or her life. For anyone seriously interested in managing stress, it is certainly worth a try. Meditation might potentially offer mystical insights—but it is also a deeply pragmatic solution to modern stress overload.

Ancient Solution, New Validation

When the word *meditation* comes up, we tend to think of a mental discipline that hailed from exotic locations such as India or Tibet. Many meditative practices did originate in the faraway realm of the Himalayas, but they have also come to us from the deserts of the Middle East, the medieval monasteries of Europe, Japan and China, and Native American traditions. For as long as humans have been aware of and curious about consciousness, we have—via slightly different paths, but with similar goals— been exploring the profound impact of quieting the mind.

In the 1970s, many Westerners were first exposed to the concept of meditation— often in the form of media images like that of the blissed-out Beatles sitting at the feet of a perpetually smiling, long-haired, robed *guru*. Lots of people were trying meditation, and many more were at least beginning to get curious about it.

Researchers interested in mind-body interactions became intrigued with meditation's potential ability to create physical well-being—for example, by lowering blood pressure—and to simultaneously create an internal sense of peace. In 1975, in a very popular book titled *The Relaxation Response*, Dr. Herbert Benson of Harvard Medical School documented the therapeutic benefits of a simple form of meditation—*mantra meditation*—in treating patients with heart conditions, chronic pain, insomnia, and many other stress-related physical ailments. The book emphasized the fact that even without its metaphysical element, and without practitioners needing to be taught by a guru, meditation had enormous healing and stress-alleviating potential.

def•i•ni•tion

Mantra meditation takes as its point of focus the repetition of a single simple sound (such as "Om") or word (such as "peace.")

The term **guru,** from the Hindu language, refers to a spiritual leader, teacher, or counselor.

By the late 1980s, with research technology having made great leaps, neuroscientists began to study meditators by taking detailed pictures (and later videos) of brain activity. With the new brain-imaging techniques at their disposal, scientists were able to gather a wealth of hard data concerning the effects of meditation on the body.

Leading the charge was Richard Davidson, director of Affective Neuroscience at the University of Wisconsin at Madison. What Davidson and his colleagues discovered, using functional MRIs (magnetic resonance imaging) and EEGs (electroencephalographs) was that meditators could regulate their brain activity, yielding more focus and composure.

Moreover—and here's the really extraordinary part—researchers found that a regular practice of meditation could, over time, actually alter the brain. This *neuroplasticity* became a focus of the studies. Although anecdotal evidence accrued over thousands of years had been pointing to the fact that meditation could, literally, change one's mind, there was now scientific evidence that it did so by actually affecting neural circuitry.

def•i•ni•tion

Neuroplasticity refers to the concept that the brain is "plastic" or malleable, and that it can be reshaped by inner as well as outer events. It signifies that the brain grows and changes depending how it is used.

The Monk—and the Ordinary Man—in the Lab

Some of the subjects studied in experiments involving meditation and brain imaging were Buddhist monks, whom researchers have called "the Olympic athletes of meditation." Because scientists wanted to know about the upper limits of brain plasticity, they looked at monks who had undertaken tens of thousands of hours of meditative practice.

These subjects consistently showed identifiably intense activity—some of the highest ever recorded—in the area of the brain that is associated with the generation of positive emotional states. (As an anecdotal aside, researchers also noted that when the monks emerged from grueling three-hour MRIs, they were beaming with joy—an atypical outcome after such a stressful procedure.)

But wait, I know what you're thinking! You're no monk, and you're hardly going to be willing or able to devote tens of thousands of hours to meditation—even if doing so meant you could sprout wings and fly around the room. So what about the effects of meditation on ordinary people?

Scientists wanted to know the same thing, so Davidson and colleague Jon Kabat-Zinn collaborated on a study of workers in a high-tech company who took a two-month meditation training program. The resulting imaging also showed substantial brain activity alterations, accompanied by beneficial changes to immune system functioning and a decline in anxiety. This strongly suggested that even those whose meditation experience was of limited duration could positively impact their health and their outlook, and diminish their stress, via regular—but not Herculean—meditation practice.

MBSR: Mindfulness-Based Stress Reduction

Jon Kabat-Zinn, founder of the Center for Mindfulness in Medicine, Health Care, and Society at the University of Massachusetts Medical School, had in fact already been working for many years with a technique call Mindfulness-Based Stress Reduction (MBSR). The program he formulated—based on a Buddhist meditation practice designed to enhance present-moment awareness by training one's attention on the breath or other simple activity—has itself yielded a vast amount of data.

For more than 20 years, MBSR has been shown to help patients diagnosed with a wide range of medical and emotional conditions from high blood pressure to psoriasis to panic attacks and anxiety disorders.

Too Tense

Meditation is not a substitute for traditional medical treatment, but as evidence from meditation research continues to mount, many doctors agree that it can be a beneficial complement to it.

Moreover, in the absence of any particular diagnosis, MBSR programs (in which people generally meditate for two relatively brief periods a day) have been shown to increase ordinary people's sense of well-being. An eight-week program of study will typically induce an increased sense of hardiness, a heightened sense of mental attentiveness, and an ability to function with efficacy in highly stressful situations. In follow-up studies, these emotional gains have been shown to be maintained three years after the initial meditation training.

Can Anyone Do It? Can I?

Can anyone benefit from meditation? More importantly, can anyone meditate?

The answer to the first question is easy: yes. Engaging in some form of meditative practice can certainly be a significant stress reducer—and overall mood and outlook enhancer—for anyone who practices on a regular basis. The answer to the second question is also easy, in theory. Yes, anyone can meditate—even you. The real question is, will you?

If you're one of those people who simply cannot imagine yourself sitting quietly and trying to focus your awareness on, well, not much of anything concrete, you're not alone. And no, it doesn't make you a bad person or an incurable Type A personality. It actually makes you pretty typical.

The truth is that there are a lot of perfectly understandable reasons why people shy away from meditation. Here are some, along with some reasons to reconsider your resistance.

"It's Not Part of My Religion"

Some people believe that meditating might represent a kind of spiritual detour from their chosen faith. But first, it is entirely possible to approach meditation as a strictly secular discipline. You do not need to be tied to any particular spiritual tradition to accrue the benefits of meditation.

Second, you might just be surprised to learn that your spiritual tradition does indeed have a contemplative, meditative component to it. We tend to think of meditation as being an aspect of Buddhism and Hinduism. Yet there is a long tradition of Christian meditation that incorporates various forms of chanting and centering prayer. Within Islam, there is a tradition of Sufism meditation, the goal of which is self-discovery and a deeper knowledge of the divine. Judaism also has a meditative component. Writings on the techniques of mysticism and meditation in Judaism were prevalent in the thirteenth century, and many people of the Jewish faith are quite interested in exploring this path today.

"I Just Can't Sit Still"

We are a very busy people, often trying to accomplish not just one task after another, but many tasks at one time. This only exacerbates our stress, but it has become such an ingrained habit that it is hard to see how to alter it.

But, other than habitual frenzy, there really is no reason that you can't sit still (no, you don't have to sit in any fancy yogic posture, either). The only way to be still is to do it. Just sit. It might well prove a challenge at first, but just keep reminding yourself that relieving chronic stress is going to involve some initial challenges. And after a while, as a new habit sets in, you will find a great reservoir of mental and emotional strength in your stillness.

"I'll Feel Silly"

Okay, then feel silly. That's hardly the worst feeling in the world—not bad at all, compared to the feeling of being totally strung out on stress hormones.

Besides, if it makes you feel less silly, remember that increasing numbers of physicians and neuroscientists—not generally thought of as silly types—heartily endorse the practice of meditation. Your meditation practice will put you in well-regarded company.

It Works for Me

"For over a year I was a 'closet' meditator. I felt self-conscious telling my friends that I had incorporated this routine into my daily life. Then friends and co-workers began remarking that I was so much calmer, so I told some of them what I had been doing. Don't you know I found that there were others doing it too?!"

—Josh, 44

"I Don't Have a Teacher"

Although many people get a lot out of working with a meditation teacher, it's not strictly necessary. There are many books and tapes available to help you master a technique that works for you. You might also be surprised to find out how many institutions, such as churches and community centers, now offer ongoing meditation classes or occasional workshops. Some hospitals offer MBSR courses as well.

Another wonderful way to expose yourself to meditation, if time and budget allow, is to journey to a spa or meditation retreat where you can immerse yourself in the experience of meditation with like-minded seekers for a weekend or a week. See Appendix C for some ideas on destinations, or visit www.retreatfinder.com.

"Meditation Is Hard"

Yes, meditation *is* hard. It's good that you are wise enough to realize it—because to many it seems deceptively easy. That latter perception can lead to being quickly frustrated as one tries to get the knack of it.

Even very experienced practitioners of meditation have days when stilling the mind is a hard—and sometimes losing—battle. The Dalai Lama himself has said as much, and this Buddhist spiritual leader has been intensively trained in meditation techniques since early childhood. But what experienced meditators know for certain, and what keeps them devoted to their practice, is that meditation offers immense rewards for those who put in the effort.

How to Meditate

So now, if you're ready to meditate, the obvious question is how to begin. As with anything, it's best to start with the basics.

There are many different schools of meditation, and each has its own array of meditation techniques. However, nearly all have in common a starting point of sitting quietly, focusing the attention on one thing, and bringing the mind back to that focus when it wanders.

Sitting Quietly

If you can't think of anywhere in your home where you can sit quietly, now is a good time to create such a space. You will find specific suggestions about setting up a small personal retreat space at home in Chapter 19, but anywhere that you can sit for a bit uninterrupted will do. Perhaps a corner of your bedroom comes to mind, or perhaps even a bathroom. During clement weather, it is also nice to consider meditating outdoors.

The main thing is to choose a meditation space where you are not too likely to be distracted by, say, a blaring TV, scampering children, or inquisitive pets. You'll also want to steer clear of areas where you'll be too tempted to engage in alternative activities. That desk where the bills are piling up, and that computer screen that tells you how many e-mails you have waiting for your reply are probably not things you want to have in your line of sight.

What to sit on is your choice. You can get a special meditation cushion, which is designed to be comfortable for extended periods of sitting. But when you're starting out you don't need to make any purchases. You can just as easily perch on a pillow, sofa cushion, folded blanket, or chair.

Although you might have seen pictures of yogis meditating in complex cross-legged postures, you don't need to worry about doing any such thing. The idea is to be comfortable so that you are not distracted by undue aches or stiffness. The one thing that is rather important is to find a seat and a posture where your spine is straight.

Too Tense

Don't be a meditation slouch. Keeping your spine relatively straight while you meditate serves two purposes: it helps to keep your energy strong and it prevents you from dozing off.

Some schools of meditation advocate keeping your eyes closed; some say you should keep them partially open, but cast downward. You can experiment with which is more comfortable for you, and which is better for your concentration. If you are wearing contact lenses, you might be more comfortable with open eyes. You might also choose open eyes if closed eyes tend to signal your body that it is time to catch forty winks.

Focusing on the Breath

Next, you will need to choose something on which to focus your attention. If your eyes are open, you can choose to gaze at an object, such as a candle or a photograph of a peaceful place, making that your focal point. But for many beginning practitioners—and experienced ones as well—the breath is the most common point of focus. It's an obvious choice because the breath is what connects you to the life-giving energy around you. Besides, breathing is something you are doing all the time, everywhere, anyhow. (You don't need to remember to pack your breath when you are traveling!)

Although we are always breathing in and breathing out, we are seldom conscious of this constant activity. During meditation, just breathe normally through the nose—no fancy sound effects or special rhythms are required—but be aware of the bodily sensations that occur as you do so.

> **Stress Less**
>
> A soothing breath meditation technique to try is breath counting. Count your breaths starting with one, and go up to the number four. Then begin again. If you lose count—as you surely will at first—simply start over.

Some practitioners "follow the breath" fully as they inhale, fill the lungs and then the diaphragm, and then breathe out, expelling the air in the opposite direction. Some find it easiest to concentrate on one particular place where they experience the sensation of the breath. For example, try focusing on the point at the top of your nose where you can feel a cool sensation as you inhale and a warm sensation when you exhale. Or try focusing your attention completely on the filling and emptying sensation in your lower abdomen.

Focusing on a Sound

Another excellent way to focus the attention is to concentrate on the repetition of a simple sound. You can say a sound out loud, or you can simply repeat it to yourself in your mind.

There is some belief that each person has a special mantra upon which they should meditate, and that this should be obtained from their meditation teacher or guru. However, this is certainly not a requirement. People have been meditating on universal mantras for quite some time.

One mantra sound you might want to experiment with is the sound *Om*. *Om* (typically pronounced in three syllables A-OH-UM) is said to be the sound of infinite creation. Whether you choose to believe this or not, there is something very soothing about repeating this sound.

def•i•ni•tion

Om—or **AUM**—from the Sanskrit, is said, by sound and form, to be the essence of all mantras, encompassing the entire universe. "A" stands for creation; "U" stands for preservation; "M" stands for dissolution.

If you are repeating the "om" mantra aloud, try doing it so that you feel the AH sound coming from your lower abdomen, the OH sound moving up your spine, and the UM sound vibrating in your head. The flow and vibration of the sound is extremely calming, and many find it relatively easy to focus on.

Another very common mantra that practitioners often use in conjunction with breath meditation is the sound SO-HUM. This is generally translated from the Sanskrit as "I am that I am." The two syllables are also said to signify the union of all energies—light and shadow, male and female, sun and moon, and so on—and so are a perfect accompaniment to inhalation and exhalation. Try repeating—silently or aloud—the syllable SO as you breathe in, and HUM as you breathe out.

If you would rather stick with a word in your native tongue that you find calming, that is also a fine way to choose a mantra. Many people simply meditate on the word *one*, and some use *peace* or *light*.

Dealing With Wandering Thoughts

Anyone starting to try to meditate always says the same thing: "My thoughts are all over the place." Then they add, "I must be doing something wrong."

When this happens to you—and it will—there is something very important you should know. This is what is *supposed* to happen. You are not doing anything wrong. The trick is to recognize what is going on, and then refocus yourself.

Our minds are continually manufacturing thoughts, as if cranking them out on an endless assembly line. They are sometimes serious thoughts; they are sometimes frivolous thoughts. Very, very often, they are anxious thoughts about what might happen in the future, or thoughts about what might have happened in the past had things gone differently than they did. Such anticipatory or retrospective thoughts often serve as a source of stress—yet we hardly notice how often we engage in them. They are like background Musak, ever-present but not much examined.

When we meditate, or attempt to, we begin to realize how our minds are continually bombarding us with these stress-provoking messages about things that might or might not occur, or that we cannot change and do not have any sway over. It's a revelation, and also an annoyance, to realize how prevalent and persistent these thoughts are. What are we supposed to do with all these thoughts, which continue nagging at us even as we try so hard to calm the mind and pay attention to the soothing rhythms of breath or mantra?

Yet in simply noticing the thoughts, you are already doing what you are supposed to be doing. Meditation is actually the process of learning to notice how the mind habitually works and to begin to become less attached to unhelpful patterns of thought. So when you become aware of a thought crossing your would-be meditating mind, just acknowledge that thought, but try not to hold on to it or embellish it and elaborate on it. Gently bring your mind back to your meditative point of focus.

Over time, you will become more adept at refocusing your mind, and at identifying less with your anxious thoughts. You will recognize them as *merely* thoughts, not necessarily reflective of reality.

Too Tense

Don't get angry with yourself for being unable to clear your mind of thoughts during meditation. That is all part of the process. Being mad at yourself won't help you let go of stress.

This is not to say that your meditation sessions—or your life overall—will be blissfully free of stressful thoughts. We cannot restrain the mind from its manufacturing process. But, with time and patience, meditation will provide you with more and more moments when you are capable of perceiving the thoughts as clouds moving across a vast, luminous sky. They come and go—the weather of consciousness, but not consciousness itself.

The Length of Meditation

Beginning practitioners of meditation are often curious about how long they ought to meditate. The answer I have most often seen given is 15 to 20 minutes twice a day. This can actually be a very demanding length of time for a novice. In my own experience teaching meditation, I have found this instructional dogma to be a stumbling block for many. Just thinking of how one might carve 40 minutes out of a busy day is daunting. And sitting for 20 minutes at a time being bombarded with thoughts from a mind that is not used to taking a breather can, at the start, be so frustrating as to discourage continuation.

My advice is to start with a mere five minutes a day—once in the morning or once at night. Do this on a daily basis for a week, and then add a second five-minute practice period. After a few weeks you can expand your sessions to 10 minutes. Then, if you like, you can move to 15 or 20 minutes once or twice a day.

Consistency in meditation practice is more important than the length of time involved. As you begin to reap the benefits of meditation, you will probably want to add more time to your sessions. But in the beginning, try to have the intent to do some small bit of practice daily.

Even if you cannot manage five minutes, you can still do *something*. Remember, your breath travels with you everywhere. So when you find you have even a few moments to pause—when you are standing in a line, or waiting for a train, or sitting at a traffic light—take a few calming, attentive breaths. You will see what a difference it begins to make.

Visualization

Akin to meditation is the practice of visualization. Visualization involves holding an image of something firmly in your mind and making that picture your focus. As in meditation, one keeps returning to the chosen image should the mind wander.

Visualization can be a very powerful element in healing many kinds of illness, and many physicians have recommended it as a complementary aid to traditional treatment of such diseases as diabetes and even cancer. But visualization is also a potent stress reliever, and is more and more commonly used to treat stress-related conditions such as tension headaches and insomnia, and even more serious anxiety disorders such as post-traumatic stress disorder.

Generally, an effective method for visualization to alleviate stress is to envision yourself in whatever your idea is of a very calming scene. This could be a place with which you are already familiar, such as a beach or lake where you like to visit or vacation. You might also find inspiration for a visualization destination by browsing travel magazines or simply by using your imagination to think up an idyllic locale in which you can see yourself feeling totally relaxed. Here are some examples:

- A beautiful grotto beside a waterfall

- The ridge of a mountainside that has views going on forever

- A field of brilliant wildflowers, all blowing in a gentle breeze

- A rustic, private tree house

- A stained-glass cathedral

- A sailing ship skimming across a deep blue ocean

- A spaceship sailing among the stars

Customizing your visualization destination gives you total control over its every detail. It can be a delightful and serenity-inducing experience to see yourself in surroundings that you equate with bliss. After you put yourself in the scene mentally, your body will respond with physical sensations that are virtually the same that would occur if the scene were really happening. And your brain will generate the same kinds of emotions. Without the trouble of boarding a plane or getting a passport or taking a week off from work, visualization allows you to take a restorative inner journey.

If it is difficult for you to envision your ideal place of relaxation, don't worry. Many experts in stress-reduction and healing techniques offer a variety of "guided imagery" audiotapes and CDs.

Guided imagery is exactly what it sounds like. Someone—usually someone with a very soothing, resonant voice and an infectiously calm attitude—verbally walks you through a scenario during which you see yourself in peaceful surroundings. You progressively relax yourself by following his or her instructions.

Some people prefer guided imagery to crafting their own visualizations precisely because the former follows a script. They find their mind is less apt to wander if they put themselves in the hands of a capable, charismatic director. Whatever form of visualization you choose, the important thing is that you will respond physiologically in such a way as to turn down the stress response.

Stress Less

Research studies performed at the Cleveland Clinic Foundation, Columbia Presbyterian Hospital, Memorial Sloan Kettering, UC Davis Medical Center, and the Pennsylvania State College of Medicine have demonstrated the positive impact of guided imagery on patients in the very stressful situation of being hospitalized. The subjects exposed to guided imagery showed statistically significant reductions of hospital stays, diminished blood loss, and reduced need for pain medications.

The Least You Need to Know

- ◆ Science is now backing up what anecdotal evidence has long said about meditation—it can actually transform the mind so that practitioners generate more positive emotions.

- ◆ Meditation has been shown to enhance immunity, have a positive impact on many stress-related medical conditions, and counteract negative responses to the stress response.

- ◆ There are many perfectly understandable reasons to resist meditation, but it is so beneficial that those objections are worth reconsidering.

- ◆ There are many different schools of meditation and meditation techniques—but most starting points have in common sitting quietly, focusing the attention on one thing, and bringing the mind back to that focus when it wanders.

- ◆ Visualizing yourself in a peaceful setting, or listening to a script that offers guidance in such an exercise, can also be a very effective way to counter the stress response.

Personal Spirituality

In This Chapter

- The impact of spiritual beliefs on stress
- The relationship of religion and spirituality
- How prayer helps in stressful times
- Pausing from worry with sacred rituals
- Exploring spiritual writings
- Finding, or forming, a faith community

Stress affects body and mind, but it can be said to affect the spirit—the nonmaterial essence of our selves. Sometimes, when we are overcome by stress, it can feel as though our life force itself is muted.

Conversely, our stress level can be affected by our spiritual beliefs and practices. As it turns out, intangibles like faith can be a powerful bolster against daily stressors and keep us from feeling overwhelmed in highly stressful situations.

The Spiritual Correlation

For thousands of years, long before the advent of modern medicine or psychotherapy, people experienced stress—sometimes to the point where their dread, frustration, and anxiety felt like too much to bear alone. At such times, they might turn to their tribal shaman, a spiritual guide and healer, who would listen to their fears, counsel them, and prescribe various rituals to free them from the "demons" that were plaguing them. The shamans, it seems, were doing something very useful. They were invoking the power of spiritual intervention.

For a long time, modern medicine and psychology—both of which strove to distance themselves from "superstitions" of the past—might have scoffed at the notion that spiritual practice and inner faith could impact one's physical and mental state. But this is no longer the case.

Modern healers have become intrigued by the power of spiritual practices and beliefs. They see this power as potentially being part of the healing process. They find that such practices and beliefs can both insulate us from feelings of overwhelming stress and help us recover from stress's debilitating effects.

New courses at medical schools are giving doctors a glimpse into this dimension of life and its impact on health and well-being. By 2002, 86 of America's 126 medical schools had adopted courses on spirituality and health.

Stress Less

A 1997 Yankelovich study found that 99 percent of family physicians, and 94 percent of HMO professionals, agree that "personal prayer, meditation, or other spiritual and religious practices can enhance medical treatment."

Harvard Medical School's conferences on spirituality and healing have for years brought together thousands of religious scholars and medical leaders from around the world to discuss the role of spirituality in the treatment of illness, pain, and stress-related conditions. Similar courses and conferences at many prestigious medical schools—including Duke University's Center for the Study of Religion/Spirituality and health—are seeing increasing enrollment.

A growing body of research supports the healing and stress-alleviating benefits of spirituality. Numerous studies have noted a correlation between people's self-reported faith, sense of spirituality, and religious involvement with their ability to cope with stress, to resist and recover from illness, and even to live longer.

Naturally, such benefits might partly be attributable to other variables related to people with spiritual interests. For example …

- Those with a religion-oriented focus often tend to make healthy lifestyle choices, avoiding overindulgence and substance abuse.

- Churchgoers' stress relief might also stem in part from the social support they receive from fellow worshippers.

- Women, who have a higher likelihood of describing themselves as spiritual, generally outlive men anyway.

But even factoring out variables such as lifestyle choices, social ties, and gender, many of the benefits remain.

All of this leads researchers to believe that part of the stress protection that spirituality offers comes from providing people with such intangibles as a coherent view of the world, a sense of meaning and purpose in life, feelings of hope, and a sense of ultimate acceptance.

Religion and Spirituality: What's the Difference?

If you are someone with strong religious convictions and traditions, attending church, mosque, temple, or synagogue on a regular basis, you might be breathing a sigh of relief about now. Well you should, for almost certainly you are accruing some stress-reducing benefits. But what if you're a person who believes in some sort of divine force, perhaps quite strongly—yet you do not participate in organized religion *per se?*

Relax. For one thing, you are not alone.

Most Americans value and desire a spiritual element in their lives, but perhaps not in traditional religious format. Demographic research tells us the baby boom generation dropped out of organized religion in huge numbers (and 32 million remain unaffiliated today). But they, and others of later generations who followed suit, often say they did not drop out because they had lost interest in this aspect of life. Rather they were seeking an alternative way to meet what they perceived as their more individual and eclectic spiritual needs.

But there is another side to this coin. National polls show that 9 out of 10 Americans believe in God and consider their belief important in their lives. Spirituality is the fastest-growing sector of the publishing industry; millions of us are snapping up books on the theme. TV shows like Bill Moyers' *Genesis: a Living Conversation* and

Hugh Hewitt's *Searching for God in America* pull in high ratings. And national magazines, including *Newsweek*, *Time*, and the *New York Times Magazine* frequently publish feature stories on faith.

Your faith might be the faith of your father—or it might not be. Perhaps it incorporates elements of numerous religious traditions—from Zen Buddhism to Taoism to the mystical Jewish tradition of Kabbalah. Perhaps it incorporates meditation or devotional aspects of yoga. Perhaps you simply find spiritual fulfillment in activities ranging from playing (or listening to) music, reading inspirational literature, frolicking with your pets, or planting flowers and helping them grow. Or perhaps you are a seeker with no particular practice, but feeling fairly sure that life contains an element of the divine, and that there is, in some way, on some level, a soul affiliated with your body and mind.

Any and all of this can serve you in your quest to find calm and peace via *spirituality*—because any and all of it enhances your ability the ability to …

- Recognize the sacred in the ordinary.

- Acknowledge a power other than your own.

- Accept and cope with—rather than deny—your problems.

- Experience awe.

- Practice gratitude.

- Spread compassion.

So don't worry if your spirituality is not something you can easily sum up "in a nutshell." And don't worry if it doesn't have a particular name. You are spiritual if you are interested in life's meaning and your role in the universe, if you are grateful for life's blessings and in awe of its mysteries, if you have ever surrendered your suffering to a power beyond yourself, or if you feel it is your duty to help others so that their suffering might be relieved.

Now the question is, what can you do to honor your spirituality? What can you do to enhance it? You don't have to do everything discussed in this chapter. In fact, faith being what it is, you don't have to do anything, other than to have it. However, the more you put your spirituality into practice, the more peaceful your outlook should ultimately become.

def·i·ni·tion

The word **spirituality** comes from the Latin root *spiritus*, meaning *breath* and referring to the breath of life. Spirituality deals with the transcendent, intangible dimension of existence but as it does so, it aids us in the life of the body and mind.

The Peace of Prayer

Prayer—taking time to directly communicate with the divine—is one of the most ancient spiritual practices. Nearly all world religions consider a form of prayer a central facet of spiritual life.

Today, prayer is the most widespread spiritual practice in America. A recent Roper poll confirms that about 50 percent of all Americans say they pray or meditate daily—far more than the number of us who attend religious services.

How Prayer Calms

Prayer is greatly effective in relieving stress because it offers mental and emotional release in addition to a sense of connection with a benevolent and transcendent power. Each of many types of prayer can be of special help in calming and uplifting us, and helping us remain stable and balanced.

- ◆ Prayers of thanksgiving remind us how much we have to be grateful for, despite whatever problems or frustrations we might be enduring.

- ◆ Prayers of adoration reinforce our sense of wonder, awe, and delight—and in honoring creation, we ourselves become more creative.

- ◆ Prayers of confession enable us to unburden ourselves and seek divine forgiveness.

- ◆ Prayers of supplication, in which we ask for divine intervention or for alleviation of our own doubts, foster humility and patience.

Prayers can be long or short, general or specific, personal or scripted. They can be simple, like the prayers we learned in childhood, or they can be complex and esoteric.

What method of prayer you choose is not nearly as important as your intent. Approaching prayer as a sacred moment, no matter how brief, will offer far more solace and meaning than doing it merely as a rote activity to which you do not give much thought.

It Works for Me
"When I pray I feel that I am not alone. I feel connected to a force that powers all of life. But I also feel connected, on a more personal level, to the people who taught me to pray when I was growing up, and whom I still sometimes pray with today. For me, this is very calming." —Stan, 44

Centering Prayer

Recently, many people have become interested in a prayer technique known as "centering prayer." Centering prayer has a great deal in common with the meditation techniques discussed in Chapter 8. Although centering prayer is by no means new, it has been newly rediscovered by Western seekers who are looking to merge an interest in Eastern techniques with their own religious philosophy.

Centering prayer, like meditation, seems extremely simple on the surface but does take effort of concentration. If you are not used to being quiet and focusing your attention on one thing, you will need to stick with it for a while to realize its positive impact.

To engage in centering prayer …

1. Sit in a relaxed and quiet place.

2. Silently affirm your faith in the fact that there is a divine presence at the core of your being.

3. Visualize this center in a way that feels right to you, perhaps with an image of a spiritual prophet or with a symbol of divinity that has personal resonance and significance (for example, the Christian symbol of a crucifix or the Buddhist symbol of a lotus flower).

4. Choose a word such as *love* or *light* that, to you, signifies acknowledgment of your most positive and compassionate emotions.

5. Repeat the chosen word silently while focusing your warm feelings toward your "center."

6. Bring your attention back to your chosen word whenever your mind wanders.

As with meditation, it is often recommended that you engage in centering prayer twice a day for a period of 20 minutes or so. But it is certainly beneficial to begin with any amount of time that you can allocate. In addition, of course, you can engage in this practice even for a few moments whenever and wherever you find it helpful in quieting stressful thoughts.

Although centering prayer is an ancient Christian prayer form, it can certainly be adapted to suit any religious beliefs or any personal ideas about the nature of the Almighty. As with all prayer, the positive intention behind the act has the most beneficial and restorative aspect.

Prayer and Healing

For millennia, many people have believed that prayer can not only heal negative thoughts and disruptive emotions, but also heal the physical body itself. In recent decades, people in the medical profession have become very interested in exploring this phenomenon—with some intriguing results.

Many scientific studies have validated the health effects of prayer and devotion. Some researchers speculate that this is no "miracle" *per se*, but rather that prayer can positively impact bodily systems—such as the cardiovascular system—by inducing a therapeutic state of mental tranquility. It's also been suggested that perhaps those who pray experience a greater rapport with their physicians because they exude greater kindness, empathy, and general affability.

But science might never be able to answer all of the questions about prayer's potentially curative benefits. Astoundingly, some studies show that ill people who are prayed *for* experience higher rates of recovery. This happens even in double-blind studies where the recipients of prayer have no idea that they are the beneficiaries of this interceding practice.

Whatever you make of this, it is certain that engaging in prayer when you are beset with stress-related illness, or any sort of illness, cannot hurt. Who knows? It might even work when all else fails.

Restorative Rituals

Another type of spiritual practice that can add a sense of order and calm to our daily lives is weaving some form of sacred ritual into ordinary activities.

Calming rituals can encompass a broad range of small and simple—but symbolically profound—activities. For example, we can …

- Start each day by stepping outdoors and breathing deeply, acknowledging the potential of the new day.

- Begin the morning with a series of stretches that celebrate the power inherent in our bodies and that also remind us to stay flexible in attitude.

- Precede breakfast or the evening meal (or both) with words of gratitude for the abundance in our lives.

- Once a day, set a fresh flower on our kitchen counter or dining room table and pause to appreciate its fragrance and beauty.

- Segue from work time to home and family time by playing an inspirational piece of devotional music—perhaps in the car on the way home.

- Transition to bedtime by turning off the lights in the bedroom, lighting a candle, and allowing our idea of a divine presence to infuse us with a sense of peace.

- End each day by noting in a journal the positive things that enrich our lives.

Rituals enable us to pause, however briefly, throughout the day. They offer a respite from the ongoing stream of thoughts, feelings, and worries that continually flow through our brains and resonate in our bodies. Rituals anchor us in the present moment, renew us, and restore freshness to our perspective.

Engaging Explorations

If you are unsure of what spiritual direction might hold meaning and appeal for you, exploring various spiritual perspectives through reading can be both an intellectually stimulating and emotionally calming pursuit.

You might choose to begin with the Torah, the New Testament, the Koran, the Hindu Bhagavad Gita, or any book that is a centerpiece of a major world religion. Countless millions find solace in such revered and respected works and turn to them, almost reflexively, in good times, in troubling times, and in times of life transition.

Too Tense

Don't worry about starting at the beginning of any spiritual tome—especially those that might be long and dense. Many seekers allow their intuition—or perhaps divine intervention—to guide them. They allow such books to simply fall open to a particular page at random. It is amazing how often "just the right passage" for the moment seems to appear.

There is no need to limit your reading to complex traditional works. You might wish to consider books by contemporary spiritual leaders and commentators (such as the Dalai Lama, Thomas Moore, or Marianne Williamson) or anthologies of spiritual works (such as *Spiritual Literacy: Reading the Sacred in Everyday Life*).

You might also wish to consider authors such as Henry David Thoreau (*Walden*) and Annie Dillard (*Pilgrim at Tinker Creek*), who view nature as the temple of the divine. Such works might inspire you to reconnect with the outdoors and, in so doing, access a source of stress relief that far too many of us have abandoned in modern times.

Make a field trip out of your search for spiritual reading material. Browse at your local bookstore or library until you find something that speaks to you and that seems to have been put in your path at exactly the right time.

The Power of Faith Community

If you belong to a community of believers that meets regularly to practice acts of worship, pray, or meditate, their camaraderie and emotional support is also likely to be an invaluable tool to bolster your body, mind, and spirit against the negative effects of stress. So if you already have the habit of attending a church, mosque, or temple several times a month, once a week, or more, you would be well advised to nurture that habit.

It Works for Me
"I have noticed that on the Sundays when I most don't feel like going to church, that when I make myself go I actually get the most out of it. My resistance to going usually means I'm feeling blue or stressed out. The friends I worship with, and the warm communal atmosphere of our church, always seem to lighten my load." —Geena, 37

Make no mistake: the gains you will accrue from regularly exposing yourself to a spiritual setting do not come from merely walking in the door. It's not only about showing up, but also about emotional participation in a caring community. You and other spiritual devotees can …

- ◆ Raise your voices in prayer and song together.
- ◆ Ponder life's mysteries together.
- ◆ Share in the guidance of a spiritual leader.
- ◆ Learn from one another.
- ◆ Join together to help others.
- ◆ Help one another.

This last point—helping one another—is an enormous benefit in terms of maintaining your health and well-being. Spiritual communities are very much in tune with the needs of their members. They know when something is wrong. (If they are used to seeing you on a regular basis and you don't show up, they will surely reach out to you.) And when something is awry, they band together to help.

Spiritual communities will happily do everything for members from praying for them when they are burdened in any way, to showing up with pots of chicken soup and casseroles when they are under the weather. One thing is for sure: when you are part of a spiritual community, if you cannot get to it, it will come to you!

If you do not have a formal religious element in your life, you might not have ready access to a group of supportive fellow seekers. But that does not mean you cannot initiate a search for such a group. Make a list of the people around whom you feel most alive and inspired. Are any of these people interested in getting together periodically to pray or meditate, or simply to discuss matters of the spirit and share questions and ideas about life's transcendent aspects?

You will never know until you broach the subject, so go ahead. You might find a number of like-minded people who would be pleased to participate in such a forum.

Taking a Leap of Faith

What if you are someone who is "on the fence" about spirituality? Like many, you might sometimes believe, and sometimes doubt, that there is a divine force in the universe. Some days you might feel vaguely connected to such a force; some days you might feel adrift.

This is not an uncommon state of mind. But if you are willing to tilt your conscious thoughts in the direction of "pro" versus "con" when it comes to acknowledging spirit, you could well benefit in terms of alleviating some of your daily concerns and frustrations.

Back in the seventeenth century, renowned mathematician and philosopher Blaise Pascal, consumed with the question of the Almighty's existence, applied mathematical decision theory to the question. In a famous philosophical gambit that came to be called Pascal's Wager, he argued that it was always a better "bet" to believe in a divine power because a positive bet would yield more "expected value" than a negative bet.

Since Pascal's time that "expected value" has, in fact, been documented by science, even if divine existence itself has not. Because we now know that some form of spiritual belief will yield a "payoff" of potential stress reduction and enhanced well-being overall, what harm could there possibly be in taking a small leap of faith?

Acting as if your life has inherent meaning—as opposed to clinging to the idea that all is random—might just serve to help you find a sense of purpose that infuses you with new energy. Having faith that everything will work out might just help you find the inspiration and strength to make it work out after all. You will never know the effects of belief until you go ahead and place your bet.

The Least You Need to Know

- ◆ Modern medicine is embracing the ancient idea that spirituality can aid in physical and emotional healing, and research supports the idea that spirituality eases stress.

- ◆ Even those who do not practice a traditional religion or attend regular religious services might be deeply spiritual in their attitudes and perspective.

- ◆ Prayer counters stress by reminding us to be grateful, rekindling awe, helping us to unburden ourselves, and honing our humility and patience.

- ◆ If you are searching for a spiritual path, reading spiritual works is a wonderful way to explore.

- ◆ Participating in a spiritual community is itself a defense against stress—if you do not belong to one, think about forming one.

- ◆ Those who are wavering with regard to whether to embrace their spirituality might benefit from taking a leap of faith.

Chapter 10

Do Good, Feel Good

In This Chapter

- How helping others eases stress
- Enlightened altruism
- The win/win of kindness to strangers
- Why, and how, to volunteer
- Avoiding the stress of martyrdom

When we feel happy and secure, our resultant good mood makes it more likely that we will help others. In the throes of this well-documented "feel-good, do-good" effect, we'll be more likely to pitch in and help a stranger in need or donate time and resources to worthy causes.

But we know now that the revere is true as well.

It's not just that when we feel good we do good; it's also the case that we feel good *when* we do good. In fact, our own selfless, helpful feelings and actions actually create a buffer against stress.

Feel Good Feedback

Remember Ebenezer Scrooge? In the classic tale *A Christmas Carol*, this selfish and insensitive man represents the epitome of mean-spiritedness when the story begins. But as the tale progresses, Scrooge's outlook is completely transformed. He becomes kind, sensitive, and generous. When Scrooge reforms, everyone around him is, understandably, calmer and happier—but did you ever notice he is significantly calmer and happier as well?

In recent years, researchers in numerous disciplines—including genetics, anthropology, human development, neurology, and psychology—have been exploring the scientific underpinnings of the idea that "doing good" is indeed a good thing *for* us. Numerous studies have examined the impact of helping others on our physical and emotional well-being.

The studies have found that when we act with benevolence on behalf of other people, we get healthier (with boosted immune functioning, fewer colds and headaches, and relief from pain and insomnia). We also live longer, and feel greater comfort and less stress. Studies also indicate that helping associated with what social psychologists term pro-social behavior (what just plain folks might call kindness) benefits not only the receiver, but also—and perhaps even more so—the giver.

The Helper's High

Whoever first said "It is better to give than to receive" was a philosopher. But had he been a scientist, he might have talked about a phenomenon known as "the helper's high." This term alludes to brain and hormonal changes that take place when we do things to support others.

Driving an acquaintance to the airport? Shoveling snow for an elderly neighbor? Stopping to pick up a sheaf of papers dropped by a total stranger? If such activities make you feel good, it is at least in part because your physiology is being altered.

Using functional MRI scans, scientists have identified specific regions of the brain that are very active during the emission of deeply empathic and compassionate emotions. These are the brain regions that we ourselves associate with positive feelings.

Helpful behavior also appears to trigger the release of the brain's pleasure-linked chemicals, such as dopamine and various endorphins, into the bloodstream. The presence of these chemicals can create a sense of euphoria and a burst of youthful energy.

In addition, a recent study has identified high levels of the "bonding" hormone oxytocin in people who are very generous toward others. Oxytocin is believed to be connected to both physical and emotional well-being, and is the instigator of what has been called the "tend-and-befriend" response, as opposed to the fight-or-flight response to stress. Best known for its role in preparing mothers for motherhood, oxytocin also helps both men and women establish trusting relationships. When we're lending a helping hand, our oxytocin level goes up—and our own negative stress is reduced.

Beyond the purely physiological side of things, caring acts and empathic attitudes make us feel better about ourselves and instill us with a sense of purpose. They also connect us to something beyond ourselves. In so doing, they alleviate an excess of preoccupation with our problems—a preoccupation that can provoke anxiety. When we're busy helping others, we're not inclined to be overcome with the act of worrying about ourselves.

> **Stress Less** _____
> Do unto others and release oxytocin. In one animal study, researchers found that oxytocin in lab rats had the effect of lowering the animals' blood pressure and levels of stress hormones as well as having an overall calming effect.

Am I Altruistic?

Acts of benevolence, compassion, generosity, and kindness fall under the collective name of *altruism*. Many say that altruism is a universal phenomenon.

Some researchers believe that the attitude of altruism played a central role in the development and expansion of our human brain, because our ancestors gained advantages by helping one another to hunt and gather food and to defend against predators. Even the seemingly simple act of keeping watch while others slept upped our group survival odds considerably. Altruism likely facilitated all forms of cooperation, including sharing and communication—key forces that shaped human evolution.

Yet although the drive to be altruistic is theoretically in our nature, it's obvious that some individuals are more naturally predisposed than others to provide help and support. The individual variance might have to do with the way in which we are nurtured as we are growing up.

def•i•ni•tion _____

> **Altruism,** from the Latin *alter,* or *other,* describes actions performed in a selfless manner for the benefit of another.

Stress Less

Helping is smart. Harvard Medical School researchers who followed Harvard graduates for 40 years identified altruism as one of the major qualities that helped graduates cope with the stress of life.

def•i•ni•tion

Ordinary self-interest asks, "What can I get for myself?" **Enlightened self-interest** asks, "What can I give to someone else" in the knowledge that such an attitude helps the giver as well as the receiver.

The trait of altruism, like all personality traits, is probably rooted in the interplay of genetics and environment. Perhaps, as some preliminary research indicates, children who were raised in a very supportive environment simply learned to mirror generous behaviors as a matter of course. They imitated helping and grew up with a broader altruistic capacity.

Altruism, however, can be cultivated at any age, by anyone. We cannot change the past, but it is never too late to change how we behave in the present.

One key to becoming more altruistic, even if you believe this is not a strong innate trait of yours, is to realize that altruism is rather a paradox. Although defined as selflessness, it actually is a form of *enlightened self-interest.* When you help someone, they are helped and you are helped. For you to become more empathic and caring is the ultimate win/win situation.

Kindness to Strangers

Obviously, everyone can use a helping hand sometimes, and it's a good idea to help and support anyone in need when it's possible to do so. Often we help those in our own immediate or extended families, both for practical reasons—their well-being impacts our own—and because we feel strong ties of love. We help our friends as well, for that is an implicit part of the bargain of friendship.

But there is no reason to limit helping to those whom we know. In fact, there is a great deal to be said—not just from a moral or spiritual viewpoint, but also from a standpoint of wishing to alleviate our own stress level—for helping complete strangers.

When you have supportive one-on-one contact with a stranger, benefits manifest for both of you. That's because the act of helping a stranger serves to break down the psychological barriers we construct between "us" and "them." To help someone with whom we have no connection is in fact to acknowledge the bonds between us all. The sense that "we are all in this together," and that we all share the struggles of the human condition, can be a healing and soothing revelation.

You might be wondering *Why should I help—not everyone does!* And, of course, you are absolutely right. Would the world be a better place if everyone helped everyone else?

Certainly. But don't get hung up on what everyone else is doing. Know that your life will be a better life if you help, and proceed from there.

How, exactly, can you help a stranger? You might not know until you start looking.

- There is the traveler who needs directions.

- There is the overburdened shopper who needs a hand with her bags.

- There is someone stranded at the side of the road with a flat tire.

- There is a seven-year-old or a seventy-year-old who needs a smile and a kind word.

The issue is not so much what you do but that you begin to become aware of others and their needs. The very act of maintaining this awareness will help you attain and maintain calm. You will be more attuned to the moment and to your surroundings, and less enveloped in an internal chorus of self-preoccupied worries and woes.

Too Tense

There's nothing wrong with writing a check to charity, but doing so won't give you the "helper's high" of pitching in and making yourself personally useful. Don't just donate money; donate time and effort.

Volunteering

Remaining alert to the needs of strangers enables you to perform so-called "random acts of kindness." In addition, you can help in less random ways by taking up some volunteer activity on a regular basis.

In everyday life, countless people—even very busy ones—choose to give up free time to volunteer. This might entail anything from preparing or serving food at soup kitchens, to cleaning up public parks and beaches, to helping elderly people with errands, to being a Big Brother or Big Sister, and so on.

Not surprisingly, studies show that volunteering has many advantages for volunteers, in addition to the people and organizations they aid. One such study showed that, all other lifestyle factors being equal, women who volunteered experienced significantly fewer major illnesses than those who did not. And two large studies found that older adults who volunteered were living longer than nonvolunteers. (One found a 44-percent reduction in early death among those who volunteered a good deal—a greater effect than exercising four times a week!) In yet another study, older adults who volunteered to give massage to infants were found to have lowered stress hormones.

Stress Less

Even dwelling on feelings of empathy and being in the presence of do-gooders might make us feel better. When students were asked to watch a film of Mother Teresa's work with the poor in Calcutta, they had significant increases in protective antibodies associated with improved immunity—and antibody levels remained high for an hour afterward. Monks who meditate on compassion show increased positive emotion-related brain activity and reduced stress levels.

There is no doubt your community is rife with volunteer possibilities. In fact, there are so many, you might easily be confused as to how to go about finding an opportunity that feels right for you. Here are some ways that you can begin to sort through the options:

- Note the issues you care about and do research. If you're concerned about a certain social problem or cause, you'll often find a local nonprofit group that needs help simply by looking in your local telephone book. Or you can do an Internet search. Contact the organizations and see what kind of assistance they need. They will be glad to hear from you—count on it.

- Find a good match. Picture yourself in various volunteer situations to find what seems like a good fit. Use your talents—*maybe that's why you are fortunate enough have been given such talents in the first place*. If you're a devoted reader and writer, you could be well suited for literacy tutoring. If you're handy with a hammer, you might get lots of satisfaction out of working with Habitat for Humanity, an organization that builds houses for the underprivileged and for disaster victims.

- Join a group. Of course you can help on your own, but becoming part of a volunteer group means you will have the pleasure of meeting kindred spirits, sharing ideas, and pitching in together.

- Offer a personal touch. Most people find that volunteering is much more satisfying when they are meeting and spending time with the people they're helping. Sure it's great to collect clothes or goods for the poor, but also think about doing something where you can get feedback and build relationships.

- Make it part of your life. Yes, you can help people in special circumstances—for example, assisting those who have suffered losses during a storm or earthquake. You can also engage in seasonal help, as many do around the Christmas and Chanukah holidays. But it's also a good idea to integrate some regular volunteer activity into your weekly schedule. Make it part of your routine.

You might also wish to consider using some of your time off from work to take a volunteer vacation. The change of locale, the people you meet, and the good you do will soothe your body and rejuvenate your spirit. Many church groups organize mission trips for such purposes. Or you can contact an organization like the aforementioned Habitat for Humanity (121 Habitat Street, Americus, GA 31709-3498) or Earthwatch (P.O. Box 403 R.P., Watertown, MA 02272). Earthwatch has volunteers join scientific expeditions, with such purposes as saving endangered species all over the planet.

Do an Internet search for "volunteer vacations" and an abundance of opportunities will spring up. After you try one, you might never go back to simply taking a cruise again—or at least you might decide to vary your vacation journeys.

It Works for Me

"We have spent much of my vacation time over the past four years volunteering at an orphanage in Costa Rica. We started doing this once a year, through our church, but now we do it two or even three weeks a year. We have never felt more fulfilled than when we are on these journeys, and we always look forward to returning. People ask us how we can 'give up' our vacation time, but we don't see it that way. We are getting so much more than we are giving—and we can't think of a better way to spend our time."

—Janet, 49, and Rick, 52

Stay a Happy, Healthy Helper

Though the stress-beating effects of helping others can be profound, anything can be taken to unreasonable extremes. Whenever that dynamic sets in, our well-being might be compromised by "overdoing." If we don't pay attention to our own needs as well as the needs of others, we can experience volunteer burnout, both in body and in attitude. In such cases, our stress levels could actually rise—and, of course, that's not what we had in mind.

There's no reason to be a martyr. It is entirely possible to help others without sacrificing yourself. But you do need to follow some commonsense strategies.

The first strategy, as with any activity—especially one you are just trying on for size—is to pace yourself. Volunteering should not cut into your work or family obligations to an extent that you ignore those obligations. Nor should it seem like a wearisome chore that causes you to ignore your other needs. If you're giving up time in front of the TV eating chips to volunteer, that's probably good. If you're losing sleep or have forgotten what your spouse and children look like, that's not so good.

In addition, if you have the sense that the particular volunteer activity you have chosen to become involved in is not a good match for you, don't be afraid to change your mind and choose another instead. The activity is not suitable if …

◆ You feel unable to employ the skills needed for the position (beginner's nerves aside).

◆ You feel demoralized by the setting.

◆ You are continually made to feel guilty for not doing more.

◆ You feel you have gotten in over your head.

◆ You feel less psychologically energized rather than more so after your volunteer activities.

It's also extremely important, when doing good and helping others, to keep things in their proper perspective. It is absolutely impossible to fix everything, help everyone, or save the entire world. In fact, it is not even possible to "save" one person. We can only support them and facilitate their journey, but each of us must finally take responsibility for our own lives.

In the course of volunteering, you will doubtless run into circumstances that you are unable to control. There will be people who do not have enough care; there will be schools and neighborhoods that do not have enough resources, and on and on. That lack of control is something you will have to accept. Compassion is not about control. It is about doing what one can with the gifts one has been given.

Trying to control people or circumstances is unhelpful and—unless you have a magic wand at your disposal—ultimately impossible. Ironically, it also creates in you the very thing you are trying to undo: negative stress. You will not only take on too much, but you will be too hard on yourself and, inevitably, feel as though you are coming up a day late and a dollar short. Remember, you did not create the situation, and you should not blame yourself for it.

Too Tense

Don't bite off more than you can chew. As William Blake said, "He who would do good to others must do it in minute particulars."

Moreover, trying to orchestrate change on a grand scale can lead us to be grandiose. Although it might still seem as though we are focusing on others in need, we will be catapulting ourselves to center stage. How can we not feel stressed with the spotlight on us? And can we still be truly aware of the needs of others at that point? Having big dreams and broad goals toward which we can stretch is fine, but what will keep you grounded and centered is seeing to whom you can be of service right now in a practical way.

Remember Self-Compassion

All spiritual traditions emphasize compassion and care for others, and many such traditions have practices for contemplating and generating compassion. These might include practices of prayer, pilgrimage, fasting, or meditation—all with a focus on love and deeply affectionate wishes for others.

In the Buddhist tradition, one such practice is called *metta*—or loving kindness—meditation. In this style of meditation on compassion, one typically sits quietly, getting centered, and then begins to bring the attention to warm feelings and words of benevolent wishes. One begins, however, by directing this benevolence toward *oneself*.

So, for example, one might silently repeat the phrase "May I be happy; may I be at peace." Only then would one proceed to directing that phrase toward loved ones, respected spiritual guides and teachers, and—finally—all beings: "May all beings be happy; may all beings be at peace."

Sometimes we have difficulty with the concept of being kind to ourselves. We dwell on our shortcomings and perceived flaws. If we experience ourselves as less than perfect—and who doesn't?—we might feel unworthy of self-love. But the progression of this loving kindness meditation illustrates how integral to kindness self-compassion is. If you don't begin by caring for yourself, you will be too tired, overwhelmed, worried, and stressed out to care effectively for anyone else. Be good to yourself and be good to others if your goal is inner peace.

The Least You Need to Know

- The evidence is in: doing good makes us feel good, and we reap benefits in terms of enhanced health and lowered stress.

- Some of us are naturally more altruistic than others, but we can cultivate altruism by remembering that when we help others it helps us—it's the ultimate win/win situation.

- Acts of kindness toward strangers take our focus off of ourselves and our worries. Stay alert for opportunities to help.

- Volunteer opportunities abound—know your interests and talents, and find a good match where you can contribute with a personal touch.

- To be a healthy helper, pace yourself and don't try to change the whole world. You cannot help others if you are not compassionate toward yourself.

Part

Restoration Through Love and Work

Relationships can be challenging, yet our connections to family and friends are critical in maintaining a sense of balance and equanimity. Work, too, can be a source of stress, yet meaningful work can be the greatest of comforts. This part of the book looks at how we can restore ourselves to a calmer way of being by recognizing and cultivating the most positive aspects of love and work.

Chapter 11

Family Ties

In This Chapter

- The tend-and-befriend response to stress
- How marital relationships impact stress
- Learning to de-stress with your kids
- How pets soothe us
- Loneliness versus healthy solitude

By definition, relationships involve *relating* to someone else—someone with ideas and agendas that might not always be similar to our own. So, of course, relationships can sometimes be stressful—especially if you approach them with the object of controlling other people.

But relationships that are positive—not perfect, but generally positive— can have a wonderfully restorative effect when life's other stressors loom large. Your family might have its foibles. Like all humans, they can make mistakes and be just plain disagreeable at times. But chances are you can count on your family members to soothe and support you. This sure beats loneliness—for isolation itself is an overwhelming stressor that we should all guard against.

Tend and Befriend

Fight-or-flight is a prevalent physiological response to stress—but it is not the only one. Another is what has come to be known as the "tend-and-befriend" response, discovered and so named by a team of researchers headed by Shelley Taylor at UCLA.

Tending involves nurturing activities toward one's family. Befriending involves creating and maintaining social networks that promote safety. Taylor emphasized that a hormonal mechanism contributes to the tend-and-befriend strategy.

The hormone primarily involved is oxytocin.

Why is oxytocin secreted in stressful situations? Perhaps because of an inherent problem with fight-or-flight: sometimes neither fight nor flight is a practical solution.

We humans have often been faced with peril that threatens us and our small children—hungry wolves around the campfire, for example. But the best strategy might not be to pack everyone up and get moving. If you've ever tried to take a hurried trip with small children in tow, you are no doubt familiar with the many logistical hurdles involved. Besides, who wants to abandon the comforts of hearth and home every time a danger looms? Why not band together and send those hungry wolves on their way?

The tend-and-befriend strategy is usually mentioned in connection with females' response to stress. In fact, females do produce more oxytocin than males. In concert with estrogen, this hormone facilitates women's bonding with and breastfeeding of their infants. But males do produce some oxytocin and in them, as well as in women, the hormone facilitates monogamous pair bonding (a.k.a. "marriage"). Oxytocin appears to be a physiological building block of many types of emotional connections in both genders.

When all is said and done, the tend-and-befriend response to stress, although activated more frequently in women, is not exclusive to females. Just as women might opt for the flight-or-flight response in certain situations, so men might opt to tend and befriend.

Too Tense

Try not to be a loner. People who are unattached to others, or who suffer unstable relationships, suffer more greatly from the effects of negative stress than those with solid family ties.

Let's not forget, too, that there is a cognitive element to any response to stress. Even when our physiology is prompting us to run away or turn aggressive, as thinking human beings we can often overrule the urge. This is especially so when we are facing a stressor that is long-term and chronic, and we have time to think about our circumstances and how best to deal with them.

When you do think about the stressors in your life, you might come to realize what a valuable resource your family can be for you—and vice versa. In times of adversity you can offer each other support, pool your resources to solve problems, and simply provide one another the kind of emotional warmth and comfort that can be a powerful stress buffer and restorative emotional balm.

The Marriage Factor

Nine out of ten heterosexual adults marry. But does that mean that nine out of ten suffer less stress as a result? If only it were so simple! What counts is not the act of being married *per se*, but the quality of the relationship. Simply placing a ring on your finger won't do the trick.

Strong, supportive relationships lower overall stress levels. They help partners cope with life's frustrations, large and small. They even increase our survival odds when a health problem strikes.

On the other hand, marital relationships that are fraught with conflict and mistrust are themselves a source of negative stress. Marital stress can be quite destructive to our well-being. Chronic marital distress can diminish our sense of self-confidence, making problems tougher to deal with. On a physiological level, it can predispose us to stress-related ailments. One study linked marital *dis*tress to dangerous thickening of the heart wall, as severe as the thickening resulting from smoking.

Stress Less

Focus on—and nurture—the positive elements in your marriage. An Ohio State University College of Medicine study determined that women and men who use positive terms to describe their marriage showed drops in the stress hormone cortisol. Among those who recounted their relationship in negative terms, cortisol levels remained constant or increased.

The reason marital distress can have such a negative impact is that it is pervasive and hard to escape from. Sadly, it also takes what should be a primary source of support—the relationship—and disables it.

If your marriage is troubled, it's of course a good idea to seek help in repairing it. But even if your marriage is a good one overall, it's never a smart idea to take it for granted. The way a couple—even a loving couple—interacts always affects stress levels. So, though it might sound cliché, work at your relationship. If you do, the benefits that you and your mate will reap will be immense. Together you can create the potential to lean on one another and live calmly together for a long, long time to come.

Calming Talk

One of the best ways to keep your marriage on a positive track, and to ensure that it will keep you on a positive track, is to pay attention to the ways in which you and your partner communicate. Talking with a spouse can give us a sense of feeling supported and, on a practical level, help us find ways in which to address specific nagging problems. But that talk needs to be of a constructive nature—as opposed to a soliloquy of whining and complaining.

If you want help with a problem, be clear about what kind of help it is that you desire. Do you want ideas and advice, do you want to brainstorm, or do you just want to be listened to and reassured? All of these are valid needs—but your partner is not a mind-reader and won't know which you're seeking unless you help him or her understand.

Remember, too, that your spouse will be unable to wave a magic wand and make your problem disappear—but often just talking about a stressful issue out loud to a receptive listener will help you objectify the situation and face obstacles with a clearer head and improved attitude.

If your spouse wants help with a problem, see if you can help him to tell you what form he'd like that help to take. Don't jump in and start giving advice unless you know that's what your spouse is after. And if you do give advice, remember that there is no law that says your spouse has to take it.

Try not to be judgmental with your partner when she is looking for your support. Maybe a solution seems obvious to you, but not to her. Give her time and space to mull things over, and remember that each of us has his or her own style when it comes to dealing with adversity.

> **Too Tense**
>
> If both partners are under stress simultaneously, communication is not likely to be optimal. If you're seeking reassurance or guidance, find a time when your partner is in an emotional place where he or she is able to provide it. If you can't seem to find the right time to talk, ask your spouse when a good time might be. It's stressful to feel ambushed.

Think it's a good idea to crack a joke when your spouse is feeling overwhelmed and stressed out? Well, maybe it is. Certainly a dose of humor can have a potent anti-stressing effect. But timing is everything. You don't want your mate to feel you are being flippant about something that is troubling him or her deeply.

If you feel like you're not getting the kind of information you need in order to be helpful, don't badger. Pose some gentle, exploratory questions to see if you can elicit more information. Ask your spouse how she might feel if such-and-such happened. Ask what options she's already considered.

Another communication element to pay attention to in your marriage is how you handle conflict. Some conflict, even in the very best marriages, is only natural. No two human beings are ever completely of the same mind all of the time. Poorly handled, conflict will create more and more stress buildup. But handled appropriately, conflict can actually strengthen your mutual trust in the long run.

If an argument is inevitable, fight fair:

- Stick to the topic at hand. Don't dig up ancient history and recount every way in which you think your partner has ever slighted you. Don't predict what he might or might not do in the future. Keep your grievance specific and don't throw in "the kitchen sink."

- Speak in the first person. The kindest and most effective way to make a point about how you feel is to start your sentences with the pronoun "I". When we barrage someone with "you did this" and "you did that," she can't help but get defensive. When you begin with "I" you are reporting what's on *your* mind, rather than accusing.

- Don't make threats. Threats and ultimatums raise the stakes and quickly raise everyone's stress level. Your partner will feel insecure if she believes you are serious about taking drastic steps that will permanently undermine the relationship.

- Don't interpret. Resist the temptation to play Dr. Freud. Don't tell your partner what they're "really trying to say." You might be psychologically astute, but in an argument your insights will be perceived as undue criticism.

- Leave third parties out. Never fight in front of others. (It makes everyone feel awkward and stressed.) Never drag an outsider into an argument and ask him to take sides.

- Watch your volume and tone. Modulate your voice. Yelling will stress your partner and only serve to stoke your anger and tension. Just as important, watch your tone of voice so that it is not dismissive or sarcastic.

Too Tense

Tone of voice can have even more negative impact on a listener's equanimity than the content of what is being said. In a study in which listeners heard voices electronically garbled so that tone was audible while specific words were not, listeners could correctly predict how well two speakers got along.

Whatever your difference of opinion, even if it remains unresolved, it's important to get beyond a quarrel. What's critical is the preservation of your bond. Even if what your partner has said or done in the immediate past has hurt you, it's important to remember all the support your partner has given you over time and all the comfort you take from his or her presence in your life.

Forgive. You don't need to let your spouse off the hook for bad behavior, or invite further behavior of that kind, but you do need to let go of grudges. Forgiveness not only releases toxic emotions but also literally calms the body. Experiment subjects asked to recall an incident where someone hurt them and then mentally rehearse forgiveness showed drops in blood pressure, heart rate, and facial tension.

Calming Touch

Another powerful way in which a strong marriage can reduce stress is by providing the comfort of touch. Lovemaking itself can have a wonderfully calming effect. As many can attest, there is nothing like a satisfying intimate encounter to take the edge off a frustrating day.

In addition to sex itself, marriage offers lots of opportunities simply to get—and give— a loving, soothing touch. Holding hands, snuggling, rubbing one another's tense shoulder muscles, even simply giving each other reassuring pats on the back, can all serve as nonverbal ways of saying, "Hey, it's not so bad. I'm in your corner. You'll be okay and, together, we'll be okay."

All human beings require affectionate touch. If we do not get it as infants, we will not thrive, nor develop optimally. But the need for loving touch does not dissipate as we grow older—to the contrary. Making physical contact with your spouse, even if sex itself is not involved, is something you should make it a point to do each and every day.

Stress Less

Don't neglect to give, and get, a daily hug—especially on days when you might not feel in a love-struck mood. Hugging calms us down and releases oxytocin. The oxytocin, in turn, makes us feel even more loving. One of this hormone's effects is to defuse memory—so if you were angry with your spouse, you'll be quicker to forget why, cool off, and move on.

Parenting and Stress

That "tending" part of the tend-and-befriend strategy strongly applies to our children. When a danger—a stressor—lurks, parents' instinct is to safeguard their offspring. Inherently, this drive itself can be said to make parenting a perennially stressful business.

There is no loving parent anywhere who does not spend a certain amount of time worrying about his or her kids. From a biological standpoint we need them to survive, for the future of our gene pool is at stake. But beyond that, we want them to stay healthy and happy, to bring home good report cards, to be socially well-adjusted, to get into a college whose bumper sticker we'll be proud to affix to our SUV.

There are no stress-free ages or stages when it comes to children; however, the younger they are the more they rely on our vigilance to keep them from harm. When they first appear in our lives, the need to look out for them 24 hours a day, every day, can be especially tension provoking. The sleep deprivation, itself a stressor, doesn't help either.

But wait! Don't give up on the idea of having children—or consider farming out the children you have—in an attempt to lessen your stress. First of all, the deep emotional bond you share with your kids will, on balance, offer you enough joy and satisfaction to mitigate many of life's frustrations. After all, so long as our kids are okay, we can often manage to keep everything else in its proper perspective.

Beyond that, you can actively resolve to interact with your kids in certain ways that will actually put you in a calmer frame of mind. Young children have a way of looking at the world that is extremely uplifting. They see things with fresh insight, and they are unafraid to openly express wonder, delight, and curiosity. Playing with your kids, getting utterly absorbed in their activities from time to time, will help you see things from a refreshing perspective of wide-eyed, stress-free innocence.

Stress Less

Although it's true that when your kids are little you will have to solve many problems for them, you'd be amazed how soon they can collaborate with you in problem-solving. You'll be less stressed, and they'll grow up the better, if you encourage them to participate in discussing options and making certain decisions.

It Works for Me

"I used to feel stressed out when things in my house weren't neat and tidy. Then I had kids and I realized I had to let that go or I would be tense all the time and miss out on enjoying them. Now I not only let them make a mess— I sometimes make a mess with them. It's therapeutic."

—Ellie, 33

Finding Peace with Your Pets

As much as we value the love, comfort, and companionship that the people in our families provide, let's not overlook those other very important family members: pets.

Just about anyone who's ever shared their home and their life with a pet can attest that the company of cats, dogs, and other furry, finned, or feathered friends can be emotionally and spiritually uplifting. Research now backs up this powerful intuitive knowledge.

Petting a dog has been shown to lower blood pressure and heart rate. Bringing a pet into a nursing home or hospital can boost people's moods and enhance their social interaction. In a UCLA study, dog owners were found to require less medical care for stress-related conditions than people who were not dog owners. And in a study from City Hospital in New York, heart patients who owned pets were more likely to survive the first year after a heart procedure than those who did not own pets.

Merely being in the presence of animal life can be relaxing. In one study, dental patients awaiting oral surgery spent a few minutes before the surgery watching a tank full of tropical fish. Their stress level at the time of surgery was found to be less than those who had not watched the tropical fish, as measured by the patients' blood pressure, muscle tension, and behavior. People who watched the fish were as calm as another group who had been hypnotized.

How the Pet Connection Calms

Why is it that the presence of pets promotes good health and longer life and helps us relax? Some argue that people who like animals or are predisposed to having pets are already of a calmer bent. Could be. But even if you haven't ever felt inclined to have a pet before, you might well want to join the club when you consider these very likely reasons why doing so could ease your stress.

◆ Unconditional love and acceptance. Pets offer us exuberant affection and accept us for who we are. We don't have to worry about "impressing" them. With them, we are free of some of the thornier issues in interpersonal relationships. What we see is what we get: love.

> **Stress Less**
>
> Help your kids develop the calming effects of compassion—get them a pet. Studies report that children who live in homes in which a pet is considered a member of the family develop greater empathy.

◆ The nurture factor. Pets bring out our nurturing instinct, which itself can be a stress reducer. They induce empathy in us, and this dynamic does as much for us as it does for them.

◆ A reason for living. Our pets depend on us and give us an incentive to take good care of ourselves—we don't want to abandon them!

◆ Exercise. Certain pets keep us moving—and that's a great stress-beater.

- An outward focus. Caring for and interacting with animals can help us focus less on ourselves. Rather than thinking and talking about ourselves and our problems, we watch and talk to and about our animals. Animals also re-orient us toward the natural world, an element whose absence in our lives can be a source of stress.

- Touch. Pets give us someone to hug, and their soft nuzzles soothe us as well. Having an animal to hold and stroke can make a world of difference to anyone, and most especially to people who would otherwise have no positive physical contact.

- Communication. Most pet owners routinely talk to their pets, and many feel there is some level of understanding and reciprocation going on. Even if talking to animals is not your thing, almost everyone enjoys watching animals' playful antics and engaging body language. There is nothing like a frisky, mischievous pet to evoke a spontaneous laugh.

> **It Works for Me**
>
> "It is hard to put into words, but when I am in the affectionate company of my pets I feel that I am in some way connected with a life-sustaining force in the universe. Caring for pets means a lot of day-to-day chores, but there is also a transcendent element in the relationship."
>
> —Karla, 29

Finally, pets can help us socialize with other people. The presence of animals somehow seems to encourage other people to talk with one another—another terrific stress reducer. Walking your dog in the park, for example, is a great way to meet a new friend.

What Pet to Get

What kind of pet can best help you feel less stressed and increasingly centered? It could be a dog—or a cat or a canary or a gecko or a goldfish. It could be any type of animal that holds interest for you. Soon that interest will develop into a healing rapport.

There are, however, three important considerations when choosing a pet.

First, find an animal that suits your temperament. Pets have personalities: some are shy, some are boisterous, and some are more demanding of attention. Consider what type of animal will work best with your own personality. Chemistry is as important with pets as it is among people.

Next, make sure the pet is suited to your lifestyle. If you have an irregular schedule, perhaps a dog who needs two or three walks a day won't fit in—although a house cat might fit in just fine.

Finally, be sure your living space can accommodate the animal. A Great Dane in a studio apartment might well end up being an all-around stressor—for you and the Great Dane both.

Solitude vs. Loneliness

Although this chapter has focused on the stress release of being with family members, don't imagine that a good way to relieve stress would be to *always* be among family members. Everyone needs a little space sometimes—both in the emotional and physical sense.

Unchosen, uninterrupted aloneness can create loneliness—that painful feeling that one's connection to others is severely lacking. But opting to be alone once in a while can give us a chance to collect ourselves and recharge our engines.

Stress Less

A withdrawn state can lead to increased stress, but having the capacity, on occasion, to choose constructive solitary activities enhances inner security.

Although the emotional dangers of loneliness are well documented, the benefits of occasional elective solitude are not so widely known. Still, they are very real.

Don't be afraid to claim a little space for yourself in a literal sense (check out Chapter 19 on creating personal retreat spaces). And don't be afraid to set reasonable limits on togetherness time. A low-stress life is a life in balance. Sometimes you need to be your own good company.

The Least You Need to Know

- The tend-and-befriend response is an alternative strategy to fight-or-flight—it involves nurturing one's family and building social networks as a means of coping with stress.

- A good marriage helps people cope with stress—it provides the mental and emotional comfort of someone to lean on.

- Parenting can be stressful business itself, but sharing wonder and play activities with your kids can create a stress buffer.

- Relationships with pets lessen stress by offering unconditional love, a chance to touch, communicate, and laugh, and even opportunities for exercise.

- Don't let the importance of relationships discourage you from also spending some quality time on your own—a spell of solitude can also soothe.

Chapter 12

A Circle of Friends

In This Chapter

- ◆ How friends calm and cheer us
- ◆ Making new friends
- ◆ Keeping the friends we have
- ◆ When friends are difficult

When we think of Bette Midler singing *You've Got to Have Friends* and of The Beatles singing *I Get By with a Little Help from My Friends,* we can all relate. Sometimes, when the going gets rough, talking to and spending time with a buddy is—without a doubt—the best medicine.

We've all also heard the lyric "People who need people are the luckiest people in the world." But the truth is it's the people who *have* people who are truly lucky—for they are much more likely to be able to bear life's stress with stamina and resilience.

Stress and Social Support

The "befriend" aspect of the tend-and-befriend response to stress originated in times when humans clearly needed other human beings for sheer

Social capital is measured by one's involvement in situations, organizations, and communities where opportunities abound for feeling like part of something greater than oneself.

practical, physical purposes. There's safety in numbers, as they say, and joining forces and resources put everyone who did so ahead of the survival game.

But forming social bonds was never simply about practical necessities—it was, and is, about emotional necessities as well. People who are socially isolated, study after study shows, are apt to suffer poorer health and to exhibit and self-report more signs of stress than those who have social support and more stores of what is called *social capital*.

Friends—other people whom we trust, with whom we reciprocate good turns, and toward whom we feel warmly—are a blessing when it comes to coping. In a number of studies, subjects were exposed to a stressor such as having to give a public talk or perform mental math. When they did these things in the presence of a supportive friend, their cardiovascular stress response was significantly lower than when they did them alone. Even primates exposed to unpleasant stressors produce fewer stress hormones in a roomful of familiar primates from their social group than in a roomful of strangers.

Friends lessen our stress by offering us ...

- Moral support. Their mere presence calms us because it reminds us someone is in our corner, and would defend us if we needed to be defended.

- A shoulder to cry on. Their understanding and acceptance makes bearable events and emotions that might otherwise feel unbearable.

- A hand to hold. Their affectionate gestures (from "attaboy" pats on the back to reassuring big bear hugs) give us the balm of positive touch.

- A receptive ear. Talking about a stressful event can temporarily arouse us, but in the long run confiding calms us. (And sometimes friends even offer good advice.)

Too Tense

Don't be shy about giving your friends—and letting them you give you—physical comfort. In the primate world, this kind of nonsexual, friendly physical contact is accomplished through mutual grooming—an act that results in blood pressure drops for both groomer and groomee.

Having friends also makes us feel better about ourselves. Our self-esteem gets a boost when we know people voluntarily choose our company (no bribes or family ties necessary!). That self-esteem boost, in turn, makes us better able to face challenges. If other people have confidence in us, we might as well have some in ourselves.

In addition to helping us feel better about ourselves, it appears that friends just make us feel better in general. People with active social networks are more apt to take better care of themselves. This could be the upshot of everything from social vanity (nothing wrong with a little friendly competition about who looks better in a Speedo) to having people reminding us to go to the doctor and to take our medicine.

Jokes aside (though humor is another stress-beating service many friends cheerfully provide) the very effect of being social seems to result in better functioning of our immune systems. You might guess you're more apt to get a cold if you're social, but you're actually *less* apt to do so because your system will be producing a higher number of antibodies.

A Knack for Making Friends

Some people wonder if the social support theory of stress relief is subject to reverse causality. In other words, they ask whether it might be the case that the kind of people who readily make friends already have the kinds of skills and attitudes that counter negative stress.

This is an interesting chicken-and-egg question, to be sure. But to lessen your stress, I suggest you work around it. Some people *do* seem to have a knack for making friends more easily than others. If you look at how they do it, then you have both new skills *and* new friends.

Finding Friendship Opportunities

So just how do friend-makers do it?

For starters, think back to your childhood friendships. In childhood, we tend to befriend other children to whom we're routinely exposed and with whom we find we can play cooperatively (that is, with whom we can have fun and share goals, without undue biting, crying, or throwing of small plastic trucks and wooden blocks).

Let's look at the first part of the friend formula first. We make friends with people that we meet up with on a regular basis.

In childhood, we are continually meeting other children in the course of each new school year, at camps, at sports activities, and so on. But sometimes, in adulthood, we find ourselves in routines that often seem to exclude the possibility of meeting new people. We get caught up in our family lives and our work commitments, to the exclusion of just about everything else.

Stress Less _____

Even if you are still in school or work for a large company with built-in social opportunities, cast a wide net for friends elsewhere as well. One friend is a good thing; two is very good; three is wonderful. A circle of friends will give you lots of emotional support, with a variety of personalities to lean on and share things with at the appropriate times.

Some of us, of course, make friends at or through work, and this is a wonderful way to defray stress in the workplace (more on this in the next chapter). But, from a sheer opportunity standpoint, work friendships are easiest to form for those who are employed by large organizations or whose work involves some elements of socializing.

Obviously, if you want to meet new people, you have to put yourself in situations where there *are* lots of other people. Ideally, you also will want to choose an environment where people …

- Are relatively relaxed.
- Will be open to talking with someone new.
- Will be open to participating in shared activities.
- Will have something in common with you.
- Are not already in impenetrable social groups or "cliques."

One thing you might seriously consider is joining a health club or gym. As Chapter 14 discusses in more detail, joining a gym will help you stay true to an exercise regimen (itself a fantastic stress reducer) while you are interacting with others who share that goal. The health club and gym atmosphere seems to be conducive to camaraderie, particularly if you take classes as opposed to pumping iron solo in the weight room. There is nothing like breaking a sweat together to relax interpersonal boundaries. Perhaps it's a primal instinct.

Another thing to try is taking a night class or weekend workshop. Here you'll meet people with similar interests and intellectual pursuits. Of course what subject you study should depend on your individual interests, but do keep in mind that if you choose a class that requires mutual participation—such as a writing or drama workshop, a cooking class, or a foreign language class—your odds of bonding with fellow students are very likely to increase.

Get involved with a worthy cause. Work with a charity, head up a PTA fund-raiser, or identify a need in your community and start an organization of your own to try to fill it. A common cause unites people and gets their juices flowing. The more success the group has, the more individuals will bask in a mutual glow of good feeling.

Get a dog. As the last chapter mentioned, pets are great antidotes to stress, but if your lifestyle can accommodate a canine companion in particular, you'll increase your chances of meeting human companions as well. Take your dog for long walks on sunny days and he or she will make introductions to other dogs and dog owners for you. Unless they are bred as guard dogs, most breeds of dogs are natural friend makers.

If you have kids, take them to places where parents stay and congregate during the children's activities. Don't drop off and run. Stick around at the ice rink, gymnastics class, Little League game, or Cub Scout pack meeting. That "we're all in this together" feeling makes for powerful parental social glue.

Have a party. Invite all your current friends and ask them all to bring some other friends you've not yet met. You're likely to enjoy the company of people your pals have pre-screened for you. Besides, if you throw a party, you'll inspire other people in your social circle to do the same.

> **Too Tense**
>
> You don't have to spend a fortune or make like Martha Stewart to host an enjoyable get-together. People usually just appreciate the opportunity to socialize. If you provide the venue and a few munchables, the rest should take care of itself. Don't be afraid to ask everyone to bring a dish. People like a casual pot-luck atmosphere.

Being Approachable

The second part of how we made friends in childhood was by "playing nice." In adulthood, we need to signal that we're open to building a mutually beneficial and supportive relationship by being approachable. If we want someone to be friendly toward us, we need to indicate that we'll be accepting, gracious, and open-minded.

Approachability is hard to quantify. It's an attitude and a "vibe" we give off when we're feeling nondefensive, curious, and trusting. Most of us can sense instinctively when someone is open to interaction as opposed to when they are totally self-absorbed or "zoned out." Rest assured that others can sense the same thing about us.

Sometimes, however, our self-awareness is not as keen as our sense of other people. There are days when we appear closed off to others without even realizing it. If you feel like no one new ever talks to you, you might be sending nonverbal messages that ask them not to.

To signal the fact that you are open and approachable …

- Make eye contact. You don't need to stare, but don't look away too quickly. Don't walk around looking down at your shoes all the time, or continually glancing at your watch. Eye contact indicates you acknowledge the presence of others and are not too preoccupied to respond to a "hello."

- Smile. A simple upturn of the lips can make all the difference in how people perceive you. If you feel silly smiling with "nothing to smile about" then—here's your chance to try out your newly acquired optimism skills—*think* of something to smile about.

- Avoid closed body language. Crossing your arms in front of your chest, folding your hands, crossing your legs or ankles, or turning your body so that it angles away from someone are all *body language* ways of saying that you are unavailable and likely to reject any friendly overtures. Conversely, when we face someone fully, with open hands and with feet planted forward, we signal availability.

def•i•ni•tion

Body language involves the communication of emotional signals through nonverbal means such as gestures, posture, and facial expression.

- Turn off your electronics. If you go everywhere with iPod headphones affixed to your ears, it should not be surprising to you that you're not meeting anyone. Even if people are shouting warm and cheerful greetings at you, you won't hear them. Being permanently tethered to your cell phone and Blackberry similarly won't do much to encourage social spontaneity. Unplug. Go on, you can do it. Notice who's around and try communicating in person as opposed to in bytes.

If you do these things, you might suddenly find that you're striking up conversations with new people hither and yon. Not all these conversations need to result in a budding friendship, but some surely could. If not, you've certainly lost nothing—and along the way two strangers have had a positive exchange that brightened their day.

Good Friend Material

How will you know with whom it's a good idea to nudge a few casual conversations into the beginnings of a friendship? Use your intuition. You might not know a new acquaintance well, but you know *yourself* very well. So evaluate the nascent relationship and be honest.

Ask yourself:

◆ Is this someone in whose company I feel animated and energetic?

◆ Does this person makes me feel better about myself?

◆ Is this someone I'd genuinely like to know more about and to share ideas with?

◆ Does the person have positive qualities I admire?

Avoid prolonged interactions when conversation feels forced. They'll be a source of stress, not a respite from it.

Imagine yourself spending an hour or two with this person and see if you think you will have lots to discuss, or if you imagine falling into awkward silence or meaningless small talk.

Keeping the Friends You Make

What is important about friendship, and what makes it such a profound source of comfort, is that both parties are emotionally invested in the bond of friendship. Without that investment, what you've got is not really a friendship, but simply an acquaintanceship—perhaps a pleasant acquaintanceship, but not a relationship that offers any measure of security. Have you ever noticed that no one sings songs about how wonderful it is that *You've Got an Acquaintance?*

In order to protect an invested relationship, or to nurture a relationship that has potential to offer both parties stress-relieving emotional rewards, it's necessary to put some effort into it. That ought not come as any surprise. After all, anything worth having merits effort and attention.

First and foremost, a friendship requires an investment of time. Friendships are based on a reservoir of mutually positive experiences. You've got to hang around together to have those, whatever form they take: playing golf or tennis together, having lunch or dinner together, taking your kids to Gymboree together, working on a project together.

All friendships require a substantial time investment up front—like anteing up the initial deposit needed to buy into certain mutual funds. The good news is that this is usually a lot of fun. And after a while, even if the demands of life distract your attention from your friendship for a while, you still have a mutually satisfying history to draw upon. However, we can't keep going back to this well forever. Friendships do require some nurturance or they will fall away. You might always feel warmly about someone you spent lots of quality time with years ago, but if it's been years since you checked in, he or she won't be the first person you'd think to turn to when you need support.

Making time for your friendships should be a consideration in your schedule, and an incentive to manage your time well. When you do organize your time well, you'll also be more able to show affection and respect for your friends by being punctual and by being able to take a few minutes to send birthday greetings and acknowledge other important events, or to simply do something to cheer up your pal when they're feeling blue. The payoff: the more you perform such affectionate acts for them, the more they should feel inspired to do likewise for you.

Too Tense

Seek out and stick with friends who hold up their end. A supportive friendship is a *quid pro quo* arrangement—it offers reciprocal consideration and compensation. If you alone are putting in all the effort, your relationship won't be a stress buffer.

Stress Less

Reflecting a friend's feelings does not mean you have to share them. If they are stressed, you only need to express understanding and concern by saying something like, "I can hear how stressful this is for you right now." Simple understanding can defuse a friend's anxiety.

It's also very important to make yourself available to listen to your friends. It's essential to offer an ear when they've had a hard day, or when they're struggling with a tough decision, or feeling overly encumbered with stressful events or difficult emotions. Even if you don't say much, just being there can be all that's required.

Being truly listened to and understood has an astoundingly calming, healing, and restorative effect on all of us, and it's beneficial to give as well as to receive this kindness.

When listening to a friend who is talking about something that has stressed or upset them …

- Ask her about her feelings, and accept her responses at face value.

- Don't try to talk her out of her feelings—she's entitled to have them.

- Reflect back what you hear so she is aware that you really do understand.

- Don't always try to tie the conversation back to your experiences—focus on her.

In a nutshell: pay attention. Many of us are in the habit of thinking of conversation as 1) talking, and 2) waiting for our turn to talk. While we're busy plotting out a response, we're missing what is actually being said. Conversation with a troubled friend should not be a contest, but rather an oasis in a stormy sea of stress.

Finally, don't forget that friends need an ear not just when they're feeling bad, but also when they're feeling good. Celebrate the good times with your friends. Congratulate them on jobs well done. Praise them, and encourage them to praise themselves when they've done something to be proud of. Feeling envious toward a friend? Keep it to yourself. Then he'll celebrate *you* when it's your turn to shine.

When Friends "Make You Crazy"

At certain times, most of us have had certain friendships that were themselves a bit (or more) stressful. Keeping in mind that no one is perfect, and that the course of true friendship, like true love, never runs smooth, we still need to evaluate from time to time when to work on the relationship and when to let it go.

The first thing to know is that people and their needs do sometimes change. Some friends might be exactly the right person to have in our lives as an outlet at one particular time, but when that time passes the friendship might fade away. This can often happen when two people are at first in similar life circumstances and their paths then diverge. For example, two people who might have been close when they were single and career-focused might have less in common when one marries and starts a family.

If you think you and a friend are not on the same wavelength any longer, there is nothing wrong with putting the relationship on the back burner for a while and letting things take their natural course. You might or might not rediscover each other, but you always will have had the pleasure of supporting one another when it counted.

It Works for Me
"There have been times when friendships I could never imagine my life without somehow slowly evaporated. No one did anything wrong. It's just that we were going in different directions. I have learned that this is perfectly okay. I think it's better to think back fondly on those relationships rather than try to force them to continue in an unnatural way. I will always value all the people in my life who made me laugh and eased my pain and just listened to me babble. I wouldn't be who I am today without their help."   —Elyse, 46

But what do we do when there is a friend in our life that we really want to keep—except we notice that, right now, he or she is behaving badly and not treating us well? We've probably all had friends who, at one time or another, started acting not so very friendly.

Perhaps they are no-shows, ignoring us, breaking plans, hesitating to make plans, and even actively choosing the company of other people over our company.

Perhaps they attempt to control us more than to listen to us.

Perhaps they are so aggressive or agitated that their presence no longer calms and reassures us, but repeatedly makes us more anxious.

Perhaps they are behaving self-destructively and will not recognize how this impacts them and those who care about them.

Perhaps they have become so self-absorbed that they no longer seem to realize that you, or anyone else, exist.

The first question to ask yourself is if this seems to be a phase they are going through—perhaps due to some extenuating life stressor of their own—or whether their behavior has become a chronic pattern. If the former is the case, your friend could be the one who needs an extra dose of understanding and tolerance right now. If you cannot muster what he or she seems to require, you might simply try putting the relationship on the periphery of your support circle for a while and seeing what happens over the course of a few weeks or months.

The second question to ask yourself is if perhaps you have changed rather than your friend. Sometimes we project what's happening with us onto people with whom we're close. Friends can sometimes unwittingly serve this purpose. Maybe it's time to do a reality check.

If you have really decided that your friend is treating you badly, you can terminate the relationship or confront the situation. If the relationship has been one you've valued, it's certainly worth bringing up whatever the issues are. Yes, these will be sensitive subjects and you will have to be diplomatic. But you will be doing your friend, and yourself, the ultimate favor by creating an opportunity to salvage the friendship.

In the end, only you will know if the relationship is worth holding on to or not. Not every friendship will last forever, but while they do last they are a saving, soothing grace.

The Least You Need to Know

- Forming friendships ups our survival odds now as in the past—but social support is as important for emotional well-being as it ever was for physical safety.

- Having friends around can help us cope with stressful situations by giving us moral support and self-confidence.

- To make new friends, remember how you did so in childhood—seek situations where you will repeatedly meet people who share similar interests and goals and with whom you can cooperate and "play nice."

- After you've established a friendship, it's important to nurture it; with an investment of time and talk, it will become an invaluable support resource.

Chapter 13

Work It Out

In This Chapter

- ◆ Whether work and stress are inseparable
- ◆ Coping with top workplace stressors
- ◆ Quick stress-busters at work
- ◆ Letting work go after hours
- ◆ Stress and the self-employed
- ◆ Matching your temperament to your job

Ask someone what's most likely to stress them out and there's a pretty good chance they'll answer "work." But ask people what gives them personal satisfaction and you might very well hear examples of things they've achieved with regard to their occupation.

We all have a relationship to our work, in addition to a relationship to the people with whom we work. This chapter is about enhancing our work relationships. Work, as challenging as it is, has the potential to be a source of positive emotions more than a source of negative stress.

Work and Stress: Synonymous?

Can work be stressful? Can a dog bark and a cat meow? *Of course* work can be stressful! We worry about work, whether we're *at* work or not, for a multitude of reasons.

We worry about our competence and about how our work will be evaluated. We worry about pleasing people, and playing politics when necessary. We worry about time pressures, more so now than ever as the world continues to speed up. We worry about competition, too. Who might be after our job? What other company might eat into our profits and impact our income? And that's just the short list of our seemingly innumerable work-related worries.

Countless surveys have documented just how stressed we feel about work. They don't always come up with exactly the same numbers, but their overall significance couldn't be clearer:

- A survey by Northwestern National Life reports that 40 percent of workers feel their jobs are "very or extremely stressful."

- A survey by the Families and Work Institute reports that 26 percent of workers report they are "often or very often burned out or stressed out by their work."

- A Yale University survey tells us that 29 percent of workers feel "quite a bit or extremely stressed at work."

To some extent, work will always provide some elements of stress in our lives. Let's not forget that work is "what we do for a living." Work is tied into our survival because it provides the income that provides the resources we need to feed, clothe, and house ourselves and to provide for our families. We're also heavily invested in work as it relates to our self-image. You can no more take all of the stress out of work and still call it work than you can take the yeast out of bread and still expect it to rise.

But, if you are committed to lowering negative stress in your life, there are things you can do to minimize your work-related worries and tension. There are also strategies you can pursue to up your potential for finding eustress (that's the positive, energizing kind) and satisfaction on the job.

Causes and Cures of Workplace Stress

The branch of psychology known as industrial and organizational (I/O) psychology has generated a great deal of research about exactly what kinds of factors and conditions make certain work environments more stressful than others. It's been discovered that people feel excessively stressed about work when their own roles and goals are unclear, when communication is poor, when they lack a sense of positive personal engagement, and when the organizations for which they work are rigid and inflexible.

Sound familiar? The foregoing problems, alas, tend to be more widespread than one would hope. So let's take a closer look not only at why such dynamics create stress, but also at what can be done to mitigate that stress.

Restoring Relevance

As with most things in life, stress often occurs at work when there is an element of confusion. It's easier to deal with situations—even difficult ones—when we know what's going on. A right-side-up world simply is more manageable than a seemingly upside-down one.

It's not so surprising, then, that people say they feel stressed at work when …

- ◆ They don't know what is expected of them.

- ◆ People around them seem to be working at cross-purposes.

- ◆ The company/organization has no clear vision or stated mission.

Specific measurable objectives (yes, even tough ones) are far more stabilizing than ambiguity. Moreover, when people work together toward a clear, challenging goal, exhilarating eustress can result.

If you are in a position to help formulate a mission and help others you work with set goals, do it. This *management by objective (MBO)* strategy has been shown to get everyone more focused and energized. It will also be a tonic for jangled nerves.

But even if you are not in a management position, that doesn't mean you cannot set clear goals for *yourself*. Can't change the situation? Change your response. Be your own island of clarity in an ocean of ambiguity.

def•i•ni•tion

Management by objective (MBO) is a workplace strategy whereby managers and those whom they manage agree about goals and also about specific actions and timetables that will enable those goals to be achieved.

To the best of your ability, manage your own time around goals that you set for yourself each day, week, and month. As you complete each one, make a legible note of it in a calendar or electronic PDA. Reward yourself upon each completed goal by taking a little time for an on-the-job stress-beating activity (see the section on "Decompressing at Work" a bit later in this chapter for ideas.)

Multi-Path Communication

Poor communication can make any situation stressful. Work, of course, is no exception. People say they are stressed at work for two primary communication-related reasons.

The first communication stressor is when they receive little or no feedback. People want to be told how they're doing. They want their progress evaluated. They want praise when they deserve it. Even constructive suggestions are appreciated.

What's difficult to deal with is a vacuum of silence, for this sends the message that those whom we work with and for simply don't care about us. The social support structure that is so important for keeping stress at bay needs to be as much a part of the work environment as it does any other environment if we are to thrive.

The second big communication-related stressor in the work environment comes when people feel they have no input in the decision-making process. You might think it would be emotionally easy to simply do what one is told without question. But it's not. People feel much more able to influence circumstances—and therefore less stressed—when their opinions are heard and considered.

Reaching a decision by consensus can take longer than simply having a decision handed down from on high. But when a decision is made, all the individuals who contributed to it implement it more quickly, feel more positively about it, and are more optimistic about the potential outcome. This remains the case even if their particular ideas did not win out in the end.

Too Tense

Communication is good, but to stay calm we need time to focus, free of incoming messages. Research conducted by a psychiatrist at King's College, London, proved that the distractions of constant e-mails, text messages, and voice mail messages are a greater threat to concentration than smoking marijuana. Set aside a particular time to check your messages. If you react to each one the moment it arrives, your stress level will soar as you are continually bombarded with questions and tasks.

In short, stress levels at work go down when communication flows in all different directions. People want to be talked to. They also want to be listened to. When both occur, everyone is less frazzled and functions better.

Personal Fulfillment

People are also stressed at work when they feel that they lack opportunities to do the things at which they excel and opportunities to grow and develop. Being stuck in a rut is a bore, which can create both depression and anxiety.

Some jobs are inherently more stimulating than others, but we all feel much more focused and more fulfilled at work when we have the chance to do what we do best for at least some part of every day. If we even spend only *ten percent* of our day exercising our strengths and talents, whatever they might be, our stress level diminishes.

But even exercising our known skills can become humdrum unless we are given opportunities to stretch ourselves. If you are lucky enough to be periodically challenged by work that will draw on your strengths and expand them, note how you feel during those times. Your level of engagement is itself a stress antidote.

If you are not periodically being offered such challenges, do your best to create them. Speak to those who can influence your assignments and express your desire to stretch yourself. Be sure to have lots of ideas at the ready as to what you might try doing next. If for any reason they are not agreeable, go ahead and stretch anyway. Show your stuff. Hopefully, others will be duly impressed—but more importantly, you'll move from stress toward eustress when you do what you love and love what you do.

> **Stress Less**
>
> Be a positive reinforcer at work, whatever your position. Catch a co-worker doing something he does well and praise him for it. This will boost everyone's morale—his and yours.

Flexible Solutions

The difficulties of juggling work and family life are increasingly stressful. Many workers have seen their stress with regard to this matter soar in recent years as they attempt to cope with not just the needs of their children, but of their aging parents. Study after study shows that workers' enthusiasm for their jobs soars when accommodations are made in the area of flexible scheduling.

If you're lamenting that your work environment is about as flexible as a steel bar, don't get too stressed out yet. Perhaps those for whom you work would be willing to consider options if you clearly lay out a reasonable plan for altering your schedule.

Be sure that the plan includes …

> **Too Tense**
>
> If your work commute is stressful, you're not alone. In New York and L.A. alone, nearly 5 million man-hours a year are lost to traffic delay. If you can flex your schedule, you'll spend less time in emotional overdrive.

- A detailed description of benefits to your employer and you.

- A specific plan about how, when, and where your work will be done.

- A proposed phase-in timetable and a specified trial period.

- A follow-up plan for assessing the effect of the actions taken.

Think they won't go for it? You never know unless you ask. More and more employers are finding it is clearly to mutual advantage to lessen their employee's schedule-related anxieties.

Decompressing at Work

Perhaps your work situation is one in which the ideal conditions of job relevance, constructive communication, personal fulfillment, and flexibility are not all they could be. Okay, perhaps they're even very nearly nonexistent. Even so, you have control over one thing that no one else can tamper with: your mind-set.

Anyone who's ever spent a day working can attest that often the difference between a good day and a bad day is your own attitude. There are any number of things you can do to bring out the potential that work has for being a positive force in your life. Many of these things involve simply taking to work with you the stress-beating skills and strategies that you are learning to put into practice in other areas of your life. Pack them with you just as routinely as you pack your lunch money and your cell phone.

Optimism Opportunities

Work offers lots of opportunities to make choices between putting a negative or a positive spin on events and your role in them. As we saw in Chapter 6, the stressed pessimist thinks of distressing circumstances as permanent; the less-stressed optimist thinks of them as temporary.

DON'T TELL YOURSELF: My boss didn't say good morning. She hates me.

TELL YOURSELF: My boss didn't say good morning. She's in a bad mood.

DON'T TELL YOURSELF: We'll never make our numbers again.

TELL YOURSELF: This was a tough quarter; things will improve.

In addition, the stressed pessimist thinks of distressing circumstances as global and insurmountable; the less-stressed optimist thinks of them as limited problems.

DON'T TELL YOURSELF: This job is boring, my whole life is boring.

TELL YOURSELF: This task is a bore.

DON'T TELL YOURSELF: I will never finish all this work.

TELL YOURSELF: There is a lot to do, one step at a time.

To keep up your optimistic edge, be mindful of the most positive elements in your work environment, whatever they might be. Focus on the areas in which you are learning and achieving mastery. Think about how you are contributing to larger goals. And— this is exceedingly helpful—value the friendships you have made through your work.

A Little Help from Your Friends

Friends are valuable in so many ways. Their impact on our well-being is well documented. But friends at work play a very special role.

In addition to being a source of encouragement and camaraderie, work pals can also be a kind of pressure valve. When you're about to blow, take a break from your endeavors and poke your head into a friend's workspace for a minute or two. Share a quick laugh, banter about your favorite sports teams, make a plan for lunch. Brief social forays like this can make tedious tasks, surly supervisors, and similar workplace pitfalls imminently easier to deal with.

Friends at work can also serve as excellent sounding boards. They'll help you to do reality checks. They're a great resource to bounce ideas off of. If asked, they'll also tell you if you're over-reacting to some minor frustration.

Too Tense

Avoid getting into situations where the only thing you do with your work friends is complain. Gripe sessions might seem like stress-relievers, and occasional ones can be cathartic. But if this is your sole group activity, you will ultimately just stoke each other's sense of distress.

Taking Breathers

Talking with friends is only one of many possible ways to improve your attitude and ease stress throughout the workday. Even very short breaks can be restorative. When you return to your work, you'll often find that energy and inspiration have replaced tension. Try …

- Taking a stretch break.

- Taking a brisk lunchtime walk.

- Watering the plants in your cubicle. (What? You don't have any? Get some!)

- Drinking a cup of calming herbal tea.

- Looking at pictures of your loved ones.

- Calling one of those loved ones to say just low much you love him or her.

Too Tense

Avoid taking too many Internet surfing breaks if your job mostly has you at a computer interface anyhow. Your body needs to de-stress by changing position. Get up and move!

Finally, when you need a breather, try breathing. Sit quietly with your eyes closed. Keep your spine straight. Put your hands on your lap, folded or unfolded—whatever's comfortable. Picture a nose on your navel and inhale through that "nose" for a count of three. As you do so, feel the breath inflating your lower abdomen. Now exhale through your "navel nose" *for a count that is longer than your inhalation*. Try five seconds or so. Repeat at least ten times, and up to thirty times if you can.

This type of breathing will initiate a "relaxation response" that is the physiological opposite of the stress response. This particular technique also has the advantage of enabling you to breathe deeply but very quietly (so no co-worker will think you're having an asthma attack). If you can't find a place to do this in your immediate work environment, take a bathroom break and find an empty stall).

Decompressing After Work

No matter how we feel about our work, most of us today face a special stressor with regard to it. We, as a society, are in jeopardy of giving our entire lives over to work. Needless to say, such an outcome would be a perennially stressful state. Work and other parts of life must be balanced, or every aspect of life—including work—will suffer.

It used to be that only a select few of us could properly be labeled "workaholics." The conventional wisdom was that such types were addicted to work. It was said that workaholics chose to work all or much of the time to keep from dwelling on unwanted emotions and to avoid intimacy in relationships. Workaholic-type addiction still exists today—but it is not the main thing that keeps most of us tethered to thoughts of work more or less around the clock.

Even for those who are not addicted *per se*, many factors make it hard to get away from work, including the following:

- Technology that makes us continually accessible.

- A global economy and global financial markets.

- Round-the-clock Internet commerce.

Moreover, we have a business culture that has come to value not only speed but also instant gratification. When does your boss or customer want the product, presentation, or "vital" piece of information they are waiting for? Now. In fact, why don't they *already* have it?

There seems no longer to be any objective discrimination between matters that are truly urgent and those that can wait. But in a world where no one is prioritizing for us we have to do it for ourselves.

Sometimes we have to be unavailable. Sometimes we have to say "no," or at least "later." Whatever your work is, you must trust yourself to know it well enough to discriminate between which matters need instant attention and which ones could actually benefit from some more time and consideration.

You also need to know yourself in terms of how you work best. Everyone has an optimum work pace that feels appropriate for him or her. It is the pace at which one can achieve a lot and be at the top of one's game without crossing that fine line over into burnout. When burnout comes, it's not just that we can't perform as well as we used to—it's also that we simply don't care as much. That, of course, doesn't help anyone. It doesn't help the people you work with or for. And it certainly doesn't help you stay calm and centered.

Know when enough is enough. Watch for signs of stress-related burnout. These include careless mistakes, poor memory and cognition, an inability to make decisions, and an apathetic or cynical attitude. Stop working for a while! The quality of your health, your frame of mind, your relationships with friends and family, and your relationship with work itself will improve as a result.

It Works for Me

"My work as a commercial real estate attorney was starting to take over my life. There was always a deal going on somewhere. I got to the point where I rarely saw the people that meant the most to me, and I hardly even knew who I was or what I cared about anymore, except that I stay on top of things at work. My health suffered, and my family life did, too, but I was able to turn things around by remembering to start each day by asking myself, 'What is it I'm working *for?*'"

—Wayne, 44

Stress and Self-Employment

It would be remiss not to mention the particular stress dilemma of those who are their own bosses. If you are an entrepreneur or freelancer of any sort, people might envy you because you can "make your own schedule" and "answer to no one but yourself." They think that your job is inherently nonstressful.

But if you are self-employed, you already know the truth: you can be the toughest boss there is *when it comes to yourself.* As boss of yourself, it can be hard to let your "employee" have any downtime. This is especially true if you are someone who is always busy drumming up your next job while also handling the current workload.

But, look at it this way: you are your own greatest asset. You cannot afford to risk your physical health, mental acuity, and emotional equanimity by subjecting yourself to an undue amount of stress without respite. Even if you love what you do, you still require a break from it to refuel.

To de-stress, you'll have to learn to internally compartmentalize work-related thoughts from other topics. You might want to pay special attention to the meditation strategies outlined in Chapter 8 to help you with this.

To complicate matters, if you work at home, you can never "go home" from work in the usual sense. To remedy this, be sure to segregate a workspace within your home and respect its boundaries. Know when to quit, and be sure to close a door behind you when you do.

Your Job and Your Temperament

There are numerous lists of "the most stressful jobs." On them you will usually find occupations that range from air traffic controller, nurse, teacher, and doctor to civil servants, call center workers, bus drivers, and home helpers. Although all of these correlate with certain statistics that indicate stress-related health risks, the truth is that some occupations are more stressful for *some people* than for others.

One person might feel that teaching is an invigorating intellectual challenge and look forward to gaining emotional satisfaction from their relationships with their students; another person might dread the paperwork and preparation necessary, feel confined by administrators and curriculum, or simply not enjoy having to hold the attention of a room full of restless, distracted youngsters.

One person might love skillfully weaving a bus through crowded city streets, shepherding passengers whom they love to say hello to every day. Another person might find her pulse racing at the very thought of maneuvering a multi-ton vehicle carrying a bunch of miscellaneous riders through perilous traffic snarls.

Air traffic control: a continually stimulating challenge or a heart-stopping roller coaster of stress? It's all in how you look at it.

Absenting truly toxic work environments with safety risks or incorrigibly abusive bosses (environments from which everyone should do all they can to extricate themselves), whether or not a particular job is inherently stressful is somewhat subjective. If you are in the process of choosing—or changing—your occupation, be honest with yourself about what level of stress you can manage and what kind of work seems rewarding to you. Make your choice based on who you are—your personality, your interests, your skills—not on statistical tables.

The Least You Need to Know

♦ Our relationship to work is complex—it can be a source of negative stress, but also a source of deep satisfaction and energizing eustress.

♦ People feel less stressed about work when their roles and goals are clearly defined, when communication is good, when they have a sense of positive personal engagement, and when the organizations for which they work are flexible.

♦ Even when you are unable to alter your work environment, you can always work on altering your attitude—so bring your stress-beating skills to work each day.

♦ Work is an important part of life, but for work and the rest of life to be less stressful, we need to construct boundaries between work time and nonwork time.

- The self-employed can be subject to a special kind of stress, because they are both boss and employee—if you're in that position, it's critical to compartmentalize your work-related tasks and your workspace.

- Some types of jobs are frequently labeled "most stressful," but in choosing or changing occupations the most important thing to be aware of is what kind of work seems rewarding to you.

Part 4

Bodywork

So far we've been looking at beating stress from the inside out. Now we'll look from the outside in. Aerobic exercise, yoga, and t'ai chi can fortify not just the body, but also the mind and spirit in the ongoing quest to cope with stress. So can keeping the playful spirit alive by enjoying a range of just-for-fun activities that keep us anchored in the moment.

The Aerobic Advantage

In This Chapter

- Why exercise is positive stress
- How exercise improves health
- How exercise improves mood and attitude
- How much to exercise
- Getting motivated
- Why sex is good exercise

Have you ever met someone who claims to feel more relaxed after they work out good and hard? Maybe that seems like a paradox to you. After all, running or jumping or cycling or what have you until you break into a sweat doesn't appear—on the surface—to be so relaxing.

But these people are on to something. Their stress-beating secret can be yours if you make up your mind to move.

Moving Against Stress

We evolved facing a lot of acute stress—watch out! Herd of charging wildebeests straight ahead!—and in response we moved. Indeed, we hotfooted it away from predators (or toward prey) if we hoped to stick around. Facing an apocalyptic stressor today—tsunami bearing down on the beach!—most of us would still be capable of moving faster and farther than we ever dreamed possible.

But as we've seen, most of the stress we face today is chronic stress, and over the long, cumulative haul our response to it is to become more sedentary. This too, is a natural state of affairs for the body. Before modern times, when we faced chronic stressors such as a long, cold winter with little game to hunt, our systems slowed down in order to conserve energy and burn less fat. Our bodies were underutilized, but that was the state in which we needed to be to facilitate survival.

Today, flat-out run-for-your-life situations are few and far between for most of us. (We should be thankful for that, of course.) And we no longer have to spend a good part of each day hunting and foraging for food. (More gratitude would be in order.) But our bodies miss the physical stimulation these situations necessitated.

When we move, we feel good. We feel alive, we feel purposeful and invigorated. When we are inactive for too long, we actually signal our bodies to conform to less-than-ideal circumstances. And that takes a toll. Sure, we might feel like we're not doing ourselves much harm when we're sitting in front of a big-screen TV on a Sunday afternoon watching football and scarfing down corn chips. In fact, such couch potato activities can feel like a great short-term fix to block out feelings of nagging stress about what Monday morning holds in store. But if lethargy becomes a way of life, our bodies start to atrophy and our moods sink.

Now we are caught in a downward spiral of inertia. The less we move, the less we feel like moving. For many of us, it would actually take nothing less than a charging herd of wildebeests—and their cousins—to make us even think about getting up off the sofa.

Besides, why should we? Exercise is a kind of stress, isn't it? It will turn on the sympathetic nervous system, raise our heartbeat, pump adrenaline into the bloodstream. All true—but nevertheless, if we exercised we would feel not distress but eustress—positive stress that offers the physiological and psychological benefits of excitement and challenge.

The Biology of Exercise

Most of us need little convincing that exercise is good for us on a physical level. In fact, most doctors maintain that if they could take the benefits of exercise and put them in a pill, they would have created a "miracle cure" unmatched by any prescription medication.

When we exercise, we signal to our bodies that we need to be powerful and efficient. Our bodies quickly get the message and comply by …

- Burning fat.

- Strengthening the heart.

- Increasing lung capacity.

- Regulating blood sugar.

- Building bone strength.

- Increasing muscle strength and suppleness.

- Promoting the growth of new brain cells.

- Increasing immune function.

Ironically, the way exercise does all of these things is by compensating for the short-term "injury"—or *adaptive micro trauma*—that occurs whenever we work out. When we make demands on our bodies, we wear them down a tiny little bit and the body then takes on the job of building itself back up to a place *better than where it was before.*

Even if I were to stop right here and tell you no more about what exercise does for you, you would probably already realize its value in terms of countering the debilitative effects of chronic stress. Because in doing all these incredible things to continually repair the body and enhance overall strength, endurance, and well-being, exercise can serve to counteract the severe physical tolls that the accumulation of chronic stress can take on us.

But I'm not stopping here. Not by a long shot.

For in our ongoing struggle to cope with stress, we can rely on exercise to add many, many more tools to our stress-busting tool belt.

def•i•ni•tion

Adaptive micro trauma is the process by which exercise wears the body down and the body then repairs and rebuilds itself in response. In the process, enzymes and proteins from physically taxed muscles seep into the bloodstream and create inflammation. The inflammation then triggers the immune system's "repair crews" to get to work.

Exercise and Mood

Back in the 1970s, when running became a national craze, many people became intrigued by the idea of aerobic exercise—the kind involving sustained movement that uses large muscle groups and relies on oxygen for energy production—not only because it might help them lose a few pounds and get great-looking legs, but because it might create in them a phenomenon known as a "runner's high."

Was it so? Certainly anecdotal evidence supported the idea that it was. Sixty to seventy percent of dedicated runners said that their exercise regimen brought on a state of pleasurable feelings. Researchers began to investigate and discovered that endorphins are indeed released during sustained aerobic exercise such as running. These "natural painkillers" not only have an analgesic effect, but also can instigate some degree of euphoria.

Stress Less _____

Blood levels of beta-endorphins have been found to increase to as much as five times their resting levels during a prolonged bout (over 30 minutes) of aerobic exercise.

Later it was discovered that endorphins alone were probably not entirely responsible for exercise's feel-good effect. When we exercise, our levels of the neurotransmitters norepinephrine and serotonin also increase. These chemicals are also said to play a role in lifting mood.

Though not every aspect of the brain chemistry of exercise is fully understood, evidence is accumulating that exercise improves mood not only in the short term, but also over time. More than a hundred studies have now been done that show exercise reduces both depression and anxiety. And many people who exercise regularly have reported being able to cope better with the impact of stressful events.

Exercise and Attitude

In addition to giving us a physiological boost that improves our mood and coping skills, exercise can give us a stress-beating mental edge. An additional benefit of exercise lies in its ability to produce the "mastery effect," i.e., in fostering a sense of personal achievement. Mastering a new skill, or getting appreciably better at an old one, makes us feel accomplished. The resulting self-confidence cheers us and enables us to deal better with all other challenges.

Exercise can also alleviate tension simply by changing our focus. A trip to the gym, a jog around a golf course, or a hearty hike in the woods can temporarily distract us from the stressors of our everyday lives. The intensely physical activity, often combined with a change of scene, gives us a break and enables us to re-enter the stream of our lives with a fresh perspective.

Finally, let's not forget about the potential benefit of exercise as a *catharsis*. Pounding the treadmill or taking an aerobic kick-boxing class can be a great physical release for pent-up feelings of frustration or anger. Mad at the boss? Piqued at the noisy neighbors? Driven to distraction by your procrastinating teenager? Purge yourself of your ire at the gym and watch your stress level plummet.

def•i•ni•tion

A **catharsis** is an experience that serves to bring emotions to the surface and release them. The cathartic experience itself is not the primary source of the emotions—it's an outlet for them.

Exercise and Self-Image

Now we come to one more way in which exercise can counter stress. It can not only make us look better on an objective level, but also make us feel much better, subjectively, about the way we look.

In our society, physical appearance and weight control are major sources of stress. For better or worse, we are a culture somewhat obsessed with self-appearance—specifically with looking thin and youthful.

Stress itself can be an impediment to looking one's best. Under stress, as we'll see in Chapter 17, most of us tend to overeat—especially sugary, starchy comfort foods. Psychological stress can also, as we saw in Chapter 3, contribute to the phenomenon of healthy people aging prematurely.

People who exercise find it easier to lose weight and to maintain a healthy weight when they achieve their goal. In addition, they can build muscle weight to replace fat (and lean muscle tissue helps to burn even more fat). The upshot is that body weight can be redistributed in some very flattering ways.

As for aging, there is more and more scientific evidence that exercise can not only help us to forestall common diseases associated with aging, but also serve to counteract the decay of the aging process.

Exercise is also great for the skin, because it enhances circulation and eliminates toxins. Here's an instance where we really don't need a lot of scientific evidence to be convinced. To look at oneself in the mirror after a hearty workout is to notice bright eyes and skin flushed with a luminous glow.

When we face the world feeling proud of ourselves, we can create a dynamic of self-fulfilling prophecy. Feeling positive about ourselves, we notice that others tend to feel and act more positively toward us. It's not that nothing negative or stressful ever happens to us when we are feeling in good form, but even when it does, our ability to rise to the occasion is remarkable, for we are not blocked by nagging insecurities and self-doubt.

How Much Exercise?

Just how much exercise should you add to your life to make it an effective stress-beating strategy? In a way, that depends. If you are not getting any aerobic exercise at all right now, the answer is: add some. If you are getting just a little on occasion, the answer is: add some more.

Minimally, many experts recommend a 30- to 45-minute aerobic workout at least three times a week. But remember, the human body is designed to move, move, move. There are many proponents of exercise who expound a six-day-a-week habit, which is not unreasonable when you consider that we evolved in a world that necessitated exerting ourselves just about every single day.

Certainly it's possible to overdo exercise, and there can be some negative consequences to doing so. For example, female athletes who exercise to extremes might discontinue menstruating (their body fat drops to a level where the body believes it is not safe to reproduce). But let's face it, most of us—buckled into our SUVs and glued to our home entertainment centers—are in little danger of getting too much exercise.

Too Tense

Consult your doctor before starting an exercise program. You might want to also consult your doctor if you plan to spend the rest of your life eating junk food and being a sofa jockey.

It is important, however, to choose your activities wisely, and to start slowly and build up endurance. It's also best not to overdo any particular exercise—because repetitive force can potentially put undue strain on joints and muscles and lead to injury (not adaptive micro trauma, but serious injury).

Getting Started

Fortunately, getting started with a fitness program that includes aerobic exercise need not be a costly or complex affair. In fact, one of the best aerobic exercises of all is walking at a brisk, sustained pace. Taking a walk also happens to be a great way to alleviate feelings of physical and mental tension.

To begin a walking program, all you really need is a good pair of comfortable walking shoes. Put them on and head out the door! It's a nice idea to vary your route to avoid boredom. And if you really want the time to fly, think about strapping on an iPod or any portable MP3 player stocked with your favorite tunes. Opt for an upbeat tempo so you can match your pace to it.

If you have a bicycle gathering dust in your garage, wipe it off, spray it with WD-40, and check the air in your tires—cycling is another great aerobic activity. Biking also conjures up, for many of us, associations with the freedom and fun of childhood. You won't need much in the way of equipment except a helmet. Don't start out on the biggest hills in town; you're not Lance Armstrong. Just pick a destination that's at least 15 to 20 minutes away, get there, and come back.

Consider swimming as another exercise alternative. It not only promotes cardiovascular fitness, but also strength, stamina, and mobility. Access to swimming pools might be more readily available than you think, so check out your local "Y," and other community pools. If you don't know how to swim, maybe now is the perfect time to learn.

Dancing can also be another great workout choice. It can be a great complement to other activities—sharpening control, agility, balance, and speed. Olympic athletes in many sports include dancing in their training.

Other great aerobic activity choices include the following:

- Racket sports (such as tennis or squash)
- Rowing
- Ice skating
- Roller blading (also known as inline skating)
- Downhill skiing
- Snowboarding
- Cross-country skiing
- Snow shoeing

 Too Tense

Don't plunge into vigorous exercise without at least a few minutes of warm-up. Stretch out your major muscle groups, holding each stretch for at least 20 seconds. A similar cool-down at the end of your workout is also a good idea.

On days when you're not formally exercising, know that you can supplement your workout by putting a little *oomph* into mowing the lawn, raking leaves, vacuuming the house, or playing with the kids. What's more, you can build up your strength and tolerance for aerobics by occasionally choosing the stairs instead of the elevator or escalator, or parking at the far edge of the parking lot (which sure beats the stress of circling and circling in search of a prime location space.)

Joining a Gym

Many people join a gym when they are thinking of beginning, or getting more serious about, an exercise regimen. You might assume this is a very pricey option, but in fact a little research just might yield some very affordable choices, including facilities such as the YMCA. If it's at all doable, do it—because joining a gym offers a lot of significant advantages.

Aside from providing equipment such as treadmills, elliptical trainers, stair machines, and weight rooms (and, sometimes, even free or low-cost child care!) gyms offer the opportunity to regularly combine exercise with social interaction. Remember that social interaction and support are, in and of themselves, very powerful antidotes to chronic stress.

At a gym, you can take classes with other workout devotees, or with similarly struggling novices. Sweating together and then commiserating around the water fountain is a great way to bond. You can also seek the worthy advice of certified professional trainers who are knowledgeable about everything from how to work a particular piece of equipment to how to make the most of your exercise time to how to prevent overexertion or injury.

Be sure to choose a gym that is convenient to your home or office and whose hours are convenient enough that you will actually go. It's easy to make excuses if you have to drive for half an hour to get there or if the gym opens after you have to leave for work or closes before you get out. Also, find a facility that is clean and appealing, even if it's not a "luxury" gym. You won't want to spend time there on a regular basis if it's not an aesthetically pleasant experience.

One common objection to joining a gym is that "I'm not in good enough shape." Let's think about that one for a minute. It's like saying you won't shop for shoes because you're barefoot. Gyms are supposed to help people get in shape. If there's a super-svelte crowd with an "attitude" at one place—okay, such snooty venues do exist—find another. If you're very self-conscious in front of the opposite sex, you might also consider joining a gym that is gender specific.

> **It Works for Me**
>
> "I read that most people who join health clubs in January as a part of a New Year's resolution stop going by April. I think they go overboard and burn out. I decided not to think of think of joining as a do-or-die 'resolution' but as a permanent change in lifestyle."
>
> —Debbie, 49

You might be reluctant to invest in a gym membership if your schedule is frequently disrupted by travel. But keep in mind that many gyms have a reciprocity program with health clubs in other cities. Ask about it. If that doesn't work out, try to stay in out-of-town hotels that have workout facilities—as many now do. Those facilities might be pretty basic, but they are better than nothing, and they will help you counteract the stresses of travel, road food, and jet lag.

Staying Motivated

Many people find that when they get into a regular exercise groove, they wouldn't dream of stopping. If circumstances do force them to stop for a while, they notice that they no longer have the level of energy that they are used to having, that their mood has taken a downturn, and that they are not as well able to cope with frustrations in their lives. At this point, the consistent benefits of exercise have become the incentive to do it.

But it does require some time for any new habit to "take." Until then, it's important to "just do it." Keep putting one foot in front of the other—literally.

To help stay on track, consider taking a "buddy system" approach to your exercise habit. Plan to walk, bike, swim, or join a gym with a friend. That way, if the motivation of one of you is flagging, the other can be the cheerleader. You'll also both be more likely to show up for your planned workout when you know someone else is counting on you to be there.

Another great way to stay motivated is to continually set incremental goals for yourself. If you've walked 2 miles, set a goal to walk a little more each day until you routinely walk 3 miles. If you've biked for 20 minutes, keep working toward 30. If you're exercising two days a week, see if you can make three or four days the new habit.

In addition to setting goals that involve working out more, you can set goals that involve working out harder. Intensifying your workout is a very efficient strategy, because you can get more out of whatever activity you're doing in the same amount of time.

To keep track of how hard you're working and help you set goals, invest in a heart monitor. A heart monitor is a device that tells you how many times a minute your heart beats.

Read the directions that come with the monitor and you can easily figure out what your theoretical maximum heart rate is. Set a goal—it's a good idea to do this with a certified trainer at your gym—as to what percentage of your maximum heart rate you want to work at and for how long. (Working at 70 to 85 percent is considered a "high-endurance mode." At first you might not sustain that for too long, but setting reasonable goals can gradually increase your endurance level and your workout efficiency.)

Finally, you can keep motivated by keeping an exercise journal. Note when you exercise, what activities you do, and what positive changes you notice. (See Chapter 22 for a suggested format.) You will be proud of yourself.

Sexercise for Stress

One last word on the topic of exercise—and that word is *sex*. As Chapter 11 noted, sex and all kinds of loving and affectionate touching can have a potent anti-stressing effect. But sex has an additional benefit as well. You might have never thought about it this way but sex can be, among other things, pretty good exercise.

Sex gets your heart rate up and burns lots of calories. A 180-pound man can burn about 10 calories for every 5 minutes of vigorous sex. Now, here's the really good part: the more you work out and build stamina, strength, and aerobic capacity, the better your sex life will be.

With a regular exercise regimen, you'll be more inclined to make love more frequently because you'll feel better about yourself and your body. (Your partner will feel good about it, too!) You'll also have the pep to do it, and do it with gusto.

The Least You Need to Know

- Exercise is eustress—positive stress that offers excitement and challenge.

- When we exercise, our bodies become more powerful and efficient, and our enhanced physical well-being will help counter the negative health effects of chronic stress.

- Exercise also impacts mood by triggering the release of brain chemicals that make us feel good, by making us feel accomplished, and by improving our self-image.

- To add more aerobic exercise to your life, consider activities like brisk walking, bicycling, swimming, and even dancing—start slowly, but stick with it.

- Joining a gym can be a great strategy for getting and staying on an exercise regimen—the gym or health club environment offers structure, professional guidance, and social support.

- Stay motivated by working out with a buddy and by setting new goals for yourself.

Chapter 15

Calming Moves

In This Chapter

- Balancing the body's energies
- What yoga is—and isn't
- Styles of yoga
- Getting started with yoga
- Calm-inducing yoga poses
- The benefits of t'ai chi

As beneficial as it is, fast-paced aerobic exercise is not the only way in which to move your body to beat stress. Moving the body slowly and with deliberate awareness can also be extremely calming. That is where the disciplines of yoga and t'ai chi come in.

Even if you have only the most vague notion—or none at all—of what these age-old practices are about, it won't hurt to open yourself up to the possibility that they have been assiduously practiced for so long in so much of the world with very good reason. After all, humans have needed stress relief for a long, long time.

Body/Mind Balance Basics

If you're reading this book right now, you're probably sitting down and have actually managed to get a moment to yourself. With any luck, you're in a spot where you can take a few minutes to conduct a little impromptu survey as to what is going on inside you.

Take a few moments to do a brief body inventory. Start at the crown of your head and work down. Bring your attention slowly across the top of your scalp, to your forehead, eyes, nose, mouth, and jaw. Now focus on your neck—is it tight?—and your shoulders, arms, hands, and fingers. Mentally note any spots where you are holding tension.

Now move your awareness across your chest and diaphragm and then up your spine until you reach your upper back. Any cricks? Now take a mental inventory of your lower body. Do you feel tightness in your stomach, groin, buttocks, upper or lower legs? How about your feet, arches, and toes? Do you notice any soreness?

Next, take a few moments to map your mind. What thoughts are nagging at you? What is making you anxious? What pressing problem is nibbling at your consciousness? Was it calling on you to pay attention to it even as, a minute ago, you were trying to turn your whole consciousness toward noticing the tensions in your physical self?

Finally, take a few moments to focus on your breath. How would you describe it? Are you taking deep breaths, filling up your lungs with air, letting the inhalation move deep down to your diaphragm? Or are your breaths rapid and shallow? Do you, in fact, notice that you are sometimes holding your breath without meaning to do so?

Now consider that the sensations of the body, the tense muscles, the short breath, and the redundant anxious thoughts, are all connected—all manifestations of the same underlying unifying energy. Disciplines like yoga and t'ai chi can help you transform this energy from stressful to serene, from agitated to calmly alert and aware.

Although different in certain ways, yoga and t'ai chi are both concerned with enhancing the totality of the mind-body system. Both also encompass—for those who are interested—spiritual philosophies. But even if you focus primarily on their physical aspects, they can have a profound overall impact on your physical and emotional state.

Practicing the disciplines yoga or t'ai chi, or both, can make you feel like you have discovered amazing forms of self-massage that, in themselves, counter stress. But these practices also serve to pull you away from your day-to-day stressed-out awareness and foster moments of self-compassion, clarity, and even transcendence. Best of all, such moments have a cumulative effect. Before you know it, the process of inward attention can help you recognize patterns of thought and emotion that might not be helpful to you and to cultivate new ones that are very helpful and healing instead.

Yoga and t'ai chi are often touted for their ability to increase flexibility. They do—but not only flexibility of muscles, limbs, and torso. They increase flexibility of our mental perspective. They increase our energy as well, and each session will leave you feeling more energized than when you began.

Open yourself up to the idea of practicing yoga or t'ai chi and you will see how moving your body with mindfulness can be like finding a doorway into personal peace.

Saying Yes to Yoga

Across America, and much of the Western world, the ancient eastern discipline of yoga is catching on with enormous cultural force. Scores of Fortune 500 corporations such as Nike, HBO, Forbes, and Apple all offer on-site yoga classes for their employees. And it seems like you can find yoga studios and health clubs that offer yoga instruction in nearly every community.

Perhaps you've already dabbled in some classes, or perhaps your dabbling has gotten a bit more dedicated. Perhaps you're just curious. Where does yoga come from? Does it require twisting yourself into a pretzel? And do all forms of yoga—of which there are many—offer the same benefits?

A Very Brief History of Yoga

The origin of yoga dates back some 5,000 years, and took place in India. Yoga is actually comprised of a number of interrelated practices—eight in all—some of which have to do with purifying the body through diet and purifying the mind through meditation.

In the West, however, the term *yoga* usually refers to *hatha* yoga, in which practitioners perform a series of postures (*asanas*) that align, stretch, and strengthen various muscle groups. The postures are also designed to enhance balance, and to open the entire spine so that energy can flow along its length more freely.

def•i•ni•tion

Yoga is from the Sanskrit word *yuj* that means "to yoke or bind." Its paramount focus is on union—the binding of opposites, and a joining of the energies of mind, body, and spirit.

Hatha yoga is the aspect of yoga that focuses on physical postures. The word *hatha* is sometimes translated as willful or forceful. But *ha* also means "sun" and *tha* means "moon"—so the word also incorporates the concept of natural balance.

While performing a series of poses, practitioners are also asked, in the hatha tradition, to bring their attention to the breath. This helps in stilling the tremors of the body as well as the mind and to be more fully present in the unfolding moment.

Yoga is not a religion. And it is most certainly not necessary to alter your own spiritual beliefs in order to practice it. Though certain styles of yoga incorporate devotional practices, one can perform them on a strictly secular level, or opt for styles of yoga that do not focus on these.

Here in the West, many recommend incorporating yoga into a physical fitness program because it is, among other things, a wonderful way to make sure our muscles are stretched and limber. Yoga's numerous balancing poses can also help us in strengthening our core and thus preventing falls.

Beyond that, many researchers have become keenly interested in yoga's power to counteract the stress response with relaxation. Controlled studies involving yoga are somewhat difficult to design, because there is significant variation in styles of yoga. Nevertheless, many researchers claim that yoga can be very beneficial in mitigating stress and its consequences. If nothing else—though there very likely is a great deal more—yoga empowers its practitioners to feel more in control of their response to stress because they are taking an active role in a regular practice meant to improve their well-being. This alone is a wonderful attitude boost.

Styles of Yoga

If you are searching for a class in yoga, you might be a little confused by some of the descriptive words you sometimes see in conjunction with it. All yoga classes will enhance your flexibility and balance, and all will simultaneously energize and relax you. But it would help you to have your priorities in mind. What would be most appealing to you? Are you looking to sweat your way into relaxation, or does a gentler, more meditative approach sound more your speed?

As you get started on your individual yoga quest, sampling is perhaps the best way to familiarize yourself with any class. However, if you have numerous options as to what style you choose, here's a little primer that should keep you from feeling overwhelmed.

All of the following types of yoga have gained popularity in the United States, and all fall under the umbrella of *hatha* yoga, the physical aspect that focuses mainly on postures and breathwork:

- **Iyengar.** One of the most popular styles of yoga around, Iyengar yoga is all about attention to detail. There is an intense focus on the subtleties of each posture. Iyengar makes use of props, including belts, chairs, blocks, and blankets, to help accommodate beginners or those with any special needs, such as injuries or structural imbalances.

  Iyengar's advantage is that you will learn to get the most from each pose in terms of overall muscular and skeletal alignment.

- **Ashtanga.** Ashtanga is a fast-paced, flowing series of sequential postures. Because it offers an aerobic challenge—a chance to generate endorphins as well as stay in shape—it has also become very fashionable. However, if you are new to yoga, note that Ashtanga devotees can be very hard core and classes quite rigorous. You might want to work your way up to this, or be sure to find a teacher who is good with beginners.

- **Sivananda.** This fairly gentle style of yoga promotes physical strength and flexibility, while incorporating a fair amount of specialized breath work techniques. It is very focused on stress release and on removing energy blockages. Classes often include a little chanting—for example, the *Om* chant (see Chapter 8), and tend to have something of a mild spiritual dimension (welcoming seekers from all religious paths).

- **Bikram.** Sometimes called "hot yoga," Bikram yoga is conducted in studios where room temperatures pushes, or even exceeds, 100° F. Practitioners say its sauna-like effect is cleansing. This style of yoga was designed by Bikram Choudhury, who sequenced a series of 26 traditional *hatha* postures to enhance the optimal functioning of every bodily system. Be prepared to perspire your way to well-being and relaxation.

> **Stress Less** _____
> Many yoga classes—especially those that are simply called hatha yoga—actually offer a blend of styles suited to the students who regularly attend. The class becomes an expression of the practitioners' abilities and goals.

- **Kundalini.** The focus in Kundalini yoga is to liberate the energy at the base of the spine and draw it upward through the body's seven energy centers, known as *chakras*. This is a very energetic style of yoga, and includes a lot of dynamic breathing and quickly repeated postures. It can provide quite a workout of body as well as mind and spirit. After a Kundalini class, practitioners are left feeling amazingly energized and fortified.

◆ **Ananda.** Ananda yoga offers a system for enhancing spiritual growth while releasing unwanted tensions. The unique part of its practice is the use of silent positive affirmations while holding poses. Class also focuses on mindful posture and controlled breathing.

◆ **Anusara.** *Anusara* means "to step into the current of divine will." It is a newer system of hatha yoga that focuses not only on body mechanics but on cultivating a transformative attitude. Practitioners' aim is to awaken their true inner nature. Each pose is conceived of as not only an exercise, but also an artistic expression of the grace in one's heart.

◆ **Kripalu.** In Kripalu yoga, practitioners are asked to hold the postures to the level of tolerance—and to gradually push that level. This deepening concentration and focus is said to result in complete release of the body's internal tensions as well as a building of mental capacity and self-confidence.

◆ **Tibetan.** Tibetan yoga is a system of movement, breathwork, and meditation that was long a mystery in the West. Its daily sequence of five flowing movements, repeated 21 times each, when the student works their way up to that number, is said to have a profound effect on self-healing and rejuvenation. Some say they comprise a veritable "fountain of youth." In 1994, yoga teacher Christopher Kilham published a modern version of these exercises called *The Five Tibetans: Five Dynamic Exercises for Health, Energy, and Personal Power.* Tibetan Buddhist monk Tarthang Tulku adapted another ancient movement practice for the modern West called Kum Nye, which is less physically vigorous and more contemplative. (See Appendix A for more information on Tibetan yoga resources.)

Too Tense

Some yoga offerings are divided into "beginner" and "intermediate" or "advanced" sections. If you are a novice, stick with the former, as you will receive extra attention and feel less self-conscious. As with any endeavor, you're apt to get discouraged if you jump in at a level that's over your head.

Regardless of what style of yoga might intrigue you, keep in mind that finding a teacher whose approach is suitable for you is perhaps the most important element in your quest. Trust your instincts. We all know the "right" teachers when we find them. They have the knack for instilling in us the sense that we can do what we set out to do, and that we are somehow rediscovering knowledge that, deep down, we might have known all along.

Starting Down the Yoga Path

Undertaking any new activity can understandably make us a bit apprehensive. New-comers to yoga can feel especially intimidated if they've been exposed to those glossy magazine covers featuring flawlessly lean and muscular physical specimens contorted into gravity-defying backbends. To alleviate the stress of starting this ultimately stress-relieving discipline, there are a few things you should keep in mind.

First, don't think you cannot practice yoga because you are not flexible. That is like thinking you can't take swimming lessons because you don't know how to float. Yoga will little by little—but probably much more quickly than you could ever imagine—limber you up, strengthen you, and provide immense improvement to your overall coordination and confidence.

Next, don't worry about getting all togged out in fancy yoga gear or buying a bunch of yoga accoutrements, like your own mat, bag, blanket, straps, or blocks. As with almost any activity, you can overaccessorize yourself into credit card debt and lose the important focus. Just get yourself a pair of leggings or sweatpants and a fitted T-shirt to start. You don't need special shoes, because yoga is done barefoot. As for all the other stuff, any yoga studio has everything you need. If you want your own mat, wait until your practice is established and reward yourself with it. (Look for one with good floor-sticking power to prevent slippage.)

Finally, as with anything, don't overdo things when you don't know what you're doing. You'll probably meet people who tell you they practice yoga daily. Be happy for them, but don't feel you have to rival them. Yoga is in no way a competitive sport.

Be realistic. If you can make yoga class even once a week, you will soon notice a benefit. Several times a week would be a wonderful goal to work toward. When you can't get to class, try 20 minutes or so at home on your own. (Many people consider 20 minutes of mindful yoga to be their morning meditation.)

> **Too Tense**
>
> It's best not to eat for two hours before yoga class. If your last meal is not fully digested, you might be a bit uncomfortable (or flatulent). If you feel too hungry or get lightheaded from not eating, try a light snack (e.g., a banana or yogurt) at least half an hour beforehand.

Some Restorative Poses

Yoga postures range from the fairly simple to the truly esoteric. But even the simplest poses can prove wonderful antidotes to muscle tension and emotional anxiety. Here is a brief sampling of a few that might prove especially helpful. (Please note, if you have back, neck, or knee injuries, or if you have asthma, or are pregnant, or have any other medical conditions, these poses might have to be modified. An experienced, certified yoga teacher should be your trusted guide.)

The Mountain Pose

Standing tall—like a mountain—can be an extremely grounding experience. In day-to-day life, we slouch. But in yoga, we can balance the body and mind by the way we hold ourselves erect.

Practitioners begin Mountain Pose by standing erect, with hips wide apart and feet parallel.

Next, tuck your tailbone, contract the muscles at the top of your knees (without locking your knees), and lift your head up from and out of your shoulders.

Now inhale, filling your lungs, as you press your palms together in front of your middle chest—with your fingertips facing up (this is the "prayer position" of the hands).

Cat and Dog Stretch

Actually a pose and *counterpose*—the cat and dog stretch is extremely relaxing for the spine.

def•i•ni•tion

In yoga, a **counterpose** is a pose deliberately sequenced after another pose to gently stretch the body in the opposite direction.

First kneel on all fours so that your knees are under your hips and your palms are on the floor—keeping your back straight and your head facing forward.

For "the cat," exhale and drop your head and tailbone as you arch your back. Pull your navel up toward your spine.

For "the dog" inhale as you raise your head and tailbone toward the ceiling, letting your abdomen drop toward the floor and your spine curve down. Your posture is like that of a friendly pup, waiting for a pat on the head.

Alternate several times between the defensive cat and the friendly dog. The routine is not only good for muscles and circulation, but is also a great emotional release.

The Cobra

Lie face down with brow on the floor. Put your hands palms down beside your shoulders. As you inhale, slowly curl your upper body—forehead, nose, chin, shoulders, and chest—upward while keeping your pelvis on the floor. Breathe deeply as you relax your arms and shoulders.

This pose should feel releasing at the lower back, where it increases circulation. The pose also expands the rib cage and—practitioners say—increases the compassionate capacity of the heart.

The Child's Pose

A good counterpose to the Cobra, the Child's Pose completely refreshes the back and spine.

Kneel with thighs on calves, hips a little apart. Bend forward and down from the hips, folding your upper body onto your knees.

As your forehead rests on the floor, extend your arms and rest them on the floor in front of you as well (with your palms facing down).

Breathe deeply and relax as this wonderful pose massages all of your inner organs. When you're feeling renewed, raise your head and resume a seated position.

The Reclining Spinal Twist

Lying on your back, with your knees together, draw both knees into your chest. Extend your arms out to your sides in a "T" position.

Now roll your hips and legs to the left. Keeping the knees together, bring them toward the floor. As you do this, turn your head to the right. Stretch and breathe for a full minute.

Now do the opposite, bringing the hips and knees to the right while turning the head to the left. Stretch and breathe for a full minute.

This pose calms the mind and balances energy flow. It also aids digestion.

The Corpse

This is the pose—also known as *Shavasana*—that traditionally ends any yoga regimen. It enables the body to rest as the practitioner fully absorbs the benefits of the practice.

Lie flat on your back with your feet about a foot apart. To help the small of your back reach the floor you can place a rolled blanket beneath your knees.

Put your arms out by your sides at about a 45-degree angle, palms up. Close your eyes, inhale and exhale deeply, and relax as you feel yourself sinking deeply into the earth.

Ideally, this pose should last at least 10 minutes. Come out of it gradually by opening your eyes and stretching hands and feet in opposite directions. Turn to one side and draw your knees in to your chest in order to lift yourself up without feeling light-headed.

Try T'ai Chi for Tranquility

Another age-old system that can help you keep in shape, enhance your well-being, and relieve stress is the ancient Chinese discipline of t'ai chi (pronounced *tie-chee*, and meaning "supreme ultimate"). Perhaps you have walked through a park early in the morning and seen people looking as if they were chasing imaginary butterflies or shooting an imaginary bow and arrow. The focused, peaceful look on their faces will tell you that they are involved in t'ai chi practice.

T'ai chi is actually a martial art—the physical and spiritual foundation of all Asian schools of self-defense. But it does not appear, or feel, at all aggressive. Rather it focuses on soft movements that strengthen the core of body and mind, balance the system's *chi* (energy), and rejuvenate one's perspective on life. The martial arts philosophy that underlies the practice is to use intelligence over force.

T'ai chi incorporates a series of slow, graceful movements. There are actually 108 movements in all, but most Westerners who practice it do far fewer movements and still benefit greatly. The movements appear, at times, to be an elegant form of shadowboxing.

Beyond being a method of self-defense, t'ai chi is nothing less than a form of moving meditation. As you master its movements, you learn to focus mindfully on your form and to hone your thoughts to a keen point of awareness. The emotional state it creates within is one of relaxed readiness. One is calm, yet ready to face anything that comes along with serene power.

Although t'ai chi, which dates back to the thirteenth century, has its roots in Taoism, an ancient Chinese religion and philosophy, its Western practice is generally secular. It is increasingly embraced by thousands of Westerners who wish to enhance their flexibility and balance—and by many doctors who particularly recommend it as a preventive health measure for older patients who fear falling and for patients with physical disabilities. T'ai chi has also proven to be very effective in lowering blood pressure, according to researchers in a pilot study at the Johns Hopkins School of Medicine.

<table>
<tr><td>

It Works for Me

"I always had a hard time sitting still and meditating. When I discovered t'ai chi it allowed me to move and meditate simultaneously. I think of t'ai chi as 'meditation for people with ants in their pants'. It has taught me to learn to pay attention to my body and to manage my fast-paced frenetic energy."
—Isabelle, 44
</td></tr>
</table>

Styles of t'ai chi vary in the West. Some incorporate self-massage techniques from another ancient Asian discipline called qigong (*chi-GONG*)—a highly therapeutic system of self-healing from which t'ai chi itself is actually an offshoot

Many health clubs, YMCAs, and community colleges offer courses in t'ai chi. If you cannot find personal instruction in your area, the discipline can also be fairly effectively learned from DVDs.

At first, don't worry about getting every movement exactly right. This is a very forgiving discipline that will reveal its many calming and energizing benefits right away, even as you are enjoying getting the hang of it. You'll know you're on the right track when you feel a sense of harmony radiating from within.

Besides, one of the really interesting things abut t'ai chi is that simply observing others doing its graceful, spacious movements induces a palpable sense of calm in the observer. If you merely watch a video of the discipline or view a class in progress, or are lucky enough to chance across practitioners in your local park, you will accrue some benefit by taking a little time to enjoy their practice vicariously.

The Least You Need to Know

- Moving the body with slow, deliberate awareness, as one does in the disciplines of yoga and t'ai chi, is an effective way to induce a sense of serenity.

- Yoga is a multifaceted ancient discipline, but in the West we usually practice its physical aspect—hatha yoga—which itself encompasses various styles.

- When embarking on a yoga practice, feel free to sample various styles until you find one that suits you—and keep in mind that finding a good teacher can be the most important element in your search.

- Yoga postures (known as *asanas*) range from the seemingly simple to the esoteric—but you don't have to twist yourself into a pretzel to alleviate muscle tension and emotional anxiety.

- The ancient Asian art of t'ai chi looks like a form of elegant shadowboxing—and although it originated as a martial art, its calming choreography is of immense benefit as a stress-relieving "moving meditation."

Chapter 16

The Process of Play

In This Chapter

- ◆ The benefits of play
- ◆ De-stressing in a state of "flow"
- ◆ Playing with art
- ◆ Playing in the garden
- ◆ Playing sports to beat stress
- ◆ Cultivating an attitude of awe

An exercise workout is in part *work*. Yoga and t'ai chi are called *disciplines*. But what about plain old play? That, too, should have a role in any comprehensive stress-relieving plan.

Any activity that offers us good, old-fashioned fun will relax us, lift our mood, and bring us back to "work" with a refreshed outlook.

No matter what your age, and no matter how busy you are, don't ever let yourself become too busy to play.

What Play Is For

Throughout the kingdom of nature, play is a near-universal phenomenon. The behavior is found in a great many animal species. This certainly doesn't need to be told to anyone who has ever raised cats or dogs. They love to play, and in some ways live to play. Dolphins play. Chimps play. When no danger is looming, and so long as food is plentiful, some creatures appear to play most of the day.

Ethologists—researchers who study animal behavior, including that of the human animal—say that play can be useful in developing survival skills, such as hunting or escaping predators. (Perhaps you never thought about a good game of "tag" in this light, but there you have it.) Play that involves mental strategizing is also useful for helping to sharpen the mind. It builds the skills of anticipating, imitating, and problem solving. Play fosters creativity, enabling the mind to wander and to fantasize.

Play can be a solitary endeavor, such as a small child twirling around and around on his own, just for the sheer joyful sensation of it. But when it is done in groups, play serves as a kind of social glue. Children bond with others and build friendships as they play—learning to share, communicate, and negotiate. They practice different roles within their social framework.

Child's play often has immediate aims—run over there, jump higher here. Sometimes it has short-term goals, as in "Let's build a sand castle." But when the tide comes in and washes away the sand castle, there are rarely tears—because the point was the fun of the building itself. Now, for more fun, another castle can be constructed. There is no long-term goal of play other than to continue playing.

Adults, whether they think to call it so or not, also play—or, at least some do. We might literally say we are going to *play* a game of golf or tennis or bridge or Scrabble. We might *work* at finishing a crossword puzzle—but that's really play as well. In such cases, our short-term goals could be to win the game or complete the puzzle. But, again, there is no real long-term goal. Play is about enjoying an experience for as long as it lasts.

Some creative play yields a product, to be sure. When we lose ourselves in painting a watercolor, writing a poem or song, molding a clay pot, or knitting a sweater, we have something to show for our efforts at the end. But if such artistic endeavors are our form of self-enjoyment, we are not interested in the product so much as the process.

> ### It Works for Me
>
> "I had forgotten the joys of play until I had children. Watching them, I was reminded that play takes our minds off any worries we might have. If you don't know how to start playing again, play with kids for a while and you'll develop a playful attitude."
>
> —Lucy, 27

For no matter where we play, how we play, or what we play, play is a mental space where we can lose ourselves. In play, we can put aside our cares and put self-consciousness on a shelf as we focus fully on what we are doing. That is why to play is to alleviate stress.

Feeling the Flow

In the 1990s, Mihaly Csikszentmihalyi (chick-SENT-me-high-ee), a professor and former chairman of the Department of Psychology at the University of Chicago, formulated a concept known as "flow" after observing painters, sculptors, writers, mountain climbers, chess players, and others who would spend hour upon hour pursuing an activity with remarkable single-minded concentration.

He noted that when people enter a state of flow they are so absorbed in what they are doing—what they are, in effect, playing at—that they completely lose track of time. What a miracle! In a world so obsessed with time and its passage (we are all consumed with meeting deadlines and beating the clock) imagine what it would be like to repeatedly step outside of stressful time consciousness.

Csikszentmihalyi also noted that the benefits of flow went far beyond the happiness of the period that one spends engaged in one's activity of choice. After being utterly wrapped up in a state of intense moment-to-moment experience, one emerges with a boost in self-esteem, and an increased sense of well-being. competence, and calm.

But does every potentially engrossing activity induce a state if flow in everyone? What if, for example, someone who feels completely inept at drawing, attempts to sit down and sketch a portrait? Frustration, that's what. The same would be the case if someone who could never sink a basketball were to decide to while away the hours by repeatedly shooting hoops. On the other hand, if a master-level chess player were to play a game with someone well below his skill level, that would not create flow either. He would, of course, be bored. In both cases, time would not seem to fly, but rather to drag.

Too Tense

When people are interrupted at random intervals and asked to report how much they are enjoying themselves, those who are passively vegetating report little sense of flow and satisfaction. Those who are actively engaging their skills feel just the opposite.

Flow takes place in that zone between the stress of feeling overwhelmed by a task that is too difficult or bored by a task that is too easy to accomplish. In this zone, we are free to do something for its own sake as our self-conscious ego virtually disappears. As Csikszentmihalyi has said of flow, "Every action, movement, and thought follows inevitably from the previous one, like playing jazz. Your whole being is involved, and you're using your skills to the utmost."

Flow is yet another of those forms of eustress we have been encountering throughout this book. It requires effort—often intense effort—and skillful awareness, but it revs us up in positive ways. It counteracts chronic distress, or negative stress, by allowing us to elevate ourselves above the ordinary and to put problems on the back burner for a while.

Playing with Passion

In order to play in a way that most effectively relieves stress, it's best to play at something about which we are passionate. It's best to find the thing that sends us into a state of flow. For some of us, a flow-inducing activity will immediately spring to mind. That might be anything from fly fishing to tango dancing, from snorkeling to writing haiku. If you are lucky enough to be able to identify what your flowing play is, you're really very lucky.

Now what you need to do is be sure to make room for it in your life. This can be difficult if you have been away from your "flow" activity for a while, as you will need to get back into a habit of prioritizing it. You will also need to help the people who are close to you understand that by pursuing this activity you are not diminishing the time you spend with them so much as enriching it. For you will come back from your flow time a more easygoing, fully attentive partner, parent, or friend.

But for some of us, that's putting the proverbial cart before the horse. Having fallen out of the habit of playing, let alone playing with a sense of passion, we need to start by dabbling and trying things on for size.

If you are not sure what your potential flow activity is, start by asking yourself these questions:

◆ What activity did I love to play at as a child?

◆ Is there some form of that activity I can incorporate into my adult life?

◆ What is something I do where I look at the clock and cannot believe how much time has gone by?

◆ What is an activity that I like more for itself than for what I "get out of it" in terms of a result?

◆ What activity is challenging enough to keep me fully occupied, but never frustrating enough so that I want to give up?

◆ During what activity do I tend not to feel silly or self-conscious—nor do I care what others think about how I am doing it?

◆ What activity leaves me with a sense of self-fulfillment, as though in some sense I was perhaps even "born to do this."

Maybe by now you are homing in on something. If not, consider experimenting, perhaps with the arts, or with gardening, or with athletics. You don't have to limit yourself to these choices, to be sure—but they are the ways that many people relieve stress by finding flow, and so they might be good places for you to start.

Artistic Play

Making art—painting, sketching, sculpting, taking photographs, or other such processes—enables many people to experience play and flow. The fact that artistic endeavors of this nature relieve stress is no surprise—it is something that has long been known to art therapists.

As we focus wholly on an artistic act, studies show, heart rate and respiration slow, and blood pressure lowers. But art's ability to calm and heal us also stems in part from how we use it to access deep-seated feelings that we might otherwise believe it is inappropriate for us to express in front of others in public (or sometimes even admit to ourselves in private).

Repressing strong feelings can lead to a buildup of emotional stress, because—believe it or not—it takes a tremendous amount of effort and strain to keep reigning in powerful emotions that we do not wish to come to the fore. Art enables people to access these pent-up emotions and to transform them, via various materials, into accessible imagery.

The artistic process is particularly effective at doing this because we tend to suspend linear thought while we work within our chosen medium. As we interact with paint, clay, or paper and pen, we lose our self-consciousness and instead begin to tap our unconscious. We find, often even to our own surprise, that the unconscious is quite adept at giving voice to our deepest thoughts and feelings by expressing them in some artistic fashion.

Another reason that creating art can provide such a calming break from day-to-day life is that art utilizes a language other than the language of words. We are continually bombarded with streams of words, not only from others but also from within our own chattering mind. Our internal monologue, as we realize when we try to quiet the mind during meditation, can often consist of a stream of self-criticism or perhaps a laundry list of worries or things we'd like to change about ourselves or the circumstances of our lives. How refreshing to turn down the volume as we lose ourselves in an artistic process.

When the artistic endeavor we are engaged in is complete, we have another bonus. Even though the actual end product is not as important as process in terms of creating flow, it does indeed feel nice to have created something—even if we choose not to show it to lots of people (or anyone at all!). Besides, who knows what latent talents we might uncover?

For people who are not able or ready to create art, visiting an art museum or looking through art books can offer ideas and inspiration. Moreover, simply viewing art—although not likely to create flow *per se*—can refresh the spirit and promote relaxation, provided it is done attentively.

Stress Less

Allow yourself to suspend self-judgment as you create art. You might be surprised at what your artistry produces, but the real benefit will come from taking a break from constantly evaluating yourself and worrying if you are "good enough."

If you are interested in trying your hand at art as a way of achieving flow, here are a few tips to keep in mind:

- Don't get hung up on buying the best materials—practice on cheap paper so you won't be concerned with "waste."

- Start with the basics—do some simple exercises like drawing basic shapes.

- Don't be afraid of abstraction—art does not have to be a literal recreation of what you see or of what already exists.

- Don't be afraid of simplicity, either—art doesn't have to be ornate or elaborate.

- Consider working in a medium you have no experience in at all, which can be very freeing.

- Consider taking some classes—they'll help you with basic techniques, help you build confidence, and allow you to meet other aspiring artists.

- Attend an art exhibit and move through it *slowly*—see if you can spot artists who might be expressing ideas similar to your own.

- Look for other venues that might offer inspiration because they contain interesting and beautiful sights—consider places like botanical gardens, bird sanctuaries, or zoos that do a good job of recreating natural habitats.

- Make a space to create art (even a small desk or fold-out table) and organize in it the things you will need ahead of time—then you can slip away during quiet moments and dive into the process.

Finally, think back to a time in your life when you were genuinely excited about making art. You might have to go as far back as kindergarten, because much of our later life does not allow a lot of time for original artistic expression. But accessing childlike glee and exuberance is one of the best things you can do to restore your creativity and relieve your anxiety.

If all else fails, just do it. Plunge in. Often artists don't know what they're doing until they're doing it. Start the process and trust that inspiration will follow. After all, what's the worst that could happen? (You weren't planning to quit your day job, were you?) You can chalk any project up to a learning experience, and you can always start over.

Playing in the Garden

As we saw in the first chapter of this book, one of the sources of modern stress stems from our sense of disconnection with nature. Isolated and insulated in our climatically controlled houses, we are oblivious to nature's cycles, and we mostly glimpse its splendors through thermal-paned windows. Environmental psychologists believe that spending time in beautiful, natural surroundings can positively influence our state of mind.

What better way to bring nature into your life, and to create flow, than to plant and tend a garden?

If you know any gardening buffs, you can surely attest to the joys they obtain from kneeling on the earth and digging their hands in dirt. (Remember making mud pies as a child?) The seeds and shoots they plant are tiny lives waiting to blossom into their full potential beauty. The gardener's watering nurtures the seeds and brings them to fruition. The gardener's detailed process of weeding and pruning gives the plants and flowers breathing room—and does the same for the gardener, who enjoys a respite from stress through an intense focus on the blossoms that are being coaxed to grow and thrive.

Perhaps you're thinking, "You need a green thumb to garden, and my thumb is black." But that is probably because you've never really attempted to cultivate a garden with any kind of attentiveness. Plants are *meant* to grow, and even if you've had some bad experiences with the odd houseplant here and there (you forgot to water it, it withered, and you felt guilty and inept), you can achieve a lot of satisfaction with a little effort when you resolve to bring nature into your life in this way.

Start small. Even if you have acres of land at your disposal, section off a small, manageable plot for your garden. If you have only a small plot of land or a window box available, you're actually ahead of the game. Biting off more than you can chew is always stressful.

If you live in an apartment and have no outdoor space, you might want to check out the availability of public gardening space—often sponsored by schools, churches, and statewide environmental organizations. But don't worry if that's not an option. You can plant a small, simple garden indoors as well as out of doors, so long as you investigate which kinds of plants thrive best in the kind of light conditions you can provide.

Now, find something to plant. It's no secret that some types of flora require more care and feeding than others. If you're a novice, visit a nursery and ask for plants that are "idiot proof"—meaning very hearty and resilient, even if they are occasionally neglected. (No, the nursery folks will not laugh at you. Lots of customers make such requests.) You can also find out about the relative heartiness of various plants by perusing gardening books and magazines—a relaxing, diverting pastime in itself.

As with other activities you are trying out in order to relieve stress, don't overaccessorize or overspend. But do invest in some basic tools such as a small spade for digging and a weeding implement. A pair of gardening gloves is also a nice idea if you are not interested in getting dirt under your fingernails—though that's hardly the worst thing in the world.

Need inspiration? Take a walk. Breathe the fresh air, enjoy the sunshine, and get the ancillary benefit of exercise as you look for ideas amongst the neighborhood greenery or the wildflowers of the woods.

Too Tense

Think about impatiens or begonias rather than rare orchids if you're creating a starter garden. Common (aptly called "garden variety") blossoms are forgiving. Delicate and temperamental flora that requires intensive expertise can prove frustrating to the beginner.

Stress Less

Growing herbs on your windowsill is another way to reconnect with nature and enjoy gardening on a small, manageable scale. Consider herbs that are known for their calming properties—such as lavender—and you will have a stress-beating bonus.

Creating your garden will afford you an opportunity to experience the flow of the moment, and will give you ongoing sources of beauty to appreciate. Another benefit is that after you have your garden, you will have the opportunity to use it as a soothing retreat space (more on retreat spaces in Chapter 19). Think about adding decorative flourishes like small garden statuary or a bubbling fountain to enhance the experience and complement the wonderful work—make that *play*—that you have done.

Sports and Stress

Many people say they deflect stress by playing sports. Getting together for their weekly game of basketball, soccer, handball, or whatever their sport of choice, they say, gets their minds off their troubles and burns off excess tension. Whether they realize it or not, when they are playing well against evenly-matched opponents and using their skills optimally, they are probably also enjoying a state of flow. Time passes without them realizing it, and their focus is intensely on what is happening in the moment.

Sports can be frustrating if they're "not your thing." Understandably, the idea of taking up a sport is anxiety-provoking if you think you have two left feet and no eye-hand coordination whatsoever. But think about this: if the state of being "sport challenged" describes you, it very likely also describes several of your friends. If you take up a sport together, you can enjoy the process of the game without feeling self-conscious. You'll get exercise, share camaraderie, commiserate, perfect your technique—or what there is of it—and laugh! That's a whole lot of eustress to be mined from one new activity.

Maybe you're just an armchair sports enthusiast, or someone who haunts the bleachers every time your kids play a Little League or Pop Warner football game. Does all that watching and cheering count in terms of deflecting stress? To some degree watching sports can relax you, provided you have the right attitude. Don't get over-invested or feel too frustrated if your favorite team, or your budding child athlete, has a bad day. It's only a game, after all. Right?

Too Tense

You won't get stress relief from sports if you convince yourself you have to be competent at all times. Watching professional athletes can teach you that everyone makes mistakes sometimes.

In any case, it's unlikely—no matter how much you might enjoy being a sports spectator—that watching others play will put you into a state of transcendent flow. No, even the Super Bowl or the World Series won't do that. To be in flow is to be busy doing. So think about what game you might like to play at—and give it a shot.

Awe Is Awesome, Wonder Is Wonderful

To enhance and nurture your ability to play and to create flow in your life, it is essential to nurture within yourself an attitude you might not have had since you were very, very young. That is an attitude of awe and wonder.

When we are stressed, we are generally in a thought rut. We are even in a sensory rut. Take our sense of vision, for example. When we are stressed, we only notice sights we expect to encounter. We are so preoccupied that we could literally walk past a purple elephant and not notice the pachyderm within our line of sight.

Allowing yourself to be surprised by new thoughts, new ideas, new sensory input, will help you break out of that rut, and give you lots of inspiration. Open your eyes! What's out there? What's new? Look at the world as if you were a child. (In fact, if you have a child in your life, walk around with them and you'll learn a few lessons.)

Stress Less

If you really want to cultivate a new perspective, try looking at the sky through a telescope. For an equally awesome experience, view a small crystal or a blade of grass under a microscope.

To keep yourself alert, try noting on a small pad of paper all the things in your immediate environment you haven't noticed recently—that new flower in the garden, the way the sun hits the kitchen window and makes a rainbow pattern. Describe what you see. If you hear or smell or taste anything new, note that as well. If you have a question about something, write it down—and then later find out the answer. Your new-found curiosity will keep your mind off your stressors and give you a new breadth and depth of knowledge about what surrounds you.

The Least You Need to Know

- Play enables us—at any age—to relieve stress by pursuing pleasurable activities that do not have long-term goals.

- When we are engaged in an activity in which we lose track of time and our skills are fully engaged, we can enter a beneficial state known as *flow*.

◆ Making art is a wonderful way to play, create flow, and relieve stress—as the process enables us to access and express feelings we might have been keeping bottled up.

◆ Creating a garden, no matter how small, is another way to enjoy the play process—and to ease stress by reconnecting with the natural world.

◆ Playing sports—when you are using your skills optimally and playing against well-matched opponents—can also put you in a flow state (but just watching sports, while a relaxing activity, won't offer quite the same benefit).

◆ To raise your potential for experiencing creative play and flow, try seeing the world anew with childlike wonder—practice noticing what's new in your immediate environment.

Part 5

Anti-Stress Self-Care

Eat well, sleep well, take breaks *at* home and breaks *from* home: that's the self-care prescription for beating stress that this part of the book will address. Though it might sound easy enough, many of us find it hard to justify a level of self-care that will keep stress at bay. Learn to do unto yourself and see the difference some simple self-care makes.

17

Anti-Stress Foods and Supplements

In This Chapter

- Eating poorly under stress
- When stress causes cravings
- Strategies for controlling cravings
- Eating right to beat stress
- Anti-stress supplements
- Making good choices simple

Eating right can help us prevent many of stress's ill effects, giving our bodies and brains the proper fuel to see us through. Yet we often overindulge in food, or turn away from it altogether, when we're stressed. Often, stress causes us to take in precisely the things that will make us feel worse and diminish our ability to cope.

Information about eating well and supplanting our diets abounds. But so does misinformation. This chapter sheds light on what works and offers a balanced approach for eating right to beat stress.

Stress and Eating Habits

Eating is something we all need to do to stay alive, but we don't simply eat when we're hungry or when our bodies need calories to keep us going. What we eat and how often we eat are highly subject to conditioning—to habit. In addition, our emotions have a profound impact on what we eat, on when we eat, and on how much we eat.

def•i•ni•tion

Stress hypophagics are people who typically respond to stress by eating less.

Stress hyperphagics are people who typically respond to stress by eating more.

Feelings of stress often change our eating habits. Interestingly, however, they can do so in two very different ways. About a third of us eat less when we are highly stressed—in technical terms, we become *hypophagic*. About two thirds of us eat more when we're stressed, becoming *hyperphagic*.

A couple of different factors help determine whether we lose our appetites or whether we scarf down every morsel in sight. One factor is the type of stress we're under. When stress is immediate and intense, appetite tends to be put on hold as the body turns its attention to pressing matters. Nutrition is important for survival, but not as immediately important as, say, fleeing from a charging bull, groping for a fire extinguisher, or deciding what to try to salvage when floodwaters are rising. Faced with an overwhelming catastrophic stressor, we're not likely to stop for a sandwich.

On the other hand, frequent intermittent stressors—the short-lived but chronic and cumulative kind many of us experience on a routine basis—tend to increase our desire to eat. In part, this has to do with how and when various stress hormones are released into our systems. In the initial grip of stress, we release lots of adrenaline, which can serve as an appetite suppressant. Later, we secrete *glucocortoroids*—a class of stress hormones that affect glucose levels and can elevate appetite. Chronic stress ensures that these glucocortoroids are cleared from our systems very slowly. The more they hang around, the hungrier we are.

def•i•ni•tion

Glucocortoroids are a class of steroid stress hormones that the brain triggers the adrenal gland to produce after initial adrenaline is released. They affect our blood sugar levels as they back up the activity of adrenaline over the course of minutes or hours.

Our individual body chemistry also has a lot to do with the eat less/eat more equation. Not everyone secretes the same level of blood sugar–raising glucocortoroids, and not everyone's liver breaks them down at the same speed.

Another factor that distinguishes stress hypophagics from stress hyperphagics is their emotional relationships with food. Many of us associate eating with the soothing of emotional upset. Even so, we try to control our urge to overindulge out of boredom or disappointment. But even those of us who make a conscious effort not to give in to emotional food triggers can lose our restraint under chronic stress. We tend to use—or rather misuse—food as a coping device.

Comfort Food

What kind of food do we want most when we're under stress? You probably already know. If you've ever had a big fight with your significant other, or been told a critical work deadline is being moved up, have you gone out and grabbed a head of lettuce or some broccoli spears? I'll bet not. You've probably gone straight for a trough of chocolate-chip cookies.

Under stress, we crave sweet and starchy foods. Our body wants easily accessible, instant energy with which to face a stressor. On top of that, our stressed-out emotions cry out for numbing. Bring on the carbs: candy, brownies, ice cream, a tall stack of blueberry pancakes with syrup!

The popular term for the kind of starchy foods we give ourselves as a "present" when we're stressed is *comfort food*. It's not a misnomer. Comfort foods are foods whose consumption evokes a psychologically pleasurable state. A rush of carbohydrates does comfort us. But what follows the rush is an inevitable crash. Then we want another rush. And another.

Eating lots of starchy comfort foods also creates another problem. We put on weight we can't get rid of so easily. The stress response stimulates us to store fat—and that storage occurs primarily around the abdomen. Eating out of stress can cause us to take on an "apple" shape, with girth around the center.

To make matters worse, it turns out, abdominal fat presents greater health risks than other kinds of fat. People with a high waist-to-hip ratio (WHR) are at a greater risk for cardiovascular diseases than are normal-weight people or even overweight people whose fat collects elsewhere (e.g., the hips and buttocks).

Too Tense

Many factors can influence our specific choice of comfort food. Frequently they are the foods we experienced as treats while growing up. But overconsumption of any comfort food—even those "just like Mom used to make"—ends up having a long-term negative impact.

They're also at greater risk for metabolic diseases such as diabetes because the fat that collects around the stomach finds its way easily to the liver, where it is converted into glucose that sets us up for insulin resistance. These phenomena have been studied in both women and men across a broad range of ages, and the findings are consistent.

Stress and Substance Abuse

In addition to eating more simple sugars when stressed, many of us turn to other substances that only make the situation worse. Chief among these are alcohol, caffeine, and tobacco. All of them offer counterproductive ways of dealing with stress.

Each of these substances has the potential to damage our overall health. What's more, stress increases the odds that we'll become addicted to our substance (or substances) of choice, that weaning ourselves from them will prove more difficult, and that we'll be more likely to experience a relapse even if we do successfully withdraw from them.

About Alcohol

When the stressors of the day are piling up, some of us look forward to that moment when we can indulge in a cocktail, a glass (or more) of wine, or a few beers. We imagine how, during those first few sips, our sense of being overwhelmed by stress will disappear. And indeed it seems to work—for a while.

On a physical level, alcohol can decrease the arousal of the sympathetic nervous system— the part of our autonomic nervous system that turns on the stress response to begin with. In some people, alcohol also has been shown to diminish the amount of stress hormones in the system. On an emotional level, alcohol blunts stress by making us perceive whatever our stressors are as not such big deals after all. If we drink enough, we might—at least temporarily—even be able to put our stressors out of our minds.

But then a backlash occurs. As our blood alcohol levels drop, we get a "cold shower" of reality. Now the remnants of the drug serve only to provoke more anxiety or depression. The solution, for far too many people, is to raise those blood alcohol levels by drinking some more. A vicious cycle can ensue, with increasing dependency on drinking.

About Caffeine

Caffeine might seem like a strange thing to reach for when we are stressed, but many of us do so. Faced with stressful feelings of too much to do in too little time, we reach for a stimulant in the form of cup after cup of coffee, or black tea, or caffeine-laden soft drinks. Some 85 percent of Americans, in fact, ingest some caffeine during the course of each day.

There's no question that caffeine can almost immediately cause a sense of recharged energy. Interestingly, for some, it even provides a temporary pleasurable rush by increasing levels of dopamine. But any such effect is short-lived. Ultimately the alertness and faster reaction time caffeine provides comes from blocking the binding sites for a calming neurotransmitter called *adrenosine*. Caffeine also raises levels of the stress hormones adrenaline and cortisol. In short, it actually exacerbates the stress response.

When the effects of caffeine wear off, we become fatigued and we need another dose of it. And because we tend to build up a tolerance to caffeine, only greater and greater amounts of it reproduce the effects we want. If you take large amounts of caffeine, you might well find your mood soaring and plummeting over and over again—hardly a sound formula for dealing with stressors. Even more troubling, researchers say that the equivalent of four cups of coffee raises blood pressure for many hours—enough to affect heart attack and stroke risk.

Caffeine is such a routine part of so many of our lifestyles that it is hard for some of us to imagine giving it up—even though withdrawal effects, usually in the form of headaches, are not terribly severe. Nevertheless, it is a good idea to monitor your caffeine use, and to especially avoid it late in the day when it can interfere with much-needed restorative sleep.

> **Stress Less**
>
> If you are going to drink anything containing caffeine, you might want to try doing so before exercise. Check with your doctor, but studies show that if caffeine isn't overused, it might enhance physical performance and endurance. Besides, the benefits of exercise itself serve as a stress reducer.

About Tobacco

Most smokers report that one reason they smoke—despite the overwhelming and irrefutable evidence that it is devastating to health—is so that they can handle the stress in their lives. They believe that lighting up a cigarette calms them.

In a way, they're correct. Smoking temporarily alleviates some degree of stress by releasing powerful chemicals into the brain. Nicotine stimulates the production of some of the brain's most potent chemical messengers, including dopamine and beta-endorphins, which create a sense of pleasure and the reduction of both anxiety and pain. It also stimulates hormones that give us an energetic kick. The brain's chemistry alters so that we feel both alert *and* relaxed.

Too Tense

If you are planning to quit smoking, don't rely on sheer willpower. Have alternative stress-management strategies in place. When the urge to smoke occurs, have a plan to take a walk, do a relaxing meditation, or call a friend for emotional support. Then act on that plan.

Ultimately, though, smoking creates more stress than it dispels. Beginning within mere minutes after each smoke, the body begins to go into withdrawal. Smokers then experience increasing anxiety, agitation, and loss of focus. The obvious "fix" is another cigarette.

Though most smokers believe they ought to quit, they dread experiencing withdrawal symptoms over an extended period of time. They also dread the emotional sense of loss they will experience and the sheer rigor of altering such an ingrained daily habit. Certainly some smokers do manage to quit, but episodes of high stress in their lives can rekindle the temptation.

Controlling Stress-Related Cravings

Millions and millions of us routinely give in to cravings for comfort foods, alcohol, caffeine, and tobacco—or some combination thereof—not only when we are stressed, but also when we think we might be entering a situation that will precipitate stress. Such cravings are hard to resist, but they are not *irresistible*.

Know Your Triggers

One of the best ways to break the habit of giving in to a craving is knowing when that craving is likely to strike. Each of us has certain stress triggers in our life. These are highly individual and can include anything from personal situations to family or work-related issues. Your stress *triggers might include* …

- Having to take a test.
- Having to give a speech or presentation.
- Working toward a tight deadline.
- Meeting new people.
- Facing a confrontation.
- Spending time with difficult relatives.
- Dealing with a demanding boss.
- Balancing (or not balancing) your checkbook.

They might even include getting on the scale or getting a check-up by the doctor. And if so, that's all the more reason to get your eating and substance-use habits under control!

After you have identified what is likely to set you running for the baked goods aisle of your local supermarket, the nearest wine shop, or Starbucks, start talking to yourself (it doesn't have to be out loud; inside your head is fine). Tell yourself that you are in control, not your cravings. Remind yourself that it is within your power to make a positive choice. Instead of reflexively going for the doughnuts/cocktail/cigarette/double latte, choose a positive calming action. This can be as simple as taking a few deep breaths. It can involve a disciplined substitution such as going to the gym instead of the nearest Krispy Kreme shop. The point is to develop enough self-awareness so that you can intervene with yourself before you opt for the quick fixes.

Don't get down on yourself for wanting a certain food or substance when you're feeling anxious—even though you recognize it won't help you in the end. The desire to soothe stress with an unhelpful substance isn't the problem; acting on it is.

Get a Hydration Fixation

If you're looking for a substance that really can help you beat stress, there is one you very well might not have thought of. It has no calories, no sugar, and is fat-free. It's just about always on hand. It's H_2O—otherwise known as water.

Water packs an amazing double punch in the quest to beat stress. First, drinking some can keep you from eating or drinking other substances that are counterproductive. It gives you something to do with your mouth and hands, and it fills up your stomach long enough so that other cravings might pass.

But equally important, water itself can actually help you feel less stressed by eliminating dehydration. Most of us don't realize it, but when we are not routinely running enough water through our systems we can suffer muddled thinking, headaches, fatigue, and irritability, among other things. Sounds suspiciously like the symptoms of chronic stress, doesn't it? Often what we physically experience as stress might be, at least in part, dehydration. And dehydration can exacerbate any circumstantial stress we are actually experiencing.

Ironically, stress itself tends to dehydrate the body, as do "pseudo" stress-relieving beverages like caffeine and alcohol. Commuting long distances can dehydrate us, and so—very severely—can air travel. Electromagnetic radiation, such as that produced by computer screens and mobile phones, might also contribute.

We tend not to drink enough water because we "don't feel thirsty." The truth is that many of us—studies say some 75 percent of all Americans—have been dehydrated for so long our bodies have forgotten how to interpret the signals for thirst. If we do notice them, we often misinterpret them as hunger.

The solution: drink up. At least eight 8-ounce glasses a day. A mere 2 percent drop in body water can affect your mental alertness and your physical stamina—both of which you need to battle stress in healthful ways.

It Works for Me

"I thought the idea of drinking water was boring. So my girlfriends and I came up with 'water cocktails'. We pour water into beautiful crystal goblets with slices of lime or lemon and colorful stirrers. We also taste test all kinds of waters, sparkling and non-sparkling, and mineral waters from all over the world. I do taste a difference, and it all makes drinking water an enjoyable ritual and a calming break."

—Amanda, 41

Try Tea Time

Another excellent choice for something to ingest when stressed are certain herbal teas known for their calming properties. These teas can be a good alternative to coffee, fulfilling the urge to have a cup-of-something. The following can be made with a tea bag in moments, or you can brew fresh tea leaves, pour your beverage into an elegant teapot, and have a mindful, meditative tea interlude:

- ◆ **Chamomile.** A natural relaxant, this tea has been a popular tea choice for stress relief since the time of the ancient Egyptians. Many still swear by its ability to simultaneously soothe and lift spirits. Some herbal teas blend chamomile with lavender. Lavender is said to relax tense muscles, and its clean, appealing fragrance is an additional soother. The combination of lavender and chamomile is especially good for upset stomach and the restlessness associated with that condition.

- ◆ **Anise.** Anise is an antispasmodic and eases tension. It's said to be especially useful for counteracting irritability that comes from a change in diet or regimen. Anise is a common remedy for premenstrual syndrome. It's also is a natural breath freshener, so it comes in handy when you're seeking interpersonal relief from stress.

- ◆ **Fennel.** Often blended with anise in calming teas, fennel is also good for detoxifying the body from any not-so-healthy substances you've been taking in.

- **Catnip.** Use of catnip as a relaxing tea dates back to old England, where it was a very popular drink prior to the importation of other teas from Asia. Taken prior to bedtime, catnip tea is widely believed to both hasten slumber and promote a restful night's sleep.

- **Peppermint.** Peppermint is more of an energizer than a relaxer. So, when you are feeling exhausted, it's a great alternative to sugar or caffeine. Peppermint assists in oxygenating the blood. It stimulates the brain and helps improve the capacity to retain facts. It works wonders for test anxiety!

Some people swear by green tea, which is known to boost the immune system and refresh the body, as a stress reliever. But be aware that green tea does contain some caffeine. It can be effective; just don't overdo it. Two cups a day is a reasonable amount, and steer clear late in the afternoon or evening.

Eating Well to Counter Stress

Now that you know many of the foods you should avoid, you might be wondering what you should be eating to counter stress. There's no single food that will act as a magic bullet to keep stress at bay or immediately calm you down when you get into an anxious state. But you can handle stress better and counteract many of its ill effects by choosing a wide variety of healthy foods.

But before we look at what to eat, let's spend a moment on how to eat. Avoid skipping meals. Even if you're in a hypophagic state, try to eat something! Also, allow yourself to have some healthy snacks throughout the day. Eating three meals and snacks is not about gorging. It is about putting enough fuel in your system to keep it functioning optimally. It's also about keeping your blood sugar from hitting peaks and valleys throughout the day (a surefire formula for irritability). Eating small portions of healthy food every few hours will also help stave off cravings for sugary, starchy comfort foods.

Also, to the extent that it is at all feasible, when you eat, just eat. Sure, you can enjoy some pleasant conversation if you're dining with others, but if you are eating alone resist the temptation to do three other things at the same time (e.g., read the paper, watch TV, check your e-mail). Eating mindfully slows your eating down, helps your digestion, and simply helps you to enjoy and appreciate your meal. That in itself can be a stress-beater.

Now, back to the question of what to eat. To keep your body sound, your head clear, and your immune system in good working order, variety is crucial. You need protein, fruits and vegetables, dairy, good fats (such as those found in nuts, avocados, olive oil, and oily fish like salmon and sardines), and whole grains.

Don't even *think* about eliminating an entire food group in order to "go on a diet." Despite recent crazes to eliminate carbohydrates, carbs are not the bad guys. But it is crucial to know which ones are which.

Good Carbs

Giving up comfort foods does not require giving up carbohydrates. But it does mean seriously limiting the wrong kind of carbohydrates—those that are quickly digested and that lead to spiking of blood sugar.

A lot has been learned lately as to what separates good carbs from bad. One difference is measured on a scale called the *Glycemic Index* (*GI*). The scale assigns values from 0 to 100 to various foods, with pure glucose at the top. Foods rated 70 and above are considered high-GI carbs and have a fast and furious impact on blood-sugar levels.

The GI scale provides a pretty good standard for choosing healthy carbohydrates, but it does present a few problems in that some healthful foods like beets and carrots scored high in GI. It turns out that these foods come off well if we also factor in another scale: the *Glycemic Load* (*GL*), which measures the actual amount of carbohydrates per serving. Beets and carrots, it turns out, score well on the GL because they contain so much water and fiber.

def•i•ni•tion _____

The **Glycemic Index (GI)** measures the amount of quickly digestible glucose in a food. Values from 70 to 100 are considered high. Those between 55 and 70 are considered moderate; those under 55 are considered low.

The **Glycemic Load (GL)** measures the amount of actual carbohydrate content in a typical portion size. High GL values are over 20, moderate are 11 to 19, low are from 1 to10.

You can learn a lot more about GI and GL on numerous websites (including that of the Harvard School of Public Health: www.hsph.harvard.edu/nutritionsource/carbohydrates.html), but don't stress about assigning numbers to everything you eat. There are actually some pretty simple general guidelines for choosing carbs that will fuel you at an even keel over those that will keep you on a stressful sugar roller coaster. Here are some suggestions:

- ◆ Stay away from the "white stuff"—foods made with sugar and flour, especially packaged snack foods.

- ◆ Eat more whole grains, like barley, buckwheat, and wild rice (see www. wholegrainscouncil.org).

- ◆ Eat more beans.

- ◆ Eat more sweet potatoes and squash.

- ◆ Forego anything made with high-fructose corn syrup.

Remember: the less processed the food, the better off you are. Foods that are highly refined and highly processed are likely to set your moods pinging all over the place. If you have to open a cardboard box with graphics that appeal to 12-year-olds and unwrap a food from inside hermetically sealed plastic wrap, chances are it has the kind of carbs you really want to think twice about.

Antioxidants

Chapter 3 mentioned the fact that people who are under chronic emotional stress also tend to be under more oxidative stress than those with a more relaxed attitude. In oxidative stress, free radicals—oxygen molecules with single missing electrons—cause cellular damage by taking electrons from molecules in healthy cells. To be clear, oxidative stress is not the kind of stress this book is generally referring to. It is purely physiological stress at the cellular level.

However, because emotional stress does seem to correlate with oxidative stress, it's a good idea to include in our diets foods that can counteract the effect of free radicals.

Those foods, in a word, are plants. Plants contain phytonutrients, protective compounds that evolved to protect our green friends from environmental damage and that can protect us as well. Most people don't eat enough fruits and vegetables. To counteract oxidative stress we need to make a concerted effort to up our intake of these foods.

Too Tense

Watch your additives! Monosodium glutamate (MSG) and hydrolyzed plant or vegetable protein are added to foods to enhance flavor, but they can also cause flushing of the skin, headaches, palpitations, and insomnia. Read labels, and if you are ordering at a restaurant tell them you want your food MSG-free.

We also need to make sure we choose the right mix of fruits and vegetables, and the easiest way to do this is by color. We need to consume plants from all parts of the color spectrum: think blueberries, blackberries, carrots, yellow peppers, ripe red tomatoes, and dark leafy greens. Picture an artist's palette, a cornucopia of color—and enjoy.

Stress-Beating Supplements

More and more, we hear claims about products like vitamins and herbs that are "specially formulated" to beat stress. Are they for real? Well, yes and no. Some supplements do have a restorative effect on us when we have been worn down by stress, and some have a reinforcing effect on our overall health and immunity, so that stress is not apt to do us so much harm. There are, however, no supplements that offer an instant cure for stress in the sense that they prevent it altogether or immediately counteract its effects.

In other words, don't expect to pop a supplement pill that will enable you to function in a state of blissful calm even though your in-laws are coming for a two-week stay. They're strictly a physiological defense strategy. That said, it's worth knowing about some supplements that can help us in balancing our systems and bolster us against physical stress.

Vitamins and Minerals

Some vitamins are rapidly depleted from our systems when we are under stress. These include vitamin C and the whole range of B complex vitamins, including B6, B12, biotin, and folic acid. A deficiency in these vitamins can lower our resistance to illness. It's also been shown that the minerals magnesium and zinc are sapped from the body during stressful times. So look for all of these in a multivitamin formula.

Stress Less

Always take your multivitamin with meals to aid absorbability. A vitamin that simply passes through you won't do you any good at all.

If you've recently been under acute physical stressors such as surgery or injuries, you might want to up your level of B vitamins. They will help you get more energy from the foods you eat. In addition to taking supplements, you can get these vitamins in foods such as whole grains and enriched cereals, lean meats, and dairy products.

Adaptogens

One of the new buzzwords in supplements is *adaptogens*. The term refers to a class of natural remedies—herbs and mushrooms—that are said to help us *adapt* to physical and even emotional stressors in the environment and to increase energy and immune function. Some of the better-known adaptogens include …

♦ **Arctic root.** Soviet scientists have confirmed that the fragrant underground part of the *rhodiola rosea* plant, which grows in high latitudes of the Northern Hemisphere (like Siberia and Mongolia), affects numerous neurotransmitters in the brain. Perhaps this is why it is said to enhance mental clarity and to have anti-fatigue and endurance-building properties. People in northern climes have long sworn by arctic root's efficacy.

♦ **Astragalus.** Obtained from the root of *astragalus membranaceus*, a plant in the pea family, this adaptogen has a long history of use in Chinese medicine. Research has confirmed its properties as an immune enhancer.

♦ **Liquid mushroom extract.** Many edible mushrooms species, such as shiitake, oyster, and maitake, are said to have immune-enhancing properties. Combinations of these mushrooms are now widely available in liquid, powder, and capsule forms. The mushrooms are said to work best in concert with one another, and some products contain more than a dozen species.

Adaptogens are considered safe and have been tested by numerous academic researchers. They contain no drugs, preservatives, or banned substances. Do note, however, that on occasion certain herbs can interact negatively with prescription drugs, so check with your doctor on that subject. Also, check the labels for dosage and do not exceed the recommended amount.

Simplify Your Eating Style

Eating well to counteract stress should not be a stressful endeavor in itself. If it's something you have to go out of your way to do, you won't make good eating a natural habit. So don't go out of your way—instead, make healthy eating your default eating style by doing some planning ahead.

Stock your pantry, freezer, and refrigerator with the ingredients for healthy meals. Invest in cookbooks and cuisine magazines that specialize in preparation of quick (30 minutes or less) nutritious fare.

Most important of all, keep snacks handy that will satisfy your need for refueling without giving in to sugar cravings. You are far more likely to grab some veggies if they are pre-cut and stored in plastic containers, and if you have some healthful dips at the ready (think salsa, made from tomatoes, and hummus, made from chickpeas). In the same spirit, keeping a bag of almonds or soy nuts in your handbag or briefcase will help you steer clear of the comfort foods in vending machines.

Can you go off your wagon once in awhile? Of course you can. But after you see the impact that eating right has on your overall ability to handle stress, who knows how much you'll really want to.

The Least You Need to Know

- Some of us eat less under stress, but most of us eat more—especially more sugary, starchy comfort foods that can negatively affect mood and health by causing blood sugar to spike and dip.

- Turning to substances like caffeine, alcohol, and tobacco are counterproductive ways of handling stress—these short-term fixes create long-term backlash habits.

- To counter cravings, know your stress triggers and have proactive alternative behaviors in place—if you need something to ingest, try water or herbal teas.

- Although there are no "magic bullet" foods or supplements that will make stress disappear, eating healthfully and choosing supplements that bolster the immune system can help us to better weather whatever stressors come our way.

- Good eating habits are easier to maintain when you plan ahead—have a variety of healthy choices at your fingertips and you'll stop reflexively grabbing for foods and substances that can exacerbate stress.

Chapter 18

Sleeping It Off

In This Chapter

- ◆ What's so good about sleep
- ◆ How sleeplessness causes stress
- ◆ How stress causes sleeplessness
- ◆ How much sleep we need
- ◆ Sound sleep strategies
- ◆ To nap, or not to nap

We so often hear about the value of a good night's sleep. Sleep, we're told, balances our physical self and recharges our mind. It seems obvious, therefore, that sleep can steel us against many of the negative effects of stress.

Yet for all the good things we hear about sleep, we're pretty willing to sacrifice it. Even as the healing properties of rest are touted, the demands of our busy lifestyles can compel us to go, go, go. Yet getting enough good-quality sleep is a must in the quest to cope calmly with life's ups and downs. It's an indispensable anti-stress strategy that we should never neglect.

Why Sleep?

Eight hours a night of nothingness. Eight hours a night of wasted time. That's how some of us view sleep. Why, we wonder, do we have to devote a third of our lives to this nonproductive activity?

But then, if we start to lose too much sleep, we sing a different tune. In addition to experiencing plain old fatigue, we feel unfocused and out of sorts. We're low on frustration tolerance and we lack much of a sense of humor. We feel, all things considered, like we're chronically stressed.

What, exactly, are we missing when we deliberately shave time off our sleep, or when we simply cannot sleep even though we want to? What on earth is sleep for?

Even scientists who have devoted their lives to studying it do not yet understand every nuance of sleep's functions. But there are many things they do know. For one, sleep is an *anabolic process*, or building process. In addition to restoring bodily energy supplies that have been depleted during the day, sleep is also the time when the body does most of its repair work on muscle tissue. One thing that happens to us during sleep is that human growth hormone is secreted. This hormone is important not only for growth when we are children, but also throughout adulthood when our tissues require repair.

def•i•ni•tion

An **anabolic process** is one in which energy is used to construct complex molecules from simple ones.

Glycogen, also called animal starch, is a compound stored in our muscles and liver that can easily be converted to energy in the form of glucose.

On a physical level, sleep also improves muscle tone and coordination. Without sleep, we're clumsy; with it we are more agile—we can run faster, jump higher, and lift a greater amount of weight. Without sleep we're more apt to get sick, because sleep also appears to boost the body's immune system.

On a cognitive level, sleep is an invaluable commodity because it helps build up stores of mental energy. Even though our brains weigh a scant 3 percent of our body weight, they consume about a quarter of our energy doing lots of thinking, creating, and problem solving. Stores of a molecule called *glycogen*, which provides that energy, are depleted during the day, but the slow, steady brain waves that occur during sleep restock our shelves, so to speak. During slow wave sleep the parts of the brain associated with arousal activity and the brain regions involved with muscle activity slow down. The areas of the brain that first respond to sensory stimulation and give it meaning are quiescent. It's not time to react; it's time to recharge our mental batteries.

Some sleep scientists believe that sleep detoxifies the brain by lowering its temperature. Whatever its exact mechanisms, sleep helps our brain think clearly. Just try doing some mental math calculations after a good night's sleep and then again after a poor one. You'll notice the difference right away.

Sleep also helps our minds by allowing us to dream. Dreams occur during a phase of sleep called *REM*, or *rapid eye movement*. During this phase the brain's frontal cortex, which helps us think in logical, sequential order, yields to our more primal limbic system. As a result, we have thoughts and images that jump all over the place and that incorporate a pastiche of ideas that range from the mundane to the seemingly bizarre.

def•i•ni•tion

> **REM, or rapid eye movement,** sleep is the phase of sleep in which we dream. During this phase there is a marked increase in metabolic activity of some brain regions—akin to brain aerobics. The regions that integrate visual information become exceptionally active, and the eyeballs jerk in various directions even though the eyes are closed.

How, exactly, do sleeping dreams help us function in our waking lives? The jury is still out on that one. Psychoanalysts have long told us that dreams are "the royal road to the unconscious," illuminating repressed wishes of which our conscious minds are unaware. Perhaps so. But sleep experts are more likely to speculate that dreams are some sort of cleaning process that sweeps the brain free of the day's sensory debris as well as an organizational process that helps us to reorganize and store gathered bits of information.

One thing everyone can agree on, however, is that dreaming is useful for optimal waking cognition. Deprive people of REM sleep and they will go to pieces much more quickly under pressure. Allow them adequate REM sleep and they will show clearer thinking and improved consolidation of information. There does indeed seem to be truth to the adage that a problem is better solved after we "sleep on it."

Chickens and Eggs: The Stress-Sleep Connection

If sleep does so many wonderful things for us in terms of balancing and recharging our bodies and minds, it's clear that not getting enough sleep is a stressor. But here's the real rub: being stressed often causes us not to get enough sleep. If we want to break this vicious cycle, let's first take a closer look at it.

When Sleeplessness Causes Stress

As we ease into the slow brain waves of sleep, the sympathetic nervous system—the part of the autonomic nervous system that revs us up—gives way to its calming complement, the parasympathetic system. As this happens, the levels of stress hormones in our systems decrease. Although this is not the case during REM sleep, it remains so during most of our sleep time.

When we are deprived of sleep, we lose the chance for the diminishment of stress hormones. In fact, sleep deprivation increases our levels of such hormones. Furthermore, we're deprived of the opportunity to replenish stores of energy in our brains. Our memories suffer, as is evident when we tackle difficult mental tasks involving recall on too little sleep (if your college final exams are coming to mind, you're not alone).

A poor night's sleep also causes the stress response to be more quickly activated during the day. Little irritants that might not bother us, or might not bother us very much, when we're well rested can suddenly seem overwhelming. And by overreacting to them we can easily create interpersonal tensions that put us in even more stress-inducing circumstances. In short: without sleep we're grouchy, and grouchy people find it hard to "play nice."

> **It Works for Me**
>
> "If I haven't slept well, my kids know I'm more likely to snap at them. I think they got so tired of tiptoeing around me when I as awake that they now know it's a priority to be quiet when 'Mom' is sleeping."
>
> —Roseann, 35

Naturally we feel flustered when we are unfocused, unable to perform well at tasks that are important to us, and less in control of our emotional reactions. We feel as though our own minds and bodies are betraying us. In a way, they actually are.

But now we're in a real pickle. The less we sleep, and the more negative stress we experience, the less likely it is that we'll be able to sleep well. And the more stressed we are about not falling asleep, the longer it will probably take to do so.

When Stress Causes Sleeplessness

Not being able to achieve release from negative stress via sleep hardly seems fair. But the phenomenon does make sense if you think of it from a strictly evolutionary, survival-oriented point of view. The parts of your mind-body system that are trying to protect you from harm don't think it's such a good idea to catch 40 winks when you're being chased by a man-eating jungle cat that had a light lunch. They want you alert and ready to spring into action.

The problem—when the stressor is a knotty work-related problem, a pending root canal, or a looming tax audit instead of a lurking carnivore—is that the stress hormones that are cascading through our systems suppress sleep nevertheless. What's more, other physical stress symptoms, such as an elevated heart rate, make it hard to get much shut-eye. Instead of drifting off, we toss and turn.

If we finally do manage to fall asleep under stress, we spend less time in restorative slow wave sleep. Instead, we skim the surface of sleep, engaging in shallow sleep rhythms during which we are more likely to be awakened by the slightest stimuli.

Too Tense

Seventy-five percent of major insomnia cases are triggered by some major stressor.

Stress can not only compromise the quality of sleep we get, but also its quality. Under stress, some slow wave sleep might occur, but even that is compromised. According to EEG (electroencephalogram) tracking, people under stress during slow wave sleep still don't manifest the brain wave patterns most necessary for replenishing energy stores.

Our profound need for sleep will eventually override most stressors, but until that happens, we are, so to speak, up the creek without a pillow.

How Much Sleep Is Enough?

So just how much sleep do we require in order to function at our best and tackle whatever life throws at us without physical, mental, and emotional deficits? The answer is—that depends.

Certainly our species evolved sleeping more than most of us do nowadays. For much of human history, we slept when it was dark. Without artificial light, we simply didn't have that many options.

Even as recently as the start of the twentieth century, the average American slept nine hours a night. But now all that has changed. We now average 7.5 hours a night—a statistic that is on its way resolutely down.

It's easy to see why sleep can lose out as a preferred activity. The things we can choose to do instead of sleep to while away those dusk-to-down hours are endless. We've got 24-hour-a-day television networks, Internet access, and all-night services that will bring to our doorstep anything from a three-course meal to the latest DVD release. If no one nearby wants to keep us company in the wee hours, we can call or e-mail or instant message anyone willing to chat from Taiwan to Timbuktu. After all, it's always morning somewhere on the planet.

Still, sleep we must, sooner or later. Some people will always choose later, but that's not necessarily a bad thing so long as the amount of sleep they are getting is adequate for *them*. The magic number of optimal sleep hours does vary somewhat from individual to individual—due, in part, to differentiators such as physical size, muscle mass, and other factors that impact metabolic rates. Extremes can range from people who require only four hours a night for optimal functioning to those who need ten hours. For most of us, however, eight hours, give or take a smidgen, seems to be a safe number to shoot for.

Fortunately, determining what the right amount of sleep is for you doesn't require hooking yourself up to any complicated electronic sensors or measuring the precise amount of adrenaline and cortisol in your bloodstream. Just be alert to the following signs of possible sleep deprivation:

- Increased daytime grogginess
- Frequent yawning
- A tendency to doze off when inactive for a while (for example, when watching television)
- Falling asleep during work or class
- Sleeping through the alarm
- A reluctance to get out of bed in the morning
- Poor attention and motivation for tasks requiring sustained concentration
- Decreased task speed
- Diminished ability to think creatively and with originality
- Memory lapses
- Decreased initiative
- Decreased decision-making ability
- Increased moodiness, depression, and anxiety
- A tendency to emotionally "explode" (yelling or crying at a slight provocation)

◆ Slurred speech

◆ Being accident-prone

If you are getting less than eight hours of sleep on a regular basis and such symptoms appear, it's time to address the possibility that you are simply not getting the kind of rest that you need. Sleep debt is cumulative in nature and prevention is important.

Too Tense

The National Sleep Foundation has suggested that intense social frustration responses such as road rage might be caused, in part, by a national epidemic of sleepiness.

Sleep Strategies

The only cure for not getting enough sleep is to get more of it. If you have been deliberately shaving time off your sleep schedule in favor of other activities that seem to take precedence, the first thing to do is to recognize the value of sleep in keeping you calm and clear-headed. Sleep is the natural counterpart to waking, part of life's yin and yang. It is anything but a waste of time. With enough sleep, your waking life will proceed more smoothly as your stress level declines.

Of course, you could already be completely convinced of the necessity for getting more sleep, but be unsure as to what to do. Different techniques work well for different people. But there are many things you can try.

Pre-Bedtime Unwinders

A warm bath before bed is a great way to relax your body and put you in the right mental frame of mind for sleep. A massage is a similarly wonderful prelude to bed-time, and if your spouse is willing (you can always take turns), even a brief back rub or scalp massage can help nudge you toward dreamland.

Soft, soothing music can also lull you to sleep—and, no, lullabies are not just for kids. Many recordings of specially composed music are designed for the very purpose of helping grown-ups drift off. Or create your own playlist and put it on your iPod, which can be programmed to turn off after a prescribed number of minutes.

In addition, white noise machines (see Appendix B) can provide soothing simulated sounds of waves rhythmically breaking, rain falling on the roof, or the steady pattern of a heartbeat. The repetitive nature of the rhythms is what does the trick for many erstwhile insomniacs.

If you like milk, drinking a warm glass of it 15 minutes before going to bed will soothe your nervous system. The milk contains calcium as well as the amino acid L-tryptophan, both of which help you relax. If you don't care for milk, try a cup of hot chamomile, catnip, anise, or fennel tea. Most health food stores also have special blends of herb tea designed to help you get to sleep. Sample until you find one that helps. If you'd like a light snack before bed, try eggs, cottage cheese, chicken, turkey, or cashews. These, too, contain L-tryptophan.

> **Too Tense**
>
> Caffeine can keep you awake, but remember that coffee is not the only drink containing caffeine. Black tea, chocolate, and cola drinks are also high in caffeine.
>
> Alcohol also upsets sleep, preventing a deep rest.

Another pre-bedtime activity that can help you sleep is doing at least 15 to 20 minutes of aerobic exercise. The activity will give your body the oxygen it needs to rest well. But do be sure you stop exercising long enough *before* bedtime to give your body time to slow down and cool down. This cool-down period varies from individual to individual, and could take from half an hour to several hours, so see what works for you.

Visualization and Relaxation

A relaxed body and mind are the essential preludes to sound sleep. To that end, you've probably heard the old advice about helping your mind relax and fall asleep by counting sheep. The secret to this calm-inducing activity is not in the sheep—one can feel free to substitute moose, ostriches, cows, or what have you—but in the counting. Simply focusing on one type of object and its repetitive imagery while counting can make us pleasantly drowsy. If that doesn't do it for you, or if you like some variety in your techniques, try any of the following:

- ◆ **The birthday cake visualization.** This is a visually oriented sleep inducer that has the added benefit of incorporating relaxing breath. Picture a large birthday cake with 100 glowing candles atop. Breathe in and think "100"; breathe out and mentally see an image of one candle flame expiring. Keep counting backwards and blowing out candles until you drift off.

- ◆ **The toe wiggle.** Lie on your back and wiggle your toes up and down 20 times, wiggling the toes of both feet at the same time. This will relax your entire body, inside and out. According to the science of reflexology, your feet are akin to a dashboard control panel for the rest of your body, because bodily energy channels known as "meridians" converge there. Wiggling the toes stimulates and then relaxes the meridians in your feet and therefore relaxes every internal organ.

- **The tummy rub.** Lie on your back and place your hand on your navel, making tiny clockwise circles as you gently glide your hand over your stomach. Let the circles gradually increase in size. When your circles reach the outside of the stomach, gradually diminish their size again until you are back at your navel. Now switch to counterclockwise circles and do the same thing again. Do this several times. You'll find it's a great way to transition into sleep.

- **Internal listening.** Lie on your back with your hands behind your head, fingers interlocked, and your palms cupping the back of your head. Now place your thumbs in your ears so that you press gently against the outer flaps and block the entrance to the ear canal. As you lie quietly you will notice that you gradually begin to hear a high-pitched sound inside your head. Concentrate on that sound.

- **Progressive relaxation.** Lie on your back, close your eyes, and begin to feel each part of your body growing heavier and heavier—sinking into the mattress. Begin with your feet, and then follow in sequence with your calves, knees, upper legs, pelvis, buttocks, torso, chest, shoulders, neck, upper and lower arms, hands, and—if you're still awake—your jaw, eyes, forehead, ears, and crown of the head.

- **Imagining morning.** Imagine that your morning alarm has gone off and it's time to get up and go to work. But you are able to steal a few more delicious minutes of sleep beforehand. Enjoying this guilty pleasure could be all the inspiration you need to help you enter the Land of Nod.

> **Stress Less**
>
> Try pre-taping your own voice giving yourself instructions during your progressive relaxation exercise. Make sure you're the tone of your voice is relaxed and soft when you make the tape. Keep the tape and a small tape player with earphones by your bedside.

Notice that many of the preceding exercises included an instruction to lie on your back. In fact, this is—in theory, anyway—the best position for achieving sleep and remaining soundly asleep. Lying on your back allows all your internal organs to rest properly. If you are one of those people who feels you must sleep on your side, see if choosing your right side is comfortable, because sleeping on the left side can cause your lungs, stomach, and liver to press against your heart, causing some physical stress on that organ. But, overall, the main thing is to be comfortable; individual preferences prevail.

Regulating Your Schedule

Making some changes in your schedule can also help you establish a regular, healthy, stress-reducing sleep pattern. Your body likes regular routines, even if your personality resists them. It likes a predictable rhythm in terms of when it's going to get up, when it's going to eat meals, and when it's going to go to bed each day. So choose a reasonable and regular time to go to bed each night and stick to it *even if you don't think you're especially tired when the time comes.*

As for getting up—yes, you should also do that at the same time each day. Weekends, holidays, and vacations included. Furthermore, when you're awake, get up. Unless it's for the purpose of some relaxing morning romance, don't loiter in bed.

As for what time you should get up, if you are about to set up a new sleep-promoting schedule, think seriously about getting up a little earlier (say 30 minutes) than you have been used to doing. You'll be more tired at night and more apt to get to sleep. You'll also be exposed to the sleep-inducing and stress-reducing benefits of more natural daylight.

Stress Less

If your sleep-inducing techniques are not working, don't just lie there. If you've been unable to get to sleep for 30 minutes, get up and do some quiet, non-stimulating activity. When you feel tired again, return to bed.

Altering your schedule might—at first—feel like a bit of a negative stressor itself. But when you do it, your body will thank you for the favor and repay it by letting you get to sleep easily. That gift will more than compensate for any small measure of perceived inconvenience.

Simplifying Your Sleep Space

One of the best things you can do to help yourself sleep is to create a bedroom environment that is ideal for doing just that and not too much else. If you have a computer in the bedroom, you'll probably be tempted to work there—so no computer. If you have a TV there, you'll probably be tempted to watch it. Watching TV is actually stimulating even though it appears to be a passive activity—so no TV. Let your body and mind identify the bedroom with sleeping (oh, okay, and one other stress-abating activity).

What should you definitely have in your bedroom? An inviting bed—firm (because that's best for supporting and relaxing your spine), big enough to stretch out in (but not so big you feel lost), and uncluttered by newspapers, magazines, or other distracting paraphernalia. If you want to splurge on something wonderful for the bed, indulge in a goose down comforter and in pillows that feel simply perfect for you. (Pillows are a very personal preference, but the Tempur-Pedic ones that mold themselves to your body shape and align your neck and spine are a great place to start investigating.)

To encourage sleep, your bedroom should be well ventilated, with a room temperature between 60 and 65 degrees. Keep the thermostat down and do your temperature adjusting inside the bed—with more or fewer blankets, or with silk long underwear.

It's also a good idea to keep the lighting in your bedroom low. It's especially sleep promoting to keep it dim for at least a half hour to an hour before bedtime. At bedtime, darker is better. Even an illuminated bedroom clock can throw off enough light to be annoying if you're having a hard time falling asleep. If you want to retain the ability to check on the time during the night, opt for a clock that lights only when you press on it.

Too Tense

Although for most of us insomnia is the result of tension, it can sometimes be a symptom of other physical disorders. Check with your doctor. If you are an otherwise healthy insomniac, he'll probably suggest habit changes and relaxation techniques before resorting to sleep-inducing prescription drugs. (And If you're not sleeping because your partner is snoring profusely, perhaps they should be checked out by a doctor.)

How About a Nap?

Finally, you might be wondering whether catching a nap during the day can be helpful in reducing stress. For some of us, the answer is yes.

Many people swear by the restorative power of brief "power naps" taken for 15 or 20 minutes or so at a time. They find that these brief interludes—which might take place anywhere from a hammock to a sofa to a seat on a train or airplane—leave them feeling refreshed.

Not everyone can manage a nap during the day, either logistically or physiologically. But if you can, go for it unless …

◆ You awake feeling groggy and disoriented rather than reinvigorated, or

◆ You notice that napping during the day makes it harder for you to fall asleep at night.

If either of these circumstances arise, forego napping *per se* and opt instead for daily downtime that consists of meditative exercises (see Chapter 8) or engaging in any focused, playful activity (see Chapter 16).

The Least You Need to Know

- ◆ Sleep restores energy to both body and mind, helping us cope better with all of life's ups and downs.

- ◆ Lack of sleep can induce stress and stress can induce sleeplessness—it's a chicken-and-egg cycle that must be broken.

- ◆ How much sleep any one of us needs will vary. Pay attention to signs that warn you of sleep deprivation.

- ◆ Strategies for inducing sound, stress-beating sleep include eating and drinking foods that contain calcium and L-tryptophan, doing relaxation exercises, conforming to a regular wake/sleep schedule, and creating a calming, uncluttered sleep space.

- ◆ Naps can help some people beat stress, but for others they disrupt overnight sleep—you can experiment with naps and see how your stress level fares.

Chapter 19

Retreat at Home

In This Chapter

- Defining your retreat space
- Sights, lights, and color in your space
- Anti-stress scents
- Soothing sounds
- Limiting media exposure
- Carrying your retreat space attitude with you

"There's no place like home." So said Dorothy in Oz, when she was weary of nerve-wracking witches and frustrating wizards. So say we all when we are inundated with the stressors of the world. One of the best self-care strategies for beating stress is to make certain that our home provides a peaceful respite where we can regroup and regenerate.

A Space for Grace

We all know the feeling of being overwhelmed from our day "out there" in the world. We've been annoyed, irritated, thwarted, and exasperated. Our commitment to maintain some semblance of calm has been tested in every conceivable way. We're over it.

Safely home at last, we unlock the door, sigh, and fling our handbag or briefcase onto a chair. Then we kick off our shoes and plop into a chair ourselves. But then … we notice something out of place or something that needs repair, and we feel we have to tend to it. We start wondering what to fix for dinner, and we canvas the kitchen cupboards for supplies. We start making lists of everything we have to do after dinner—open the mail, pay the bills, do the laundry, and, of course, get everything ready so that we can go out into the world tomorrow and do it all over again.

What's happening here? We were so happy to seek the haven of home, but we have almost immediately turned home into another source of stress. Sure, we have to tend to our home and our home life, but we also have to ask ourselves the question: Are we in charge of our home or is our home in charge of us?

Relaxing at home in order to counter the stressors of the world *is* possible. But it doesn't seem to happen as often as it should. It would, however, happen much more frequently if we had a defined space where relaxation would be the primary goal. Call it a space for grace: an area, no matter how small or humble, where we could get away from it all, and peacefully reconnect with ourselves without actually going anywhere—except perhaps up or down the stairs.

Affirming Familiar Space

Don't get all stressed out about putting an addition on your home, or renting a bigger apartment. It's not necessary.

An at-home getaway space might be something you already have, or for which you already have the makings. Think about whether any of the following spaces are the places toward which you naturally gravitate when stress starts to get to you, and from which you emerge revitalized, feeling "like yourself" again:

- **The garage or basement workroom.** Putterers everywhere find relief amidst bolts, nuts, screws, drills, saws, heavy-duty power cords, and car- and lawn-care products. Hours can feel like mere minutes as body and mind slip into the relaxing rhythms of tinkering. If puttering is for you a kind of play that relaxes, a garage or basement workroom could be the space that you define as your stress-beating retreat. Never mind the oil stains on the floor: think of them as awe-inspiring art. But do respect your retreat space by organizing it to some degree, perhaps discovering what's in those unopened mystery boxes from two moves ago. Give yourself space to maneuver in your space, and so maximize its relaxing potential.

- **The garden.** It might be a postage-stamp-sized backyard, but if its trees, shrubs, and flora put you back in touch with the natural world and turn your frame of mind from stressed to serene, then the garden could be your perfect retreat place. Tend the soil, and so tend your soul, with loving care. And if you live in a climate where year-round enjoyment of the garden is not possible, think about cultivating some indoor plants in an inside retreat space that reminds you of what awaits in spring.

- **The bathroom.** Although arguably the most functional room in the house, the bathroom is increasingly used by many world-weary folk as a sanctuary from stress. Well it should, for it can offer a range of sensual benefits like no other room. Adding a few touches such as scented candles and soaps, light dimmers, candles, and bath pillows can transform the most basic bathroom into a spa-like environment from which you'll emerge revitalized. If you're lucky enough to have your own bathroom, make the most of it. If you have to share, allocate a cupboard or drawer to your stress-reducing paraphernalia so you can instantly remake the environment as you need to. Choose a retreat time when you're least likely to be interrupted by family members who need to use the facilities.

> **Too Tense**
>
> If you're lucky enough to have a whirlpool bath—great for relaxing tense muscles—don't forget to use it! Surveys show that the average homeowner who installs such a bath only uses the whirlpool feature seven times.

If any of these spaces, or another that especially relaxes you, is your pre-designated haven, it's important to acknowledge it as such. Treat it—and by extension, treat yourself—with respect and loving care. Keep it clean and inviting. Rather than spend time in it on a haphazard basis, see if you can integrate a time each day when you access it. Work toward at least 15 to 20 minutes, and ideally more. Tend and nurture your retreat space, and it will nurture you in return.

Creating New Space

If you can't identify an at-home retreat environment that you already enjoy, don't stress out about it! Look on the bright side: you get to create one from scratch.

You don't need an entire room: a corner will do. Find an area in your house or apartment that is somewhat out of the main traffic flow. It might be an area that already has a natural definition (such as a bedroom dormer, a space beneath the roof that is built out to accommodate a gable), but if not, you can create a partitioned space anywhere through the use of decorative room dividers.

Room dividers for virtually every décor and budget are readily available (see Appendix B). Many are made of natural materials, such as wood, wicker, and woven palm, but various fabrics in a wide range of shades and patterns can also be used for this purpose. Room dividers are ideal for creating a retreat space in a smaller home or apartment, because the space can be easily reclaimed as needed for other purposes by simply folding and removing the light-weight screens, which then fit handily into a closet.

How much space you should stake out depends on how you see yourself using the area. If you'd like to stretch out, be sure there is room to do so without feeling cramped. If you'd like to sit and meditate or read or listen to music, you might be able to make due with an even smaller space. In general, it's a good idea to make sure that at least one dimension of the space is as wide or long as you are tall (for example, my space is a dormer in my home office, which measures 6 feet by 3 feet and is more than adequate).

If your space is cluttered, de-clutter it. If it's dusty, dust it. If it has a window in it, get out the glass cleaner. If you'll be sitting down in your space, be sure you have an extremely comfortable chair on which to perch—or consider a meditation cushion, which can be surprisingly comfortable and provide a good deal of back support.

def•i•ni•tion

Feng shui is an ancient Chinese discipline dealing with the design and layout of dwelling places. In its modern form, much of it focuses on arranging objects in the home so as to allow one to live in balance and harmony.

The items in your retreat space can be arranged according to your personal aesthetics, along with practical considerations. However, if you'd like some ideas and inspiration about ridding yourself of stress by channeling the energy in your space in the most soothing and beneficial way, consider consulting a book about *feng shui*, such as *The Complete Idiot's Guide to Feng Shui*.

Serene Sights and Lights

To make your space as serenely soothing as possible, place in it a few objects that you consider especially lovely to look at. Consider paintings and prints that engender a sense of peace in you. They needn't cost a fortune, and can even—perhaps preferably—be something you or someone you love has created (perhaps with this very space in mind). Photographs can serve a similar function. Wall hangings are a wonderful adornment for a retreat space, because the use of fabric integrates an element of texture.

Feel free to place in your space a variety of items that serve no purpose other than to be pleasing to your eye. These might include seashells, stones, woodcarvings, pottery, and glassware. There are no rules about what to include, but including too many things will lead to a cluttered feel. If it is hard to leave some objects out, don't—but do rotate them in turn with others. This way you'll often have something new to appreciate every so often.

Peaceful, sensual lighting is another means of de-stressing your retreat space. Harsh lighting is a known stressor, and there's no reason to expose yourself to it here. Almost any light—including overhead chandeliers and track lighting—can be hooked to a dimmer, which instantly regulates light intensity with the turn of a dial.

Some people also find it very soothing to replace white light bulbs with pink ones. Everything looks rosier—literally and metaphorically—in pink light.

> ### It Works for Me
>
> "A few years ago, I started collecting kaleidoscopes. I find it incredibly restful to turn them and gaze at the ever-changing, colorful patterns. They are a wonderful addition to any retreat space."
>
> —Abbie, 33

> ### Too Tense
>
> Avoid fluorescent lighting in your retreat space—and anywhere else you can. The intense environmental stimulation produced by fluorescent lights and their accompanying electromagnetic fields is considered by many to have a draining, stressful effect.

You also might want to have some candles in your retreat space. Just a few can fill any room with an ethereal glow. Candles are so inexpensive and versatile that you can feel free to experiment with different shapes and sizes. Candles should be placed thoughtfully so that melted wax does not become an annoyance.

Calming Colors

The colors you choose to adorn your space is a very personal matter. Obviously, you want to be surrounded by colors that you like and that make you feel good. But most of us like many colors, so you might want to gear your selections to those that have inherent calming properties.

Although you might never have thought about it before, some colors are more likely to rev us up, and others are more likely to soothe us. Color creates a psychophysiological response within us, exerting an influence over both our bodies and our minds. This makes sense because colors are by nature interwoven with perception. What we call colors are actually electromagnetic radiation vibrating at different frequencies. Each color coordinates with a particular wavelength on the electromagnetic spectrum.

Warm Colors

At the red-orange-yellow end of the spectrum, colors stimulate and excite us. These so-called warm colors speed up our heart and nervous system. They do so to such a degree that a room with a relatively low thermostat temperature will still feel hot to us if it is painted red.

When we are exposed to warm reds, oranges, and yellows, our state of mind is stirred up as well. We feel active and alert. We also feel a sense of speed, and have the perception that time is passing quickly.

Needless to say, continual exposure to warm, stimulating colors will not have an overall calming effect. In fact, too much exposure to them can be stressful and emotionally draining.

None of this is to say you should not use warm colors in your retreat space. But do consider them more as accent colors than colors with which you want to paint an entire wall.

Another way to make use of reds, oranges, and yellows in your space is to add a white tint to them. Red with lots of white can become a soft pink; orange and white, a calming coral; and yellow and white, a pale, pleasing buttercup.

Cool Colors

At the opposite end of the electromagnetic spectrum are the so-called cool colors: blue, indigo, and violet hues. As we move down the spectrum, we find these colors have increasingly shorter wavelengths. They slow down our pulse and heart rate and, as a result, are soothing and calming.

When a room calls out for a calm atmosphere, blue is an especially popular color choice. Blue seems to recede from us, rather than advance toward us as do reds and yellows. It is also culturally connected to feelings of safety, constancy, and contemplation.

Do be careful, however, not to decorate your space exclusively in blue. Used judiciously the color evokes serenity; used overwhelmingly it can induce melancholy—that's why we sing "the blues."

Stress Less

The color green, evocative of nature, can be a wonderful addition to your retreat space palette. But be aware that green, which lies in the middle of the electromagnetic spectrum, behaves in a versatile way. Yellow-greens are stimulating; blue-greens are more soothing.

Neutrals

Neutrals like whites and earth tones can also be wonderful stress-reducing color choices for a retreat space. White calls up emotional associations of purity, innocence, and peace. Of course, we should actually refer to white in the plural—whites—because there are many shades of white, as anyone who has ever looked at a paint sample chart is aware. If this seems like one of those instances where too many choices can drive you a little over the edge, just know that as long as you stick with one white, you can't go wrong. Bluish whites are cool and soothing, but yellowish whites, which look like luminescent pearl, are also quite serene.

Beiges and browns are aptly named earth tones, because they call up images of the natural world: wood, bamboo, autumn leaves, and sand. Even the names of such shades are soothing: fawn, chestnut, oatmeal, mahogany. Browns and beiges are also reassuring because they engender associations to the restorative aspects of hearth and home, such as wicker baskets filled with warm bread and terra cotta bowls of steaming soup like Mom used to make.

Soothing Scents

How should your space smell? Well, obviously it ought to smell good. But to really reduce stress, consider applying some of the principles of aromatherapy—the use of *essential oils* from plants to enhance health and spirit. Aromatherapy is a holistic therapy because the oils it employs have psychotherapeutic effects as well as physiological effects on the body. Aroma can alter a stressed-out mood and outlook—quickly. As we inhale certain *essential oils* that are known for calming properties, there is a direct link to the limbic system of the brain via the olfactory nerve. The oils can trigger the secretion of neurotransmitters such as serotonin or encephalins that calm or uplift us.

def•i•ni•tion

Essential oils are necessary to the biological processes of the plants and trees from which they are extracted, and also provide scent. These oils can be taken from herbs, flowers, woods, and spices. In their purest form, they are highly concentrated.

Scent is a very personal matter, because scents are powerful agents of memory recall. Therefore, one scent might have a particular calming association for you that it does not necessarily hold for someone else, and vice versa. In general, however, it's widely agreed that the following scents have stress-reducing potential. If you're looking for the right scent for your space, these (alone or in combination) are a place to begin:

- **Bergamot.** This golden oil with a citrus scent is refreshing and calming.

- **Lavender.** Lavender's clean pure aroma, with a bit of bite, is reputed to encourage balance in the entire nervous system. It has been used to alleviate tension headaches and tense muscles, and to sharpen overwhelmed minds.

- **Roman chamomile.** Bright, crisp, sweet, and fruity, the scent of Roman chamomile blends well with that of lavender for a double dose of stress reduction.

- **Sandalwood.** This is an extremely calming and earthy scent, renowned for alleviating emotional tension and stress-related insomnia.

- **Vetiver.** In India and Sri Lanka, vetiver oil, with its sweet, woodsy aroma, is widely known as "the oil of tranquility."

- **Ylang ylang.** Made from the flowers of a large tropical Asian tree, this fragrant yet fresh and delicate scent has an entrancingly soothing exotic note.

Too Tense

Don't overdo aromatherapy: less is more. Also, practice thoughtful care when using essential oils. All essential oils are for external use only, and should be properly diluted. Tips for beginners are available at www.aromaweb.com.

Additional stress-reducing scents include jasmine, rosemary, orange, cedarwood, clary sage, and rose. Trying several is a relatively inexpensive indulgence and so is a practical way to be good to yourself.

There are many ways to introduce essential oils into your retreat space. You can purchase a diffuser to spread them into the atmosphere; you can spray them from mister bottles, or—if your retreat space happens to be a bathroom—you can try adding them to bathwater from which you can then inhale soothing vapors while you soak.

Other ways to add calming scent to your space are with scented candles or incense, both of which are also available in a wide variety of stress-reducing fragrances. Incense sticks burn safely and cleanly with the use of "ash catchers." Many catchers are made of carved wood and serve as attractive decorative touches for your retreat.

Stress-Less Sounds

What should you listen to in your retreat space? Perhaps only the sound of silence. If you choose to sit quietly with your own thoughts, prayers, or meditations, that alone is sufficient. But if you'd like externally soothing sounds in your space, consider the following:

◆ Pre-select CDs you want to listen to and enjoy them—consider low-key instrumentals, spiritual chants, recordings of the sounds of nature, and other listening experiences you might not have tried before.

◆ Relax to the soothing rhythms of a white noise machine, which can replicate sounds such as waves, wind, and rain. (If you are using one in your bedroom as a sleep aid, simply transport it to your retreat space as needed.)

◆ Purchase a miniature meditation gong or a Tibetan "singing bowl" that will enable you to demarcate the beginning and end of your retreat period with a series of sonorous chimes.

Now, do yourself a real kindness and turn off your cell phone. Don't worry—whoever is calling will leave a message if it's important. In addition, get ready to enjoy some time free from the ubiquitous drone of the media.

A Media-Free Zone

In the first chapter of this book, we looked at the impact of continual media overexposure on stress in the modern world. The 24/7 news cycle pumps up our stress response by providing more negative stimuli than our brains and nervous systems can possibly handle. Media exposure also tends to fill our minds full of unrealistic and unattainable images—such as the highly stylized faces and figures of fashion models and movie stars—and feed our craving for more and more consumer goods. Our unfulfilled desires to be "perfect" and have "everything" are themselves a source of continual frustration and stress.

So give yourself a rest and respite. Use your retreat space as a media-free zone. That's right: no TV, no radio, no high-speed Internet connection (and no slow-speed one, for that matter). Whatever part of the day you choose to spend in your at-home retreat should be devoted to uplifting input only. That means you need to be in control of it. Think of it as going on a media diet.

When you are on a weight-loss diet, you judiciously plan what you will eat each day. You deliberately eliminate junk and include a reasonable amount of nutritious fare. A media diet is the same. Eliminate junky, stress-inducing media chatter and blather. (Sometimes simply turning off the TV makes one breathe a sigh of relief. Try it.)

Like beginning any diet, beginning a media diet is tough. Many of us are at least somewhat addicted to a continual backdrop of news noise and computer screens full of minute-by-minute updates on everything from traffic fatalities to battle casualties to stock market quotes to sports scores to storm paths. When we first stop the addictive behavior, we might actually find ourselves having to deal with cravings.

Stress Less

If you'd like to read in your retreat space, savor something timeless and inspiring. Instead of the local tabloid or the obligatory newsweekly, consider a book of poetry, perhaps, or a collection of essays on an engaging—albeit unnewsworthy—topic.

On a weight-loss diet, we want one—just one—candy bar; on a media diet we want one—just one—bulletin. But gradually, the cravings will pass. And just as you can't grab a candy bar if there isn't one in your cupboard, you can't flip on the TV in your retreat space if you don't have a TV there.

Taking regular breaks from media exposure invariably teaches two lessons that have a tremendous stress-lowering effect: the first is that whether we pay attention to the news or not, the world goes on; the second is that there is very, very rarely anything we can do to change the news. Yes, we need to be informed in order to be responsible citizens and to manage business and personal decisions—but we also need to set limits and choose how, when, and by whom we will be kept informed.

Restricting our media fare restores a sense of control over what we *can* do, which is a better way to manage our response to world events and marketplace messages. In doing so, we are better prepared to positively impact our own lives and the lives of those immediately around us.

After you get used to a daily media-free period, you will probably notice that you are making better, less compulsive, choices about what media fare you do let back into your life.

Ideally, you'll become aware of how often the news repeats itself, and pace your exposure accordingly. Moreover, you'll choose to expose yourself to media outlets that don't fuel the fires of stress by sensationalizing the news.

Your new relationship to the media—one in which you are in the driver's seat—is but one of the many carryover benefits that can result from a daily dose of your retreat space.

It Works for Me

"I used to get up in the morning and turn the TV news on before I even brushed my teeth. I'd fall asleep to the eleven o'clock news at night. Now I go on a media fast from about 8 p.m. until 8 a.m. Late at night and early in the morning, I spend quiet time in a quiet place. When I decide to tune in again, I know the decision as to when and how much to tune in is mine."

—Ben, 48

Coming Out of Your Space

When you exit your retreat space, aim to keep your transition a smooth one. Yes, all your home and work commitments are waiting for you. Maybe family members are literally waiting for you, too, thinking *Hey, isn't it time you rejoined us?* All the more reason to ground yourself.

Perhaps you'd like to stop for a moment and conduct a momentary ritual such as bowing or saying a short prayer. Maybe you'd just like to just breathe and stretch. Whatever you do, take a moment to acknowledge the time you've spent gathering yourself in body, mind, and spirit. Then affirm that you will carry with you the sense of serenity you have achieved.

Take what you've learned while in stress-free solitude into other parts of your house and your life. If you've tamed your media habits there, you can do so elsewhere. If you've gotten your mind to quietly focus there, you can do so in other venues. If you've come away from your retreat space with a good idea or a resolution to do better, put these ideas and resolutions into practice.

Finally, during the course of each day, allow your thoughts to occasionally settle on the prospect of your awaiting at-home retreat space. Doing so should serve as a shortcut signal to your brain and body, allowing them to take a breather from tension.

The Least You Need to Know

- It's natural to want to go home when the world stresses us out, so be sure that at least part of your home is a stress-free haven.

- A haven at home can be a retreat that already exists, or one that you decide to create from scratch. You don't need a lot of room to craft a renewing retreat space.

- What you see in your space is important—choose art objects with care, keep the lighting gentle, and work from a palette of calming colors.

- Scent can have a powerful impact on mood and attitude—experiment with aromas known for their stress-reducing properties.

- Choose some serene sounds and make your retreat space a cell phone-free and media-free zone—messages and "news" will be there waiting when you emerge.

- When you emerge from your retreat space, carry your newfound calm along with you.

Chapter 20

Jumpstart Journeys

In This Chapter

- ◆ Can we really "get away" from stress?
- ◆ Finding a relaxation destination
- ◆ Stress-busting packing strategies
- ◆ Coping with travel hassles
- ◆ A stress-less re-entry

Often when we feel stressed we say "I need a vacation." The idea of getting away from everything that frustrates us is as appealing as can be when we've "had it up to here."

In truth, getting away from it all doesn't usually turn out to be a complete cure-all. However, as this chapter will show, choosing the right kind of journey and planning for it well can be both a relaxing interlude and a way of laying groundwork for further stress reduction when we return.

What Getaways Can Accomplish

Much of the stress we experience is connected to our daily routines—the commute, the commitments, the concerns about crossing myriad items off our "to do" list. When we think of a getaway vacation, we think—ideally—of a period of time when we're freed from any such demands. We also think of pleasing surroundings that are soothing in themselves—a rustic cabin in the woods, perhaps, or a cozy ski lodge, or a casual seaside resort.

It's tempting to imagine that we'll not only enjoy ourselves while we're gone, but also come back a "new person." Alas, expectations of vacation perfection and a resulting total personality transformation can be unrealistic. Heaven on earth probably doesn't exist. Besides, wherever we go, we do tend to take some baggage—and I don't mean just the suitcase kind. Most of us find it difficult to leave behind all of our sources of stress, because we usually take some of our anxious attitudes along with us as faithfully as we take our toothbrush.

As for coming back a totally reinvented person, that's also not likely to happen. If a vacation could transform us completely and irrevocably, one per lifetime would be all we'd require.

However, there's a lot to be said for carefully chosen getaways. Taken on a regular basis, and guided by realistic expectations, they can accomplish a great deal:

- ◆ They can slow down our frantic pace.

- ◆ They can temporarily relieve us from some of our time-consuming, frustrating chores.

- ◆ They can provide space and time to reflect on our priorities.

- ◆ They can begin to recondition negative habits.

- ◆ They can teach us new stress-beating skills that we can adapt to our daily life.

If we journey with loved ones, we can reconnect with them on a deeper level, restoring the healing power of our relationships. If we get away alone, we can get reacquainted with ourselves, discovering new activities—or rediscovering old ones—that can sustain us in times that are less idyllic.

Stress-Reducing Destinations

In order to maximize the stress-reducing potential of our journeys, it's best to begin with the end in mind. Consider the kinds of vacations that you are able to take, given whatever constraints of time, budget, and distance apply. But consider, too, which type of vacation is most likely to instill in you a calmer perspective on your daily post-vacation life and to offer you the tools and positive energy that you can carry back with you along with whatever T-shirts you purchase and photographs you take.

While planning, stay open to all options—even those you might not ever have seriously considered before. All vacations come to an end—but your lifelong journey toward mental, emotional, and physical equanimity can get a real jumpstart at the right place.

Pampering Spas

Perhaps nothing calls up the notion of banishing stress—at least temporarily—more than a trip to a spa. Just close your eyes and think "spa" and notice what images come up: you're lying on a massage table having your back rubbed in just the right spot, you're luxuriating in a whirlpool or hot spring, maybe you're taking a mud bath or getting a facial—complete with refreshing cucumber slices perched atop your weary eyelids. It feels so good to imagine all this that just planning a spa trip can be a mini-vacation in itself. (You can get a great overview of spa offerings at www.spafinder.com.) But don't stop there, because everything you've imagined is even better when you get to your spa destination.

If it's stress-beating massages you're after, most spas offer them in astonishing variety. There's Swedish massage, specifically crafted to relax muscles by applying pressure to them against deeper muscles and bones, and rubbing in the same direction as the flow of blood returning to the heart. There's deep tissue massage—including the methods known as Feldenkrais and Trager—that focuses on the body's deeper muscles and connective tissues. There's *shiatsu* massage, which incorporates acupressure and other techniques to manipulate the body's *chi* and remove energy blocks by stimulating pressure points. Then there's my personal favorite, stone massage (also known as thermotherapy), which combines heat, cold, and pressure, in the form of smooth hot and cold stones that are applied to various parts of the body.

Too Tense

Any type of massage can directly relieve stress-related physical symptoms like tension headaches and sore neck and shoulder muscles, as well as indirectly reduce our emotional anxiety level and create a sense of calm and well-being. But no matter what type you choose, communicate with your massage therapist as to what feels best. Don't be shy! A good massage professional will respond to any customization you require during the treatment.

As for "taking the waters," many spas offer various forms of *hydrotherapy*. In Europe, and increasing in North America, there are numerous health spas offering different types of "water cures." If you've ever so much as plopped into a hot bath at the end of a long, hard day, you know the stress-beating impact that water can have on stiff, fatigued bodies and frazzled minds.

def•i•ni•tion

Hydrotherapy means "water healing." It refers to any water or liquid-based treatment, such as soaking in natural hot and cold springs. Back in the fourth century B.C.E., the Greek physician Hippocrates was among the first to prescribe hydrotherapy.

For variations on this theme, look for spas that offer volcanic mud baths or even wine baths. The nutrients in the former and the antioxidants in the latter have a revitalizing effect on the skin, but that's not all. Few things resurrect a playful spirit like glopping around in mud. As for wine's role in stress-busting, it's more beneficial to soak in it than to drink too much of it.

Spas offer a host of other pampering services that can restore a visitor from head to toe, with everything from herbal facials to foot reflexology. Many also offer more esoteric fare, such as *chakra*-balancing energy adjustments. But just as relaxing as any particular treatment is the fact that guests can amble around for most of the day in robes and slippers completely free of self-consciousness. And people are generally as warm and friendly as can be, because everyone's there for the same reason: to chill out.

But being nurtured and supported is not all a truly good spa journey will offer. Most such places pride themselves on inspiring guests to take better care of themselves when they return home. Between all your coddling, be sure to attend some exercise classes, as well as talks and workshops on topics that will aid you with stress management. Beyond that, pay attention to how you feel when you eat light, healthy, nutritionally balanced spa meals, get plenty of rest, and treat yourself with some loving kindness.

Meditation Retreats

Have you tried meditation yet? As Chapter 8 detailed, meditation practice has been shown to have extraordinary potential for countering the stress response. But there's no question that beginning and sustaining a regular practice can be challenging. For this reason, a meditation retreat could be just what a seeker of stress reduction needs.

A retreat, which can last a weekend, a week, or more, will enable you to practice meditation free of many of the distractions of everyday life. It will give you the opportunity to meet others with goals similar to yours, and to avail yourself of the wisdom of teachers who are adept at meditation techniques.

The retreat format will vary from place to place, but in general there is a structured schedule that alternates periods of practice (perhaps sitting and walking meditations), instruction, and discussion (perhaps including a one-on-one meeting with an instructor). The atmosphere tends to be relaxed and low-key. Some meditation retreats even offer extended periods of *noble silence* to facilitate practice and reflection (and no fair resorting to your iPod).

A meditation retreat should build your capacity for focused attention. Along the way, be prepared to stretch your capacity for stillness, but know that you will be doing so in an emotional environment where whatever obstacles you face can be safely and carefully examined. As a stress-beating bonus, you can anticipate being in natural and serene surroundings, eating healthful (often vegetarian) food.

def•i•ni•tion

Noble silence is a period of formalized quietude, in which practitioners refrain from verbal, visual, and written communication with one another. Those practicing noble silence are even encouraged to take care with the opening and closing of doors and other routine activities that generate a certain level of noise. The overall effect is a highly peaceful interlude.

Be aware that although all meditation retreats are spiritual, some are more rooted than others in particular spiritual or religious traditions. Some are also more oriented than others toward beginning practitioners (and many offer beginner's introductory weekends). Doing thorough research before you go will prevent unsettling surprises.

Yoga Vacations

For a journey that merges inner life and outer activity, consider a yoga vacation. Yoga retreats are offered in virtually every style of yoga (some accentuate breathing techniques, some more strenuous postures, and some a more rapid pace). You don't need to head off to India or Katmandu (though you can if you like). Yoga retreats are found all over the world—some much nearer than you might have imagined.

Yoga resorts feature—no surprise—lots and lots of opportunities to learn and practice yoga from teachers who are devoted to the art. Between sessions, enjoy peaceful surroundings, nutritious fare, and the companionship of a diverse group of fellow guests dedicated to nurturing and calming both body and mind.

Stress Less

Finding a meditation or yoga retreat that suits your style of practice, spiritual tradition, and level of experience will ensure a pleasant and worthwhile trip. The website www.retreatfinder.com is useful for discovering what's available.

Active Adventure and Learning Journeys

Exercise and play are both important for stress reduction. For those interested in physically playing and staying in shape as well as reconnecting with nature in the great outdoors, an active vacation is a wonderful choice. The sky's the limit on what activities you can sample. They include …

◆ **Bicycling tours.** You can bike anywhere and everywhere from California's wine country to the green hills of Vermont to the French or Italian countryside. You don't need to be Lance Armstrong. Reputable tour operators offer everything from easy explorations to epic journeys. A good organization will match your fitness level to your ride—and will have a van available if you find it less stressful to take some time off from more difficult stretches.

◆ **Camping.** Just plain old camping in the woods is many people's idea of the perfect respite from modern-day stress. No tour-operator needed—but do be sure you have the equipment necessary to be safe and comfortable while you're cooking around a fire and sleeping under the stars—far from urban air, noise, and light pollution.

◆ **Golf or tennis camps.** If memories of the carefree summer camp days of your childhood make you smile, you'll be glad to know that the camp experience can go on … and on. In these specialized sports camps, you can take up a sport you've always wanted to learn or perfect your golf swing or tennis strokes. Learn tips from the on-staff pros and trade them with fellow enthusiasts in the spirit of camplike camaraderie.

◆ **Multisport tours.** It's possible to blend hiking, biking, kayaking, and water sports in many breathtaking and invigorating locations that include the Shenandoah Valley, the Rocky Mountains, and the canyons of the American Southwest. Comprehensive multisport tours are great for alleviating potential travel stress among companions and families because everyone gets to pursue his or her favorite activities.

◆ **Walking tours.** A good walk is a wonderful stress reducer. On these vacations, walks across nearly every scenic spot on the planet are offered for walkers of every level and preferred pace. You can hike the backroads of the American countryside, traverse the English moors, or trek the foothills of Nepal and Bhutan. To prevent physical and emotional stress along the way, find a seasoned walking tour company that offers daily route options for all levels, knowledgeable guides, and the backup you need when you're ready for a break.

If your idea of play activities is a bit lighter on the pure physical elements and a bit heavier on cerebral ones, there are many journeys that can offer you a chance to unwind while you acquire or refine skills in everything from photography to pottery-making to cooking every imaginable type of cuisine. You can immerse yourself in language instruction, take up poetry writing or watercolors, sculpt in marble, or make a film. Best of all: you might find something so engaging and relaxing that you will continue to make time for it and take pleasure in it when you are back in your day-to-day life.

Beach- and Deck-Potato Vacations

Sometimes the first thing that comes to mind when we think of undoing the stress in our lives is "vegging out" on a beach or, perhaps better yet, on a luxurious cruise ship that ferries us from one beach to another. Far be it from me to say this isn't a suitable idea. Doing nothing much while soaking up some rays might be just the stress-beating ticket—especially if you are susceptible to winter weather and light deprivation stressors.

A word of caution, however, is in order. Such vacation destinations have been known to create in some of us the urge to overindulge in pleasures that might feel good in the moment, but lead to even more stress in their aftermath. Eating too much, over-indulging in alcohol, or sitting in the sun until you can grill sausage on your chest will send you home overstuffed, dehydrated, and feeling like you need—yes—a vacation. Moderation is a sound strategy in all such settings.

It Works for Me

"I used to think of vacations as a place to 'go wild'. I had pretty healthy habits at home, but while away I put them on hold. Eating, drinking, and partying half the night was fun while it lasted, but when I came home I was 'fried.' Now I use vacation as a time to expand on my good habits while also trying new things and having a great time. I still enjoy a vacation with a party-type atmosphere, but I see I can contribute to that atmosphere with my attitude alone."

—Bill, 50

As for doing "nothing," even that has its limitations. When you're tempted to wake up from your nap or look up from that good book I hope you've remembered to pack, try sampling some of the inherently stress-reducing activities that most cruise ship lines and beach resorts now include in their day-to-day fare. Even though you haven't signed up for a full-fledged yoga vacation, for example, you can probably sample a yoga class or two in such venues. You can also perhaps take a class in sushi making or napkin folding or some similar diversion. And you can certainly work out at the fitness center. When nothing else appeals, there's always the option of a long beach walk or deck promenade. Mindfully breathe in the fresh air and relish the natural world around you.

Simplify Your Packing

After you know where you're going, you face a perennial travel dilemma: what to take. As part of keeping your journey as stress-free as possible, follow this rule of thumb: the less you take, the less stressful your journey will be.

Certainly, the less you take on an airplane trip, the less you have to cope with searches and delays. But even overpacking for a car vacation—where you're tempted to throw in the proverbial kitchen sink—is a nuisance when you get where you're going. The fewer items you pack, the less weight you have to schlep around. Starting a vacation with a strained back and aching shoulders won't enhance your relaxation experience. Besides, the less you have, the less is likely it is to be lost, damaged, or stolen.

Most of us could do with some serious paring of our packing selections. It's usually the case that after you're packed, you can eliminate half of what you're taking and still have more than enough.

Many travel guides and Internet sites offer sample packing lists geared to gender and to the type of trip for which one is packing. These are handy checklists to investigate. In addition, there are a number of general stress-reducing packing principles that will make your life easier and keep your mind's focus on the restorative aspects of your trip.

Too Tense

Standard advice is to limit airplane packing to one carry-on bag. That's good advice so long as you are sure your bag meets your airline's carry-on criteria. Check online ahead of time, because carriers vary. Also, don't overstuff. Swinging around an unwieldy bag can make you, not to mention fellow passengers, cranky.

First and foremost, remember that it's not necessary to "dress up" to impress people you meet on vacation. No one is going on vacation to be impressed—or, if they are, they're not the sort of people you ought to seek out for R&R. Besides, you'll most likely never see most of these people again. And lastly, if anything is going to make people admire your travel wardrobe, it will likely be its practicality and simplicity.

Next, pack your clothing in color-coordinated layers. Imagine yourself as a mannequin you're going to be dressing from the inside out. Each layer should fit comfortably atop the one beneath it, adding warmth as temperatures fluctuate along your journey. Most items should be in neutral shades. Although some accent colors are fine, remember that earth tones, dark blues, deep greens, and blacks have a lot of versatility and can be easily mixed and matched.

Shoes? Here's where many of us stress out and surrender our packing sanity. There are dress shoes and sandals and flip-flops and specialized footwear for almost every imaginable type of sports activity (except yoga, which is done barefoot—something else to recommend it). Our general packing rule for shoes seems to be "if the shoe fits, throw it in." But then we are stuck carting around a sack full of the heaviest wardrobe item we've got. Instead, think in terms of a beige or black leather comfortable walking shoe, maybe a pair of Tevas, and a pair of athletic shoes. You get to wear one pair as you go, so make those the heaviest ones.

Stress Less

If you feel you really need to pack dress shoes and lots of fancy clothing, you might ask yourself if this vacation destination is truly a stress-beating one.

As for toiletries, there are three rules that apply:

- Think small. Stock up on tiny tubes of toothpaste and miniature cans of shaving cream so you'll always have some handy to toss in a bag.

- Take health and hygiene basics only. Floss is good, medications are mandatory, but a sack full of beauty creams can be left on your dresser. (The vacation itself should make you glow!)

- You can get most things almost anywhere. Unless you are off to spend a month penguin-watching in Antarctica, chances are there's a drugstore nearby.

Electrical grooming aides like blow dryers and curling irons are best left right on your dresser. If there was ever a time to try your hair *au natural*, a stress-free vacation is it. Who knows, you might like it. If not, aim your digital camera at the scenery—and don't forget to pack your sense of humor.

Coping with Travel Stress

I wish I could tell you that when you are en route to your chosen destination you will instantly lower your stress level. But the realities of modern life being what they are—with security concerns, delays, overcrowding, and just plain old rudeness—it's almost a certain bet you're going to encounter some potential travel frustrations along the way.

Here's where it helps it have a positive, optimistic attitude.

Relax, Don't React

Travel stressors are a given, but how you respond is a choice. If you've taken the trouble to plan a stress-reducing trip, it is never too soon for you to start the internal part of that journey.

Stress Less

Within your carry-on bag, carry a Miniature Calm Kit. In it, keep a good book, an MP3 player or iPod loaded with your favorite stress-relieving music, a small vial of aromatherapy balm (in lavender or other soothing scent), and an eye mask to aid catnaps.

There's a little travel game you can play to amuse yourself—in much the same way you used to play Hangman or "I Spy" on long family car trips. I like to call this game "No Reaction." The goal is simply to remain calm—preferably calm *and* smiling—no matter what happens.

Being stuck in a serpentine line at the airport is actually conducive to practicing nonreactivity. It offers a chance to do some deep meditative breathing. If you'd rather choose another activity, be sure to pack a really engrossing paperback book.

It's a good strategy to be very, very nonreactive by the time you get to the security checkpoints. Because security procedures are largely random, you never know when you might be the one to get "wanded" or to have the entire contents of your luggage scrutinized. You can rest assured that the more agitated you act, the longer this will take and the more thorough the search will be. On the other hand, the more cooperative and calm you are, the faster you can move on to your destination. And the nicer you are to security personnel—who, after all, are just doing their jobs—the less stressed everyone around you will be.

When you're actually on your way, keep on not reacting—except with calm and compassion. Don't clench your teeth and angrily buzz the flight attendant if you're seated near a crying baby. Don't fuss if the person seated beside you needs to get in and out and in and out. Don't moan if you realize you've already seen the movie—remember you have your great book, right?

If you're driving yourself, as opposed to flying, remember that traffic happens. Slow down when you have to and stay within the speed limit even when things are moving along snappily. And don't forget to let the other guy into your lane once in a while. You'll get there when you get there, right?

As for arrival at your destination, don't stress out if things aren't exactly the way you pictured them. They rarely are. The truth is your journey might be a lot better than you could have possibly dreamed, but it takes time to get accustomed to any new venue.

To Connect, or Not

Now for one of the big questions that face the modern traveler seeking stress relief: Should you, or shouldn't you, check your voice mail and e-mail while you're away?

In the best of all possible circumstances, the answer is no. Ideally, your journey should offer a respite from the demands of your job and other obligations. However, as a practical matter, some of us find ourselves unable to relax and let go if we are nagged by thoughts of all the things that could be going wrong at home or at our workplace. So even if it seems somewhat paradoxical, some people are less stressed with a slight tether remaining. If that describes you, so be it. But do keep that tether as lax as possible.

Disconnecting—completely or almost completely—without anxiety or guilt is possible if you take some steps ahead of time. First, be sure to leave outgoing messages on your work phone numbers that say you are away and when you will return. If you are not checking messages, say so, but also leave contact information for someone whom you have designated to handle problems while you are gone or contact you in the event of a genuine emergency. (Make sure it's someone who does not consider the question "Where do you keep your paper clips?" a genuine emergency.)

If there is no such trusted designee available, or if you truly feel you have to check in on a particular pressing matter, limit your checks to one a day and keep them short. Rather than bringing your own laptop computer, which you might be tempted to overuse, go to an Internet café or use a hotel business center computer (there are even online centers at most spas and on most cruise ships these days). Yes, this can be expensive— *and that's the point!* You won't be tempted to stay logged on indefinitely when every minute gets tacked onto your escalating bill.

> ### It Works for Me
>
> "I found many of my co-workers were not paying attention to my 'out of office' e-mail replies. They kept bombarding me with e-mail even though they knew I was away. So, I changed my 'out of office' message by adding, 'If you don't contact me during my vacation I won't contact you during yours.' It works like a charm."
> —Lauren, 42

Another good reason to leave your laptop, Blackberry, and yes, possibly even your cell phone at home is cord buildup. Wireless, ha! All such devices still require charging, and therein lies a knotty problem. Plugs and chargers take up lots of valuable suitcase space, and always seem to require extensive disentangling at the least opportune moment. Besides, getting home to find you've left a charger plugged into a hotel wall outlet is an all too common stressor in itself.

One, Two, Three ... Re-entry

Sooner or later, of course, getaways end, and we must acknowledge that all the things from which we got away are waiting back home for us. Some aspects of this might make us happy. We're glad to reunite with family members or other friends and loved ones left behind. We can't wait to be greeted by our faithful pets. We smile at the thought of sleeping in our own bed.

But we also know there will be a stack of mail awaiting us, and messages to respond to, baskets of laundry to do, and refrigerators to fill with groceries. And let's face it: even though the dog might jump up and down with joy when we walk through the front door, the cat could well give us the cold shoulder for a while.

Work? Yes, there'll be some. More than when we left, no doubt. How are we ever going to handle all of this? Was it a dumb idea to go take a break in the first place? No! But there are things a traveler can do to make re-entry less stressful.

First, if at all possible, time your return so that you have a full day at home before heading back to work. Coming home on a Sunday night might seem like a good idea when you want to stretch out your getaway, but rather than maximizing your gains, being rushed from the moment you re-enter your household can well diminish them.

Stress Less

During your re-entry transition, write down something you learned during your journey that can help you lighten you stress load. If you like, pair this written note with a photograph from your trip. Have this keepsake handy when you go back to your daily routine.

Think of your day between your vacation and your workaday world as a transitional period during which you can take time to relish the things you missed about home even as you catch up on errands and chores. Take a little time to reacquaint yourself with your at-home retreat (revisit Chapter 19 if you have not created yours yet). Tell someone how much you missed him or her while you were gone.

Many people return from a jumpstart journey lamenting that it is time to return to "real life." But, remember, the period of time you have just completed was as "real" as any other part of your existence. Cherish it for the opportunity that it *was*, and *is*. A smooth, thoughtful transition, during which you continue to be as kind to yourself as you were on your trip, will help you face your everyday life with newfound calm and creativity.

The Least You Need to Know

- A well-chosen getaway can help slow down our pace, provide space in which we can examine our priorities, and offer opportunities to learn or enhance our stress-beating skills.

- Take your time and enjoy exploring options for your journey—consider destinations that have the potential to continue to de-stress your life even after you leave.

- Simplify your packing—it's easier on your back and your brain, and you need less stuff than you think you do.

- All travel involves some potential frustration, but you can start your vacation from stress early by not reacting in negative ways.

- Plan carefully before you go so you need spend no time, or minimal time, checking voice mail and e-mail back home.

- After the getaway, the things from which you got away await you. Transition smoothly during "re-entry" and you'll return renewed and fortified.

Part 6

The Stress-Beating Workbook

The proof of the pudding is in the eating. It's time to put your newfound knowledge and skills into action. This workbook section of the book guides you through self-evaluation and planning as you move forward into a calm, focused, and healthful future. Get your pencil ready, and prepare to beat stress on a permanent basis.

Chapter 21

Crafting a Personal Plan

In This Chapter

- A review of the stress response
- Noting your stress triggers
- Mapping your attitude
- Doing a relationship check-up
- Checking in with your body
- Evaluating your self-care

In the first 20 chapters of this book, we've looked at how the stress response operates and at what you can do to beat stress. Hopefully you have already begun to make some positive changes. Now it's time to get seriously proactive.

In this chapter, you're going to be asked to take a look at habits in your life and create some benchmarks—some starting points of reference—for yourself. What causes you feelings of distress? How are your mental, emotional, and physical habits impacting your stress levels? How sound are your stress defenses?

There are no "right" and "wrong" answers to any of the questions you'll be asked to respond to or lists you'll be asked to make. As you proceed, there's just one important guideline to keep in mind: be honest with yourself. You won't easily make changes in the future without gaining awareness of where you stand right now. So take a deep breath, relax, and go for it.

A Brief Review

When we sense a threat at any level, we are pre-wired to respond with certain bodily reactions that comprise what's known as the stress response. The stress response kicks up our level of mental alertness and physical readiness, so we can do what we need to get out of harm's way. Overall, stress is a normal, integral part of our survival mechanism. We come by it honestly; it's part of our genetic make-up.

Too Tense

Don't knock Mother Nature. The stress response has been naturally selected. If there were any members of the human race way back when who were not programmed this way, they most likely didn't live long enough to pass their genes along. All of the really laid-back cavemen probably got eaten by lions, tigers, or bears.

Ironically, however, in the modern world we have created, the stress response can sometimes harm us more than the stressor it's meant to protect us from. That's because many of our stressors are not acute situations from which we need to flee or toward which we need to turn and fight. Many of them are chronic frustrations: the unpaid pile of bills on the desk, the daily commute, the overcrowded schedule, a hard-to-please boss, a taxing personal relationship. And many times we ignite the stress response by merely thinking about problems or potential problems. Our mind-body system reacts to a situation that hasn't even happened.

When we are perpetually stressed, the things that happen in our mind and body can sap our vitality and our health. That's because a vast amount of that energy that would normally maintain emotional balance and repair physical problems is diverted toward keeping us in a fight-or-flight mode.

In short, we're lucky to have a pre-wired protection device to help us when immediate danger looms. But chronic stress is a danger in itself. We can all benefit from learning methods of remapping our response to chronic stress.

Know Your Stress Triggers

Although chronic stress is a universal problem, what causes such stress for each of us is a highly individual matter. What might be a source of chronic stress for one person might not bother another very much—if at all. In some instances, what provokes tension in one person might even provoke exhilaration in another.

Knowing which kinds of circumstances or events are likely to trigger your stress response will help you begin to get stress under control. This is the first step in developing greater awareness of how you react and respond. When you understand when you are most vulnerable, you can begin to take steps to take better care of yourself.

So think about what frustrates you and makes you tense. When is it you are most likely to feel physical, mental, or emotional pressure? For example, do you feel very stressed when you are up against a work deadline, when you are balancing your checkbook or filing your taxes, when you are interacting with a particular person, when you are faced with a particular task (preparing dinner, making a presentation)?

In the following spaces, list your top stress generators. You do not have to list them in any particular order, nor do you have to fill in all of the spaces. If you leave any blank spaces and think of something to add later, just come back and fill it in.

My Stress Triggers

1. _____
   _____.

2. _____
   _____.

3. _____
   _____.

4. _____
   _____.

5. _____
   _____.

Now, look over what you have listed. Remind yourself that you might or might not be able to alter these circumstances. You might or might not be able to avoid them. But there is always something you can do: you can work on modifying your response to them.

You can take a preventive approach by mobilizing a healthy defense so that the stressful event does not take too great a toll on you. You can also take a recuperative approach, by devoting the time and expending the self-care effort needed to recover from a stressful episode.

Examine Your Attitudes

Now it's time to take an attitude reading. In the next few sections, you'll be asked to notice the habits of your mind. Once again, be honest. No one is watching except you! The more honest you are with yourself, the more progress you will make in the five-week program outlined in the next chapter.

Silver Lining Search

An upbeat, optimistic attitude is a potent defense against stress. One way to recognize your tendency toward optimism is to see whether you can find a positive element to focus on in a stressful situation.

To assess your optimism, look at stress triggers you identified in the previous exercise. For each one that you can, identify some aspect of the situation that makes you feel good. For example, if you identified the act of preparing dinner for your family every night as a stressor, you might write "I'm glad to have this time each day when my family gathers together." List your answers below.

My Silver Linings

1. _____
   _____.

2. _____
   _____.

3. _____
   _____.

4. _____
   _____.

5. _____
   _____.

Was that easy, somewhat difficult, or perhaps very difficult? Notice any resistance you have to taking a "glass half full" approach to life. This reluctance is merely a habit of thought. As you consciously address altering such habits, your stress level will plummet.

Laugh Tracking

Laughter is a form of eustress. It jumpstarts a cascade of positive sensations in body and mind. Chapter 7 suggested you begin a Laugh Log, noting how many times per day you create this positive dynamic. If you did not do so earlier, now's the time. If you *did* do so before, now's the time to do so again so that you can see if your laughter quotient has increased.

This time, our exercise includes a new element. Note the number of times per day you find yourself laughing, and also the number of times you made someone else laugh. Sharing laughter enhances social bonds—another powerful stress reducer.

The Laugh Tracker

	My Laughs	Making Others Laugh
Monday		
Tuesday		
Wednesday		
Thursday		
Friday		
Saturday		
Sunday		

If you noticed some days when your laugh numbers were low, ask yourself what was going on. Did you let your frustration or pessimism get the best of you and lose your sense of humor? Now think about what you were doing on the days when your laugh factor was high. Were you around certain people, engaged in certain kinds of activities, or was your attitude just different? Identifying what makes you have a laugh-filled day or not can go a long way toward instilling more stress-beating laughs in your life.

It Works for Me

"The good news for me about keeping a laugh log was that I realized I was laughing more than I thought. I just had not been stopping to notice or to savor how good it felt. Also, I noticed that now that I am paying attention to how much I laugh, I am laughing even more. Awareness did the trick."

—Evan, 32

My Faith Factor

Faith can have a decided impact on reducing stress. Spiritual beliefs calm and empower us, so it's good to become aware of what we believe. This next exercise asks you to do just that, by filling in the blanks after the starting phrase "I have faith that …"

Stress Less _____

For ideas and inspiration on beliefs, visit www.npr.org/thisibelieve/about.html. This National Public Radio site features "This I Believe" essays where contributors from all walks of life and all spiritual persuasions write about the beliefs that see them through.

If you practice an organized religion, it might be relatively easy for you to enumerate some of the things in which you have faith. For example, you might say you have faith in your church, or in the power of a particular prayer or ritual. But if you do not practice a formal religion, this exercise is just as important—perhaps more so. Think about what it is you have faith in and write it down. Some examples: "I have faith that most things work out for the best"; "I have faith that there is some kind of benevolent force in the universe"; "I have faith that when you do good things, good things come your way."

I Have Faith

I have faith that _____
_____.

I have faith that _____
_____.

I have faith that _____
_____.

Let these statements of faith be your affirmations as you work on lessening negative stress in your life. They can sustain you when you feel overwhelmed. If you have had a hard time coming up with statements of faith, keep this as a goal and see if you can come back and fill in the blanks as your stress-beating program progresses.

My Do-Good Diary

Next, we have a Do-Good Diary. Doing good makes you feel good, and reduces your stress level. Not coincidentally, it makes your corner of the world a less stressful place for everyone.

What good deeds are you doing? Keep track for a week and see. These deeds can include anything from a small kindness to a stranger to organized volunteer activities to extra support given to a co-worker, friend, or loved one.

Daily Good Deeds

Monday	_____
Tuesday	_____
Wednesday	_____
Thursday	_____
Friday	_____
Saturday	_____
Sunday	_____

There's no need to feel guilty and stressed if you do not have an entry for every day. Remember, this chapter is about benchmarking. If you have spotted an area in which you can improve, make a resolution to do so.

Relationship Reconnaissance

Reconnaissance involves examining and exploring an area, with an eye toward increasing your strengths in that area. That's what you'll be doing in this section on relationships. Relationships with our family and friends, as well as our relationship with work, can sometimes be sources of stress, but we need also to learn to recognize their crucial restorative potential.

My Support Structure

An alternative to the fight-or-flight response is to counter stressors by tending and befriending others. This exercise simply asks you to acknowledge those people in your family and circle of friends whom you can count on in times of stress—and who, in turn, can count on you. You do not need to have a "perfect" relationship with those listed here. Imperfection is the nature of human relationships.

As you list these loved ones' names, you don't need to write anything about them. Simply pause for a few moments after each name and allow yourself to experience the feelings of warmth and gratitude you have toward them and the desire you have to protect and defend them.

I Can Count On You

1. _____
   _____.

2. _____
   _____.

3. _____
   _____.

4. _____
   _____.

5. _____
   _____.

Even though there are only five spaces here, this list can, of course, be as long as you like. Don't be afraid to write people's names in the margins. Get yourself additional sheets of paper as needed. The more the merrier. Social support is a powerful stress antidote. If you have not filled in all the spaces, think about how you can expand your social circle. Revisit Chapter 12 for ideas.

I'm Working On It

Lots of us have a love/hate relationship with work. It can be stressful in some ways, but very satisfying in others. In the following exercise, you're asked to enhance the potential of your work experience by noting not only your job stressors, but also your job soothers. For example a job stressor might be "tight deadlines"; a job soother might be "supportive co-workers." A job stressor might be "long hours"; a job soother might be "opportunities to use my talents and learn new things." List as many as come to mind for each category—scribble in the margins if you like.

Job Stressors and Soothers

Stressors	Soothers
_____	_____
_____	_____
_____	_____
_____	_____
_____	_____

Checking In with Your Body

The stress response resonates throughout our complex body-mind system. We can't ignore the benefits of moving our body if we're going to mitigate stress. Are you giving your body a chance to work out and work off stress?

Am I On the Move?

Happily, we can beat stress by physical means that include a wide variety of activities. Whether you're walking, running, swimming, doing yoga or t'ai chi, or any number of other body moves, you are unleashing brain chemicals that have profoundly positive effects. Ideally, you'll end up making bodywork a lifelong habit. For now, however, just take a benchmark of where you are. Note what activities you do each day for a week and for how long you do them.

Too Tense

The body adapts to the physical activities you do. After a time, you might not realize the benefits of exercise as intensely as you did at first. This means it's time to mix it up. Add something new, or do current activities harder or longer.

My Moves

	Activity	Time Spent
Monday		
Tuesday		
Wednesday		
Thursday		
Friday		
Saturday		
Sunday		

What you do is a choice, but a mix of many physical activities is best because it will strengthen your body in numerous ways and keep you from getting bored. Look over your list and see if you can add some variety. Also, consider whether it's possible to add more days per week or to devote more time per day to moving.

Way to Play

Working out is good for stress reduction—and "playing out" is good, too! Now take stock of the things you do that put you in flow—the state where time flies when you're having fun. Include artistic activities, playing sports, gardening—anything and everything that is a way that you play.

Days I Play

Monday   _____

Tuesday   _____

Wednesday   _____

Thursday   _____

Friday   _____

Saturday   _____

Sunday   _____

Playing tends to be an area where a lot of people leave blank spaces—on this page and in their lives. We have constructed a world in which we are all so busy that we neglect to play. If you filled in any spaces at all, give yourself a big pat on the back, and keep it up. Think about possible ways you might add even more play interludes to your life. If you did not list anything, you're not alone—but do revisit Chapter 16 for ideas on "going with the flow." Don't neglect this potent stress-beater.

Be Aware of Self-Care

Your caring attitudes toward others will help you feel more centered, but don't forget to care for yourself as well. After all, if you don't do that, you won't be calm and collected enough to really be of service to anyone else. These next check-ups will help you evaluate if you're being a good friend to yourself by looking after your diet and sleep habits, and by giving yourself opportunities to unwind.

Mindful Nutrition

Too often we eat unconsciously in a misguided attempt to suppress feelings of stress. But what we choose to eat (like sugary fats) or drink (like excessive caffeine or alcohol) only makes matters worse by creating a physiological stress backlash.

Many nutritious foods will help bolster you against the ill effects of stress, but the first thing you'll need to do is to eat consciously. For this exercise, use your own pocket calendar or electronic PDA. For one week, make a notation in that calendar every time you eat or drink. Write down what you eat and drink. Also, give yourself a "+" every time you are eating out of genuine hunger. Give yourself a "–" every time you are eating because you feel stressed, bored, or fatigued. Now, notice what it is you are eating during the times when you have assigned yourself a minus sign. Ask yourself if these foods are doing you more harm than good. What can you substitute for them? See Chapter 17 for ideas.

It Works for Me

"It's the foods I eat when I'm not thinking about food that aren't good for me. If I am eating mindlessly, thinking about all the things I have to do next, I eat the wrong things and I eat way too much. When it is time to eat, I try to make that my only activity. I try to spend time enjoying the food. This helps me calm down and I know it is better for my body."

—Corrine, 38

Getting My Z's

Getting enough sleep is critical if we are going to manage stress wisely. Too little sleep saps our physical, mental, and emotional defenses. Because the amount of sleep that's needed varies somewhat from individual to individual, it's hard to tell whether you are getting enough simply by tracking your hours. Instead, keep track for a week of how you feel when you awaken. After 10 to 15 minutes of being awake, check off the words that apply to you.

Too Tense

Not sure if you're sleep deprived? Sit down and close your eyes for ten minutes. Set an alarm clock. If you're asleep when it rings, you're sleep deprived.

The Morning After

	Mind Alert	Body Energetic	Mind Groggy	Body Fatigued
Monday	_____	_____	_____	_____
Tuesday	_____	_____	_____	_____

continues

The Morning After (continued)

	Mind Alert	Body Energetic	Mind Groggy	Body Fatigued
Wednesday	_____	_____	_____	_____
Thursday	_____	_____	_____	_____
Friday	_____	_____	_____	_____
Saturday	_____	_____	_____	_____
Sunday	_____	_____	_____	_____

If you're not awakening with a fresh, invigorated perspective, you know that getting a greater quantity of good quality sleep is a goal worthy of paying attention to. See Chapter 18 for tips about falling and staying asleep.

My Break Times

Last but most assuredly not least, take a look at your life in terms of how often you get to take a break from its many pressing demands. Simply fill in the remainder of these sentences:

The last time I spent some time alone at home, meditating or just relaxing, was

_____

_____.

The place in my house that I go to retreat is _____

_____.

My last restorative vacation was when I _____

_____.

For my next restorative vacation I am planning to _____

_____.

How many of these blanks were you able to fill in? If the answer is none—and for many people it is—you need to focus on taking some time to refuel. Look at Chapter 19 for inspiration on creating a retreat space at home, and at Chapter 20 for ideas about brief journeys that can get your stress-management program off to a wonderful start.

Signing Up to Show Up

If you have done the exercises in this chapter, you now have a pretty good idea where your particular areas of concentration should be as you begin the five-week program outlined in the next chapter. Now it's time to commit. Before going forward, and if you feel prepared, read and sign the statement below.

I, _____, am committed to lessening the level of chronic negative stress in my life and to coping better with stressors I cannot lessen by modifying my response to them. In order to do this, I am willing to pay greater attention to and to take greater responsibility for my attitudes, my thoughts and beliefs, my physical habits, my relationships, and my time.

Signed, _____

The Least You Need to Know

- To review: although the stress response is a survival mechanism—and one we should be grateful to have—our modern circumstances often cause it to run amok.

- Recognizing your personal stress triggers is the first step toward countering stress overload.

- Find out where you stand with regard to your attitude—if you are lacking optimism, laughter, faith, or a habit of doing good deeds, plan to pay special attention to these areas to increase your stress-beating potential.

- Look at your love and work relationships with an eye to their restorative power—your odds of beating stress rise as you notice and tend your support systems.

- Move quickly, move slowly, move for the sheer fun of it—look for opportunities to devote more time to your body, and your entire mind-body system will benefit from the release of brain chemicals that counter stress.

- Don't just tend and befriend others, but also tend and befriend yourself—notice any gaps in your self-care and prepare to patch them by eating and sleeping well, and by taking breaks at and away from home.

Chapter 22

The Five-Week Stress-Beater

In This Chapter

- Adjusting your attitude in Week One
- Uplifting mind and spirit in Week Two
- Nurturing relationships in Week Three
- Tuning in to your body in Week Four
- Nurturing yourself in Week Five

Only five weeks until you have much more control over your response to stress? Try it and see. This chapter contains suggested goals, strategies, and helpful exercises to get you there. Ideally, you should use the program to build momentum, so that the practices of the first week continue into the second week, and so on.

One caveat: don't let this program or its timetable become a source of stress for you. That would certainly be counterproductive. All the goals herein are ideal objectives. You alone can factor in your personal circumstances and your available resources. Be reasonable and consider your own needs. If something doesn't feel right for you right now, move on to another strategy—or be creative and improvise your own based on all of the things you have learned throughout this book.

Above all, be kind to yourself and stay in touch with yourself. If you put in the initial effort, your body and mind will respond in ways that tell you when you're on the right track.

Week One: Attitude Adjustment, Goals, and Strategies

In the first week of this program, the overriding goal is for you to adjust your attitude so that you are less inclined to default to negative thinking habits that increase distress and lessen resilience after a stressful episode. In other words, the goal is to lighten up and be more positive!

Select a date to start your program and, for the following seven days, incorporate as many of the following strategies into your life as you can:

- **Separate molehills from mountains.** This week, whenever a daily frustration sets off a major stress reaction, flip open your calendar to one year from the date. Ask yourself if the outcome of this particular situation will have made one bit of difference in your life. If the answer is no, it's a molehill. Note your revelation in your current calendar by writing the code *MH*, and move on.

- **Take a time out from time.** Is time always of the essence? There's a difference between wanting things to work out and feeling compelled to have them work out on your precise timetable. To practice taking a more fluid approach to time, spend one day this week not wearing a wristwatch. No fair checking your cell phone for the time every five minutes, either. When you need to know the time, ask someone. You'll soon wonder: "Why am I so obsessed with the time?"

- **Stay open to serendipity.** Take a chance on something this week—something small and whimsical is a fine place to start. Buy a lottery ticket, or enter a contest or sweepstakes. It doesn't matter if the odds are astronomically against you; what matters is your willingness to stay open to entertaining the possibility of good fortune.

Too Tense _____

Most people tend to begin new regimens on a Sunday or Monday, but pick a day that feels right for you. Some people prefer a Friday or Saturday because they have time over the weekend to unwind and to try new things.

Stress Less _____

Many positive outcomes occur only after a period of confusion. If you feel anxious because you cannot foresee outcomes, try this affirmation: *everything is exactly the way it should be right now.*

- **Make lemonade from lemons.** Well, not literally—instead, consciously recall a time in your life when things looked grim but in fact turned out well. Write about that experience and keep this note to yourself someplace where you can easily access it.

- **Start a laugh library.** Clear off a bookshelf and stock it with books and DVDs that you consider surefire laugh generators. Set aside at least an hour this week—and in all the following weeks—to dip into your laugh stacks. Continue to expand your laugh library.

Many of these strategies are even more effective and fast-acting if done along with a friend. You can compare notes and exchange advice. For example, if you and a friend both start laugh libraries, you can check out one another's favorite materials.

Week One Thought-Stopping Exercise

Negative thoughts can be persistent little nuisances. But they are just mental habits, *not facts*.

To stop negative thoughts, set a timer and allow yourself to have those thoughts for three full minutes. When the timer rings yell "Stop," or—if you prefer—pinch yourself (or yell and pinch). Take a 30-second break during which you breathe deeply. Begin the negative thoughts again for a two-minute interval, breathe, then do a one-minute interval.

Do this exercise each day for a week. At the end of this time, you should be able to give yourself the "stop" or pinch cues whenever you want to interrupt a negative thought pattern.

Week One Reactions

In the following space, or in a journal you create, write your reactions to the strategies and exercises you have tried during Week One. Make a note of which ones worked best for you. Note also any that you have not attempted yet but would like to attempt in the future.

_____

_____

_____

_____

_____

_____

_____

_____

Week Two: Mind/Spirit Lift, Goals and Strategies

In the second week of the program, the main goal is for you to cultivate some habits of mind that enable you to transcend everyday stressors. These include habits of mediation, personal spirituality, and good works. In other words, the goal is to uplift your consciousness so that you can be calmer.

Incorporate as many of the following strategies into your second week as you can manage:

- **Watch your breath.** For a minimum of five minutes each morning shortly after waking or each evening shortly before bed, sit quietly and focus on your breath. Have the sense that you are "watching" your breath as an objective observer. As thoughts interfere, and they will, say—in your mind—"Thank you. I'll think about you later." Then return your focus to the breath.

- **Choose a calming word.** As the week progresses, choose a word to focus on and to repeat internally as you breathe. Select any word that signifies peaceful-ness to you (perhaps _peace_ or _centered_ or simply _one_). Think of this word as your personal stress-alleviating mantra. Practice saying the word to yourself to trigger a relaxation response whenever tension strikes.

- **Institute a gratitude ritual.** Create a brief ritual (even 60 seconds will do), during which you plan to pause each day and express gratitude for the positive things in your life. This might take the form of a silent or spoken prayer, or a notation in a journal, or simply some time spent appreciating the beauty of an object selected specifically for this purpose. Perform the ritual in the same way every day—that's what makes it a ritual.

- **Perform unexpected kindnesses.** Helping someone in distress is good, but what if no obvious situation presents itself? To make certain to get your daily good deed in, this week create an opportunity to perform one such deed each day. This requires being extra alert to others around you. Ask yourself: What would make them smile? What would turn their stressful attitude into a more contented one? You might proffer a small, spontaneous gift, a gallant helpful gesture, or simply a sincere compliment.

Don't expect to be levitating by the end of Week Two. Don't expect to have discovered the meaning of life, either. But do expect to have cracked open a window into a new mind-set that, ultimately, can radically alter your perspective and your reactions to stress.

Stress Less _____

For some very effective technological assistance in learning to breathe deeply for relaxation, try a device called the Stress Eraser (www.stresseraser.com). The palm-sized biofeedback machine tracks your pulse rate as you inhale and exhale. Its easy-to-read visual display charts when you are in a state of physical and mental stress or calm. Though not inexpensive, this biofeedback device does such a good job of training you that you will soon be able to pass it along to a friend.

Week Two Visualization Exercise

If you can find 20 minutes for a meditative type exercise once or more this week, try this one, which is based on a *qigong* favorite:

Lie on your back, with arms and legs outstretched, V-shaped, at about a 30-degree angle from your torso. Inwardly repeat to yourself, "I am inside of the Universe, and the Universe is inside of me." Breathe deeply into your lower abdomen and picture a ball of golden light. See it expanding until it encompasses all of you. Imagine floating and resting in that golden light as it envelops you.

Repeating "I am inside of the Universe, and the Universe is inside of me," keep breathing deeply as you imagine the light contracting and nestling once again in your lower abdomen.

Keep repeating this sequence for 20 minutes. It's a good idea to set a timer so that you are not distracted by wondering how much time has passed.

Week Two Reactions

In the following space, or in a journal, write your reactions to the strategies and exercises you have tried during Week Two:

_____

_____

_____

_____

_____

_____

_____

_____

Week Three: Enhancing Love and Work, Goals and Strategies

In the third week of stress-beating, the chief goal is to enhance your relationships with family, friends, and co-workers, and to get more enjoyment from the process of your work itself. As you do so, you will maximize the potential for the love and work elements in your life to bolster you against stress.

- **Listen up.** Once each day this week, make it a point to ask someone in your life how they're doing. But don't do it in the usual cursory way that really indicates you just expect a standard answer of "Fine." Sit down, make eye contact, and give him the sense you are prepared to listen. Then do so. Don't jump in with tales of how you are doing. Don't offer advice unless asked. Just let him know that he's being heard and that you care.

- **Map your body language.** Many of us are unaware how our body language discourages people from communicating with us. Draw a picture of yourself (stick figures will do) in a "closed" posture, with arms and legs crossed and eyes averted; draw a picture of yourself in an "open" posture with open arms, uncrossed legs, eyes forward. Put a smile on that second drawing. Set three times each day to check in on your body language. Which drawing do you resemble?

◆ **Converse with a stranger.** Go ahead, you can do it. When you find yourself in a situation where you and someone else are "in the same boat"—e.g., waiting to pick up your kids from an activity, or waiting for a class to begin—start up a casual conversation. If the situation is one that is likely to be repeated, this could be the beginning of a friendship; if it's a one-time situation (e.g., standing in line at the grocery), it's still great practice for expanding your social support circle.

Too Tense

In successful human interaction, timing is often everything. If you're in the mood to listen, but someone is not in the mood to talk, be patient and pick another time. Don't expect people to conform to your timetable—even though you might want to "check something off your list." They don't know you have a list, now do they?

◆ **Identify your work passion.** The most meaningful 10 percent of what you do at work gives you 90 percent of your feelings of calming flow. But do you know what that is? Make a list of everything you do and rank your work-related endeavors in terms of how much they utilize your talents, engage your full attention, and make you feel competent and proud. Vow to spend at least part of each workday focusing on your passion.

◆ **Motivate someone you work with.** When people around you feel positive about what they are doing, they are less stressed and the entire atmosphere becomes somewhat less tense for all. Praise someone sincerely each day, and reinforce his or her efforts.

◆ **Offer acknowledgement.** Each day this week, be sure to thank someone for something he or she has done for you. It might be a tangible thing ("Thanks for packing my lunch.") or an intangible thing ("Thanks for being such a great husband/wife/mom/kid/friend and being there to cheer me up when I need it.").

When you begin Week Three, your relationships will be imperfect. When you end Week Three, they will *still* be imperfect. But you'll come away with greater appreciation for everything positive the love of family and friends and the joy of meaningful work bring to your life.

Week Three Response-Slowing Exercise

Conversation is, allegedly, about taking turns. Yet we're often in the habit of using conversational listening time not to listen, but to formulate our response. In doing this, we often "talk over" one another, miss most of what people are saying, and unwittingly create stressful miscommunications.

During Week Three, try slowing down your reaction pace. Silently count to three before reacting to someone else's statement or question. At first this will seem like a long time to you, but no one else will perceive it that way—except that, on a subliminal level, it will get them to slow the pace of conversation as well. Everyone will be calmer, and conversations will be more productive.

Try this technique for at least one conversation each day and notice how it calms your interactions.

Week Three Reactions

In the following space, or in your journal, note your reactions to the strategies and exercises you have undertaken during Week Three.

_____

_____

_____

_____

_____

Week Four: A Calm Body Tune-Up, Goals and Strategies

In Week Four of this program, the prevailing goal is for you to focus on conditioning your body to better withstand stress and to recover more quickly from stress. It can't be stated too strongly—exercise and play drive stress away!

This is a very active week, but more importantly it's the beginning of a more active lifestyle. Over the upcoming seven days, do as much of the following as you can:

- ◆ **Write movement into your schedule.** Plan to do some form of physical movement six days this week. Yes, six. This does not mean you have to run 10 miles a day. Just plan something that will get you up and moving—even a brisk 20-minute walk around the neighborhood counts. If you put movement in your day planner you will have a better chance of following through. (As much as possible, keep the time of day consistent. This week is about forming physical habits that will stick.)

- **Mix it up.** Varying your exercise obviously keeps you from burning out and getting bored. The less obvious but very important stress-beating benefit of variety is that it simulates a more natural way to move. We did not evolve doing 30 minutes on the stair machine each day. We ran, jumped, leapt, lifted, hauled, and hunted. The body functions optimally and the mind stays sharp when we recreate this natural dynamic.

- **Do *something* outdoors.** Speaking of natural dynamics, schedule at least one of your exercise ventures to take place outside. Hike, bike, ski, jog, walk, and expose yourself to the stress-lessening ambience of Mother Nature as you do so.

> ### It Works for Me
>
> "I enjoy taking my workout out of the gym. Recently I gave up my golf cart in favor of walking the course."
>
> —Gene, 33

- **Add music.** To add *oomph* to an aerobic workout, or added relaxation to a yoga or t'ai chi session, find music to suit your activity. Music itself has tremendous stress-relieving properties. Combining it with movement is a double stress-beater.

- **Watch a yoga or t'ai chi tape.** If you've never done yoga or t'ai chi and are timid about trying a class, rent a DVD and watch it. Simply viewing these practices has stress-relieving benefits, and you might well be inspired to participate.

- **Go with your flow.** In addition to scheduling exercise time, set aside at least two one-hour periods this week to delve more deeply into a hobby you already enjoy or into finding a hobby.

Keep in mind that there is no law that says you have to do any of these activities alone—during Week Four or ever. Make a play date with a friend. Work out together, take a long hike together instead of a long lunch. Play a game of squash. You'll enjoy the benefits of socialization as a bonus.

Week Four "Objections to Exercise" Exercise

If you have objections to adding exercise to your life, go ahead and get them out of your system. Write them down; make a big, long list.

"I was an unathletic kid—picked last for teams in gym class."

"I have two left feet."

"I have no time."

"I don't look good in workout clothes."

Now, next to every objection, write the words, "Exercise is a surefire stress antidote" three times.

Week Four Reactions

In the following space, or in your journal, jot your reactions to the strategies and exercises you have tried during Week Four.

_____

_____

_____

_____

_____

Week Five: Self-Nurturance, Goals and Strategies

In Week Five of this program, the main goal is for you to focus on taking better care of yourself. In doing so, you'll develop habits that will strengthen your stress defenses and prevent you from creating vicious stress cycles. You'll focus on eating better, sleeping better, and planning at-home and away-from-home retreats from your hectic schedule. Over the next seven days, pursue as many of these strategies as you can:

♦ **Cut the sweet treats.** For this week, stop adding extra sugar, honey, or syrup to your food and avoid packaged foods with sugar in their first four ingredients. Try fresh fruit for dessert and use it to sweeten non-sugary cereal.

♦ **Up your Bs and C.** If you are not taking a multivitamin supplement that includes minimum daily requirements of vitamins C, B12, B6, biotin, and folic acid, start. These vitamins are depleted during stress—when we most need our defenses up.

Too Tense

Be a careful label reader. Sugar is called by many names, including fructose (often listed as high fructose corn syrup), sucrose, glucose, dextrose, maltose, and lactose.

- **Cut your caffeine.** Limit this stimulant to 200 milligrams daily—the amount recommended by the American Medical Association. An 8-ounce cup of brewed coffee has about 135 milligrams, instant coffee 95, and most teas and colas about 30 to 40.

- **Plan your fare.** Plan and shop a week of healthy meals at the start of the week. You'll make less impulsive choices and simplify your daily routines.

- **Unplug the bedroom TV.** Or, move it out altogether. If you can't tolerate that notion yet, just vow not to view TV from bed this week and watch what happens.

- **Identify a home retreat space.** Find the space in your home where you will create your at-home retreat (see Chapter 19 for ideas on how to do so). This week, begin the creation process by talking about your plans with those you live with and by sketching out ideas for the space.

- **Research a journey.** Do some Internet research and create a "blue sky" list of destinations you'd enjoy trying for a relaxing and restorative vacation. For now, this is an armchair journey. Don't concern yourself with prices or logistics. You are brainstorming.

By the end of Week Five, you should have developed the habit of taking good care of yourself. It's not a selfish agenda, but one that will ultimately benefit you and those around you. At week's end, let's hope you have a new best friend: you.

Week Five Mindful Eating Exercise

Enjoy a silent, mindful meal. Prepare a simple, nutritious meal; arrange it pleasingly on a plate, sit down, and enjoy it. If you are alone, turn off the TV/radio/CD player. Do not read the paper, or anything else. Look at the food, take in its smells before tasting, feel gratitude for it, chew and taste every bite, and don't take another bite until the food is swallowed. When the mind wanders, bring it back to your repast.

You can also choose to eat a silent meal in the company of family or friends. Agree ahead of time when the meal will take place and what the rules are. You can begin with a joint silent blessing if you like. Afterward, you can talk about what your silent dining experience was like.

Week Five Reactions

In the following space, or in your journal, write your reactions to the things you have tried during Week Five:

_____

_____

_____

_____

_____

Don't Forget Spontaneity

Although each of the five weeks has been laid out one at a time, in linear fashion, feel free to take a more freestyle approach to this program if that suits you. If it feels too intense to add the new habits of each week to the ones of the preceding week, it's possible to try a week-at-a-time sampler approach, seeing which anti-stress strategies have the greatest impact on you. Likewise, if you feel strongly that you'd like to take the weeks in a different order—perhaps starting with new exercise habits and self-care before trying meditations and visualizations—do so.

Want to mix and match? Go ahead, be spontaneous.

If you give most of these strategies a fair shake, regardless of which you do when, you will have, by the end of a five-week period, a new outlook and a new understanding of just how much you can do to contain the stress factor in your life. That's all that really counts.

The Least You Need to Know

- ◆ Week One of stress-beating involves readjusting your mind-set with optimism and laughter.
- ◆ In Week Two, add meditation, personal spirituality, and good works.
- ◆ Week Three is a time to continue by enhancing your relationship skills.
- ◆ In Week Four, add an exercise and play components to your program.
- ◆ In Week Five, eat, sleep, and chill out—you deserve it.

Chapter 23

Holding On to New Habits

In This Chapter

- ◆ The challenge of maintaining gains
- ◆ Why resistance to progress is natural
- ◆ Overcoming resistance to progress
- ◆ Detaching from your symptoms
- ◆ Confronting your excuses
- ◆ Why persistence pays

This might not be the first time in your life that you have enthusiastically committed to a program of some sort of self-reinvention. Some of us take stock periodically and decide it's time for a change. Some of us wait until conditions get nearly too tough to bear and then decide it would be less painful to change than to leave things as they are. But most of us, whatever our motivation or timetable, decide at one time or another that we have had enough and we attempt to revise our habits.

Then we notice that our initial efforts and enthusiasm might flag. Habits die hard. That's why they call them habits. This chapter explains why we sometimes slide backward and get stuck in old habits that we thought we had discarded. It also offers ideas about how to get unstuck.

Week Six Until ... Forever

If you have been practicing this book's stress-beating program for the past five weeks, you have likely noticed that a number of things have begun to happen. As a result of your attitude and mind-set adjustments, your relationship work, your bodywork, and your self-care, certain internal dynamics are shifting. Among the stress-alleviating changes you might be experiencing, you've noticed that ...

- You are living more in the present moment.

- You are observing your anxious impulses without immediately acting on them.

- You are experiencing a greater sense of connectedness with other people.

- You are more tolerant.

- You are not dwelling so much on minor irritants.

- You are not so concerned with "fixing" everything or with having everything be perfect.

From a physical standpoint, you are probably feeling more energetic, and less wound up. Perhaps, every once in a while, you are experiencing moments of near-buoyancy. I don't mean to say you're feeling six feet off the ground, but you're certainly somewhat uplifted in body and spirit.

This all must seem pretty good, right? So why is it that sometimes you are not doing the things you now know you have the power to do to counter negative stressors in your life?

No, I don't have a crystal ball or a magic mirror. I just know you are backsliding sometimes because you are human.

Stress Less

Not perfectly "cured" yet? Welcome to the human race. Forget about following this program—or doing anything else—completely consistently and flawlessly.

The reality is that none of us make progress toward significant goals by following a linear path. Sure, we move ahead for a while—often with a great burst of speed at the start. But then we do a little side step, pivot, maybe even spin for a while, and even back up before moving forward again.

If you want to continue managing the stress in your life, you'll have to accept this little dance as a part of the process. It's natural; it's inevitable. So what!?

The only way a little sidestepping and backward movement can harm you is if you misinterpret this organic process as signifying an ending rather than a routine transition. When you accept it and understand it, you can manage stress from Week Six until forever.

Getting Stuck: Resistance Rising

Let's say you have been sailing along on a sea of calmness, centeredness, and clarity for weeks. Subtle rewards begin to accumulate. You make decisions more easily. You sleep more soundly. You feel different, the world feels different. It's all good.

Then—all of a sudden—you "lose it." Something happens or, more likely, a few things happen at once. Your computer program develops a glitch, your kids get chicken pox, your accountant says you owe back taxes. You start gnashing your teeth, and you feel like you're coming down with a cold. Your mind goes in circles. You worry and fret, fret and worry.

Clearly, the honeymoon—that brief period of bedazzlement with something new and alluring—is over. Your old habits are coming to the fore; your stress-beating regimens seem like silly distractions.

What, go to the gym *now?* Meditate *now?* Drink a cup of chamomile tea and forego that doughnut *now?* You're too busy stressing out to keep up your new routines, right?

Well, wrong. We all regress under stress now and then. That makes sense, because stress ignites our primal impulses—not our higher thinking. You have to think your way out of this pickle, and you can.

When we stop moving forward in pursuit of our goals, it can feel as though we've run into an invisible wall of resistance. You can't scramble over the wall. But you *can* get around it. The trick is to incorporate the resistance itself into your stress-beating strategies.

Getting Unstuck: Resolving Resistance

Think of your resistances to continuing your new habits as a wake-up call. The times when resistance manifests itself are precisely the times when you need to redouble your efforts. Meet your resistance head on. Work hardest at beating stress when you least feel like it. *Practice self-calming strategies most when you're not in the mood.*

No, it's not easy. But there are many things you can do to help get over the hump.

Forget About Guilt

Resistance days are bound to happen. They are facts of life. There's no use feeling guilty about them. In fact, feeling guilty but doing nothing to modify your behavior is just another form of resistance itself.

If you've committed a "sinful" omission to your stress program, you could sit around chastising yourself. *What a miserable lout I am*, you could say. *What's the use, I just don't have what it takes.* Woe is you, right?

But such self-accusation will only make your situation more stressful. Remind yourself that you are not a bad person, but rather a perfectly normal person with bad habits. Objectify the situation. What's done is done. You can't go back in your time machine and change it. But you can stop feeling sorry for yourself and do something positive.

Monitor Your Morning

On "not in the mood" days, a vitamin pill usually taken with breakfast might go un-swallowed. The morning jog might get put off "until later." Your eager dog might get only the most cursory of walks, or be let into the backyard with a half-hearted apologetic shrug from you. Uh-oh. That's all indicative of a little too much lethargy. Be vigilant, and notice the early warning signs of your resistance. When your day starts out this way, you know you are setting yourself up for a downward stress spiral.

> **Stress Less**
>
> If your morning routine feels too crowded to add stress-beating rituals, gradually change your schedule so you get up earlier. Set your alarm 15 minutes ahead, and then a few days later add another 15 minutes, and so on. If this cuts into sleep time you feel you need, go to bed earlier.

Morning can be an exceptionally productive time, because we are refreshed from sleeping and most open to the creative part of our mind. Always allow time in your morning for one or more stress-relieving routines. Make this part of your morning "system." Interweave them with all the other things you have to do to get ready, like brushing your teeth and getting dressed.

Be Wary of Time Leeches

Resistance is shameless. It will appropriate just about anything in your day-to-day life to divert you from your stress-beating attitudes and enterprises. It will try to convince you that pressing chores require your full and immediate attention, and that you should tend to them now in lieu of, say, taking a few deep breaths, or sharing a laugh with a friend, or making it to that yoga class.

Our modern world is full of potential time leeches anyway. It's all too easy to be seduced by ...

- The Google search that leads you down all sorts of diverting byways.

- The television show that leads directly into another television show.

- The new software you are prompted to download *right now*.

- E-mail, e-mail, and more e-mail.

- Magazines—even the ones you cancelled that seem to keep coming anyway.

- Clutter—there's always a mess somewhere.

- Shopping—there's always something more you can buy.

- Gossip—especially the derogatory kind.

- Unopened mail.

- Opened mail that you put in a pile instead of a file.

- 24/7 news feeds.

- Office politics and silly sucking up.

- Obsessing about your weight and personal appearance.

Too Tense

TV network programmers have started segueing from one show into another without a commercial break, in an attempt to seduce viewers into pursuing seamless entertainment. Nice trick. To fight back, set your VCR or TiVo to record only the shows you want to see. Then watch them—and only them—at your convenience.

It Works for Me

"Talking to my friends is calming and enriching—depending on what we talk about. I have found that negative gossip creates a negative, stressful climate."

—Louisa, 29

To counter time leeches, prioritize. Write down everything you need to do and assign it a value from 1 (top) to 5 (forget about it!). Make sure that each time you do this some stress-beating endeavors get a 1. That does not mean that nothing else gets a 1, but stress-beaters have to be right up there.

Now, get going. Don't procrastinate on those 1s. Twos are next. Threes are for spare time only. Fours and below—well, some things have got to go.

Say No to Nay-Sayers

Occasionally people in your family, in your circle of friends, and in your work environment can actually help to activate your resistance. They might not consciously mean to do so, but nevertheless, they do.

You might hear comments like:

What do you mean you're meditating? You look like you're just sitting there doing nothing.

Why are you going to the gym? You just went yesterday. Are you having an affair or something?

Oh come on. Get off that healthy eating kick. What a bore. I don't want to have a double mochachino and a brownie all by myself.

You might even hear specific complaints that the people around you are uncomfortable with your new, calmer persona. After all, everybody has gotten used to you being one way, and any change—even one that you consider positive—can be unsettling. *Who do you think you are?* they might ask.

Depending on how suggestible you are, and how much credence you give the people speaking to you, you might be all too easily swayed. *Hey*, you might think, *I'm not really being myself when I'm this calm person.*

Puh-lease. Once again, you need to remind yourself that what others have gotten used to was merely a system of rote behaviors and reactions on your part. You are still you—a more authentic you than ever—when you refuse to let stressors pull your strings.

When others try to talk you out of your new way of being, don't bother getting angry with them. That will only cause—you guessed it—more stress. Just know you've thrown these folks a little off balance and that they will recover. This is not your problem to solve. Meanwhile, setting the best stress-beating example won't hurt them—or you.

Right Strategy, Right Situation

This book has offered a wide array of stress-beating strategies. It would be unreasonable to expect yourself to perform every one every single day. That expectation alone would be a massive stressor.

Individuals vary with regard to what coping skills work best for them. And any single individual will typically have a range from which they like to pick and choose. Pick the right strategy for the right moment. Trust your instincts.

- If you are confused or depressed along with being stressed, social support could be the perfect remedy.

- If your stress has an element of anger or frustration, vigorous exercise could be just the right cathartic outlet.

- If you're being overwhelmed and overcommitted, you might need time in your personal retreat space.

- If you're feeling physically run-down from stress, you might need to focus more on what you're eating and drinking.

- If you're bored and uninspired from too much of the same old same old, you might need some playtime to resurrect your creative spark of eustress.

If you try one strategy and it doesn't seem to be doing the trick for you, try another. Stay flexible. During times of stress, mustering the inner strength to keep trying until you get it right can be challenging—but it's exactly the approach that's needed.

Giving Up Your Symptoms

We can't leave the topic of resistance without mentioning the fact that sometimes this phenomenon occurs because we become so attached to our own symptoms of stress that we are reluctant to give them up.

It might seem hard to give credence to the idea that we are actually attached to stress symptoms. After all, they include everything from tight neck muscles to loose bowels, from short tempers to long, sleepless nights, from churning minds to totally mindless living. Nevertheless, it's a fact that symptoms sometimes give their sufferers what are called secondary gains—peripheral benefits that offer some advantage.

One type of secondary gain might simply be that of earning ourselves some attention. Having people feel sorry for us, commiserate with us, and tell us how many stressful burdens we appear to be shouldering can be an odd kind of comfort. What we might not realize is that it would be much more of a comfort to engage with people in more positive ways. The type of attention we get based on displaying stress symptoms is a mere band-aid compared to the sustaining healing that comes when we work at re-solving those symptoms and when others come to recognize our efforts.

Another type of secondary gain from stress could be that being stressed out all the time gives us an excuse for ignoring other pressing matters in our lives. If we continually tell ourselves that "one more stressful straw will break our back" we might, for example, feel justified in not noticing that our kids are growing up without our spending much time with them, or that our finances are in disarray, or that we haven't had a medical check-up in years.

It Works for Me
"My too stressed, too busy attitude was my way of signaling everybody to 'stand back.' I had to come to terms with that. Once I gave up sending that message, I had sources of strength and comfort opened to me that I had never realized were there." —Eric, 44

In the short run, it might seem like it's easier to ignore such matters, but in the long run there's not much point in kidding ourselves.

Symptoms become a part of our physical and psychological make-up. They're like a pair of eyeglasses we're used to seeing perched on our nose, or a pair of worn, frayed jeans we've grown accustomed to sporting day after day. But don't make the mistake of thinking your symptoms define you. It is when you are willing to relinquish them that you can see who is truly underneath.

Know Your Wake-Up Calls

No one knows you better than you. No one but you can recognize your resistance to beating stress as well as you can.

Treat each resistance as a wake-up call for corrective action. Note here, over the upcoming week, all the reasons—all the "good excuses" you have for not continuing with your new habits. (There's plenty of room for at least one a day—two on some. However, if you need more room, don't be shy. Use extra paper or a journal.)

My "Good Excuses"

1. _____
   _____.

2. _____
   _____.

3. _____
   _____.

4. _____
   _____.

5. _____
   _____.

6. _____
   _____.

7. _____
   _____.

8. _____
   _____.

9. _____
   _____.

10. _____
   _____.

After you have these excuses in black and white, an interesting phenomenon will happen. They will begin to lose their power.

That's right, just keep looking at them. Is this all you've got? Ask yourself if these excuses seem worthy of undermining your dedication to lessening stress. If not, acknowledge that they exist, thank them for showing up to teach you something about yourself, and get back on track.

A Reservoir of Calm

Though you will doubtless have times when you slip and slide, the key to lessening stress throughout your life is to keep this important goal in mind and not give up. Patience and persistence will pay off.

Bit by bit, the intellectual resolve with which you started this program will transform into gut instincts. New habits will supplant old ones. Now, when stressors appear, you will not meet them with an already overtaxed body and mind, but rather with a quantity of calm in reserve.

Remember, the stress response is a neat trick of nature. But it's often overkill in today's complex world. It is possible for a calm, centered approach to prevail. Allow it to become your second nature.

The Least You Need to Know

◆ Progress toward significant new goals doesn't follow a linear path—there is always some backsliding to be expected.

◆ The times when you feel most resistant to continuing your stress-beating practices are precisely the times when you should be sure to do them.

◆ Resistance to progress takes many forms, including guilt, procrastination, allowing your time to be sucked by nonessentials, and listening to people who try to dissuade you from new habits.

◆ We can also resist positive change because we are attached to negative symptoms (perhaps our stress has given us attention for physical symptoms or excuses for avoiding other important issues in our lives)—so it's time to get unattached.

◆ Persistence pays—replace old habits with new and you will have a reservoir of calm to draw upon when unexpected stressors appear.

Appendix A

Resources for Further Reading

Bennet-Goleman, Tara. *Emotional Alchemy. How the Mind Can Heal the Heart*. New York: Harmony, 2001.

Benson, Herbert. M.D. *The Relaxation Response*. New York: Harper Torch, 1976.

———. *Beyond the Relaxation Response*. New York: Berkley, 1976.

Brussat, Frederic and Mary Ann. *Spiritual Literacy: Reading the Sacred in Everyday Life*. New York: Scribner, 1996.

Cohen, R., and F. Ahearn. *Handbook for Mental Health Care of Disaster Victims*. Baltimore: The Johns Hopkins University Press, 1980.

Cousins, Norman. *Anatomy of an Illness as Perceived by the Patient*. New York: W.W. Norton, 2005 (new Ed, Edition).

Crowley, Chris, and Henry S. Lodge, M.D. *Younger Next Year: A Guide to Living Like 50 Until You're 80 and Beyond*. New York: Workman, 2004.

Dalai Lama and Renuka Singh. *Path to Tranquility: Daily Meditations by the Dalai Lama*. New York: Viking, 1999.

Dalai Lama and Howard C. Cutler, M.D. *The Art of Happiness: A Handbook for Living*. New York: Riverhead, 1998.

Dillard, Annie. *Pilgrim at Tinker Creek.* New York: Harper Perennial Modern Classics, 1998. (Reprint edition)

Dossey, Larry, M.D. *Healing Words: The Power of Prayer and the Practice of Medicine.* San Francisco: HarperSanFrancisco: 1997.

Epstein, Mark, M.D. *Going to Pieces Without Falling Apart.* New York: Broadway Books, 1998.

Goleman, Daniel. *Destructive Emotions: How Can We Overcome Them?* New York: Bantam, 2003.

Hendricks, G. *Gracious Breathing: Breathwork for Health, Stress Release and Personal Mastery.* New York: Bantam, 1995.

Jamison, Kay Redfield. *Exuberance: The Passion for Life.* New York: Alfred A, Knopf, 2004.

Kabat-Zinn, Jon. *Full Catastrophe Living: Using the Wisdom of Your Body and Mind to Face Stress, Pain, and Illness.* New York: Delta, 1990.

———. *Wherever You Go, There You Are: Mindfulness Meditation in Everyday Life.* New York: Hyperion, 1994.

Khlasa, Guru Dharam S., and Darryle O'Keefe. *The Kundalini Yoga Experience: Bringing Body, Mind and Spirit Together.* New York: Fireside, 2002.

Khalsa, Shkata Kaur. *Kundalini Yoga: Unlock Your Inner Potential Through Life-Changing Exercise.* London: Dorling Kindersley, 2001.

Kilham, Christopher. *The Five Tibetans: Five Dynamic Exercises for Health, Energy, and Personal Power.* Rochester, VT: Healing Arts Press, 1994.

Lasater, Judith, Ph.D., P.T., et al. *Relax and Renew: Restful Yoga for Stressful Times.* Berkeley: Rodmell Press, 1995.

———. *30 Essential Yoga Poses: For Beginning Students and Their Teachers.* Berkeley: Rodmell Press, 2003.

LeShan, Lawrence. *How to Meditate.* New York: Little Brown, 1974.

Luks, Allan. *The Healing Power of Doing Good.* Lincoln, NE: iUniverse, 2001.

Man-Ch'Ing, Cheng, and Robert W. Smith. *T'ai Chi: The "Supreme Ultimate" Exercise for Health, Sport and Self-Defense.* North Clarendon, VT: Tuttle, 2005.

Matthews, A.M., *The Seven Keys to Calm: Essential Steps to Staying Calm Under Any Circumstances*. New York: Pocket Books, 1997.

Moore, Thomas. *Care of the Soul: A Guide for Cultivating Depth and Sacredness in Everyday Life*. New York: Harper, 1994. (Reprint)

Moran, Elizabeth, Joseph Yu, and Val Biktashev. *The Complete Idiot's Guide to Feng Shui* (Second Edition). Indianapolis: Alpha, 2002.

O'Connor, Richard, Ph.D. *Undoing Perpetual Stress: The Missing Connection Between Depression, Anxiety, and 21st Century Illness*. New York: Berkley Books, 2005.

Provine, Robert R. *Laughter: A Scientific Investigation*. New York: Viking, 2000.

Rinpoche, Sogyal. *The Tibetan Book of Living and Dying*. San Francisco: HarperSanFrancisco, 1994.

Sapolsky, Robert M. *Why Zebras Don't Get Ulcers* (Third Edition). New York: Henry Holt, 2004.

Seligman, Martin E.P., Ph.D. *Authentic Happiness: Using the New Positive Psychology to Realize Your Potential for Lasting Fulfillment*. New York: The Free Press, 2002.

———. *Learned Optimism*. New York: Alfred A. Knopf, 1991.

Siegel, Bernie. *Love, Medicine, and Miracles*. New York: Harper & Row, 1986.

Thakar, Vimala. *Blossoms of Friendship: Yoga Wisdom Classics*. Berkeley: Rodmell Press. 2003.

Thoreau, Henry David. *Walden*. Boston: Houghton Mifflin, 1995. (Reprint)

Tulku, Tarthang. *Kum Nye Relaxation: Movement Exercises*. Berkeley: Dharma Publishing, 1978)

Weil, Andrew, M.D. *Healthy Aging: A Lifelong Guide to Your Physical and Spiritual Well-Being*. New York: Alfred A. Knopf, 2005.

Williamson, Marianne. *Illuminata: A Return to Prayer*. New York: Riverhead, 1995. (Reprint)

At-Home Retreat Resources

Meditation Supplies and Instruction

3 Pound Universe

www.3pounduniverse.com

The store takes its name from the weight of the brain (3 pounds); its tapes, CDs, and supplies are geared to take it to a higher, calmer realm.

Center for Mindfulness in Medicine, Health Care, and Society

www.umassmed.edu/cfm/mbsr

508-856-2656

Mindfulness meditation practice tapes from this well-known University of Massachusetts Medical School-based MBSR center.

DharmaCrafts

www.dharmacrafts.com

1-800-794-9862

High-quality meditation cushions, benches, bells, gongs, incense and incense burners, wall hangings, Japanese screens, rice paper lamps, and a beautiful collection of spiritual statuary. A "teachings" section of the web-site offers an extensive selection of audio and video instruction.

Equinox Gifts

www.equinoxbooksandgifts.com

1-877-870-7369

A wide array of gongs, bells and chimes, malas (prayer beads), traveling altars and altar cards, singing bowls, finger labyrinths, and more.

Four Gates

www.fourgates.com

1-888-232-7414

Meditation furniture (including "back jack" chairs for those with back problems), kimonos, robes, and other loose, natural clothing, and a nice collection of tapestries, among other delights.

Samadhi Store

www.samadhicushions.com

1-800-331-7751

Cushions and benches, gongs and incense, and calligraphy and flower arranging (ikebana) supplies. A wide selection of books, audio, and video.

Well Baskets

www.wellbaskets.com

1-800-763-3488

Resources for the health and wellness of mind, body, and spirit. The CDs utilize healing techniques such as guided imagery, meditation, and breathwork.

Wild Mind

secure.wildmind.org/store/customer/home.php

1-877-763-3488

An appealing assortment of supplies, some quite practical and interesting, including a Guided Meditations for Busy People CD and an invisible clock meditation timer.

Zen By Design

www.zenbydesign.com

1-866-903-0328

An elegant collection of meditation chairs (portable and stationary) that are said to promote spinal alignment. Select fabrics from an array of Thai silk brocades.

Soothing Sounds

Amazon.com

www.amazon.com

Type "soothing sounds" and/or "sacred sounds" into the Amazon search engine for a variety of calming music, chants, and even birdsong.

The Ear Plug Store

store.yahoo.com/earplugstore/whitenoisecds.html

1-918-478-5500

Shop here for an array of white noise CDs and white noise machines.

Isabella Catalogue

www.isabellacatalogue.com

1-888-481-6745

Offers a wide variety of chants on CD.

Pure White Noise

www.purewhitenoise.com

Choose from a broad selection of calming sounds including waves, wind, rain, distant thunderstorms, and the like. Three-pack variety selections are also available.

Aromatherapy

Aromatherapy.com

www.aromatherapy.com

1-800-877-6889

Shop here for a variety of quality essential oils, including calming lavender and chamomile, and for diffusers to spread them throughout your space.

Aromaweb

www.aromaweb.com

Oils, blends, diffuser candles, and fans. The site also features a wonderful article archive on aromatherapy.

The Incense Company

www.bytheplanet.com/Incense/incense.htm

1-888-543-9294

An astounding array of incense and terrific starter sampler packs; e.g., "Flowers and Spice" and "Harmony and Zen."

Incense Galore

www.incensegalore.com

Unique, hand-dipped incense—long-lasting and fresh. Gift combination packs available.

Candles and Lighting

Illuminations

www.illuminations.com

1-800-621-2998

Every conceivable style of candle—tapers, votives, jar candles, etc.—in every imaginable color and scent. Also, a plethora of candleholders and other accessories.

More Than Light

www.more-than-light.com

1-866-228-9132

Unique illumination and light-spreading products; e.g., glass oil candles, colored-flame candles, and exotic tea light stands.

Screens/Room Dividers

Home Decorators

www.homedecorators.com

1-877-537-8539

A large assortment of room dividers. Search by style (Oriental, Victorian, contemporary), fabric, color, or finish.

Oriental Furnishings Club

www.orientalfurnishings.com

914-592-6320 or 203-853-7553

A wide collection of elegant screens in assorted sizes and materials.

Tatami Room

www.tatamiroom.com

866-465-4068

Traditional and contemporary screens. While you are at it, check out their lamp collection.

Gardens

Garden Retreat

www.gardenretreats.net

1-800-940-1170

Everything necessary to create a garden retreat in the style of your dreams.

Smith & Hawken

www.smithandhawken.com

1-800-940-1170

Upscale items for the well-appointed garden.

Yoga and T'ai Chi Accessories and Instruction

Gaiam

www.gaiam.com

1-877-6321

Yoga wear, yoga mats, bricks and straps, instructional videos, and CDs.

Marie Wright

www.mariewright.com

1-800-217-0006

Great-fitting women's yoga wear: tops, bottoms, and unitards in a rainbow of colors.

Om Time

www.omtime.com

1-877-688-4631

Men's yoga clothing: shirts, shorts, tops. Women's clothing, too, as well as mats, props, and bags.

The Patience T'ai Chi Association

www.patiencetaichi.com

Step-by-step instructional videos.

Spring Forest Qigong

www.springforestqigong.com

1-888-860-2319

Offers a comprehensive, easy-to-follow program (on video or DVD) for healing and calming. The program has four extensive levels, but you can begin with the "Small Universe" sitting meditation CD that aims to remove tension and blockages from the body's energy pathways.

World T'ai Chi and Chi Gong Day

www.worldtaichiday.org

1-913-648-2256

Videos, DVDs, CDs, and books, t'ai chi fans and swords, and Asian lifestyle products.

Yoga Journal

www.yogajournal.com

1-800-600-9642

Shop for CDs and DVDs, including a three-CD step-by-step practice system that includes a set of illustrated posture cards. If yoga has caught your interest, consider subscribing to the monthly *Yoga Journal* magazine.

Anti-Stress Destinations

Spas

Amansala

www.amansala.com

Located on the remote beach of Tulum, Mexico, the boutique-type eco-resort Amansala is best known for a six-night program that is limited to 25 men and women. In between aerobic power walks on the beach, yoga, and meditation, you can enjoy a calming swim in nearby freshwater swimming holes.

Canyon Ranch

www.canyonranch.com

1-800-742-9000

Every Canyon Ranch experience is an opportunity to explore your potential for the highest possible quality of life. Canyon Ranch has resorts in the Berkshires and in Arizona.

Mirabel

www.Mirabel.com

1-866-MIRABEL

This Scottsdale, Arizona, spa is renowned for its gorgeous setting and comprehensive fitness programs.

Rancho la Puerta

www.rancholapuerta.com

1-800-443-7565

A truly unique spa resort, Rancho la Puerta, just South of the Mexican border about an hour from San Diego, "the Ranch"—as devotees call it—provides a variety of different activities for you and your partner, including artistic workshops, nature walks, meditation, and an astounding variety of fitness workouts. The beauty and sage-infused fragrance of the surrounding land will transport you to a realm that transcends the ordinary.

Spa Finder

www.spafinder.com

212-924-6800

Browse this worldwide online directory to find your ideal spa vacation.

Meditation/Spiritual Retreats

Angel Valley Spiritual Retreat Center

www.angelvalley.org

1-800-393-6308

A nondenominational organization located on the edge of breathtaking Sedona, Arizona. The 70-acre property is surrounded by National Forest where renowned Sedona red rocks radiate their magic. The retreat offers a perfect environment for individuals, whether in a personal or group retreat. Accommodations include creekside guesthouses, creekside cabins, and teepees.

The Chopra Center

www.chopra.com

1-866-260-2236

Located at California's La Costa Resort and Spa, The Chopra Center is a health and wellness retreat that integrates the mind-body techniques and Ayurvedic (Indian healing) principles set forth by internationally acclaimed author and philosopher Dr. Deepak Chopra.

Earth Sanctuary

www.earthsanctuary.org

1-425-637-8777

Washington State's Earth Sanctuary is an excellent environment for personal renewal and spiritual connection, whatever your spiritual path. Accommodations are immediately adjacent to a 72-acre nature reserve, meditation parkland, and sculpture garden.

Esalen

www.esalen.org

1-831-677-3005

A kind of "mind spa," this legendary Big Sur paradise was founded as an alternative education center blending East/West philosophies. It offers a broad array of workshops in everything from meditation to sensory awareness to dealing with psychological issues.

The Expanding Light Retreat

www.expandinglight.org

1-800-346-5350

Located in Northern California's Sierra Nevada foothills, this retreat offers meditation, yoga, and great workshops.

The Garden at Thunder Hill

www.gardenofone.com

1-518-797-3373

This retreat—describing itself as a "personal research facility"—is located on 120 acres of forest, streams, trails, and natural beauty in the Albany, New York, area. Paths through old orchards and even older forests hold the promise of serenity and simplicity.

Green Mountain at Fox Run

fitwoman.com/mindfulness_retreat.htm

1-800-448-8106

At this Vermont retreat, discover and practice techniques of visualization, meditation, and journaling to help yourself let go of stress and bring peace and self-care to your daily life.

Mount Monresa

www.manrsasi.org

1-718-727-3844

At this Jesuit retreat house on New York City's Staten Island one can stroll a rustic landscape and pray in the warmth of a traditional chapel. A professional retreat staff will help you focus your inner journey.

Omega Institute

www.eomega.org

1-800-944-1001

This peaceful oasis in Rhinebeck, New York, offers a plethora of retreats and work-shops to expand mind, body, and soul.

Our Lady of Peace Spiritual Life Center

www.our-lady-of-peace-retreat.org

1-401-783-2871

A Rhode Island retreat in the Christian tradition, the Center seeks to enable people to re-encounter their spirituality in their personal lives. It offers individual and group retreats, and a hermitage is available for private retreats.

Retreat Finder

www.retreatfinder.com

1-800-889-6906

If you are on a quest for inner peace, this site helps you find what you're after. Search also for yoga resorts.

Seven Circles Retreat

www.sevencirclesretreat.org

1-559-337-0211

Located in beautiful foothills just outside Sequoia National Park, this retreat is situated on 24 acres of scenic hills filled with native oak and manzanita. Visitors can take a short hike to view sunrise over the snowcapped high Sierra, watch sunset over a peaceful countryside, or experience the awe of a panoramic view of the night sky with brilliant constellations and the Milky Way. The website has an ongoing list of retreat events and programs.

Zen Mountain Monastery

www.mro.org/zmm/zmmhome

1-845-688-2228

This upstate New York meditation training center provides Zen training for people of all ages and spiritual backgrounds. The "Introduction to Zen Training" weekend is a great way to get your feet wet.

Yoga Destinations

Kripalu Center for Yoga and Health

www.kripalu.org

1-800-741-7353

The nation's largest yoga retreat center, in the Berkshire Mountains of Massachusetts, offers workshops with master teachers, along with fitness activities and healing arts services. Volunteer workers can stay in dormitory-style accommodations and attend classes free of charge, so consider this cost-saving option.

Mahalo Hawaiian Retreat

www.mahalohawaiianretreat.org

1-877-703-7453

Nestled in the tropical rain forest of Hawaii, this retreat complements yoga instruction with a hiking program.

Sewall House Yoga Retreat

www.sewallhouse.com

1-888-235-2395

This small, personalized yoga retreat in Maine provides daily yoga, massage, and great food.

Sivananda Ashram Yoga Retreat

www.sivananda.org/nassau

1-242-363-2902

This yoga retreat lies on five acres of tropical beauty on Paradise Island in the Bahamas. It offers year-round yoga vacation, trainings, and symposiums.

Unique Yoga Retreats

www.uniqueyogaretrets.com

1-408-377-3746

Based in San Jose, California, this retreat offers all-inclusive retreats for the yoga enthusiast that also feature culinary, artistic, and athletic experiences. They will design custom programs for groups.

Yoga in the Pines

www.yogainthepines.net

1-972-393-6281

This weekend retreat is serenely tucked away in 30 acres of pine trees in East Texas.

The Yoga Lodge on Whidbey Island

www.yogalodge.com

1-360-678-2120

The Yoga Lodge sits on five secluded Washington State acres, complete with a yoga studio. Personal and group retreats can be customized.

Cruises

Celebrity Cruises

www.celebrity.com

1-800-647-2251

Celebrity cruises offer first-class ambience at affordable rates. In addition to fine dining and entertainment, they offer great fitness centers, acupuncture, and spa services.

Royal Caribbean Cruises

www.royalcaribbeancruises.com

1-866-562-7625

Royal Caribbean cruises are a bit more casual than those of Celebrity, though both lines are owned by the same parent company. Passengers are assured more activities than they can possibly get in, but don't forget to save time to be a "deck potato."

Windjammer Cruises

www.windjammer.com

1-800-327-2601

If you've never felt the calm that accompanies weathered teakwood beneath your soles, now's your chance. Windjammer's spacious decks are a focal point of activity. Atmosphere onboard is relaxed and comfortable.

Windstar Cruises

www.windstarcruises.com

1-877-STAR-SAIL

The Windstar passenger sees the world from the serenity of a sailing ship with luxurious accommodations, a casual yet elegant atmosphere, and exquisite service and cuisine. The ships are small, with far fewer passengers than large ocean liners. This means less crowding and less stress.

Active Adventure and Learning Vacations

Carolina Tailwinds

www.carolinatailwinds.com

1-888-251-3206

Bike America the beautiful, including the Shenandoah Valley, the Outer Banks, and—for real aerobic enthusiasts—the Blue Ridge Mountains. This organization knows how to balance exercise with relaxation. Trips feature exquisite cuisine and comfortable, charming inns.

Country Walkers

www.countrywalkers.com

1-800-464-9255

Burn off that stress by walking across Montana, Wyoming, Utah, and Maine—or Chile, Bhutan, New Zealand, and Crete. For over a quarter of a century this organization has enabled travelers to experience the most breathtaking sites in the world, on foot. Trips include accommodations, three meals a day, and between-hike transport by bus, boat, train, plane, gondola, or funicular.

Scott Walking Adventures

www.scottwalking.com

1-800-262-8644

Change your mind-set entirely as you immerse yourself in the world's most beautiful venues with like-minded inquisitive and environmentally aware travelers. You can choose from trips that are as easy as a fall foliage hike to as challenging as a trek across Iceland.

Shaw Guides

www.shawguides.com

1-212-799-6464

For those who want to relax and learn, this organization offers comprehensive world-wide guides to educational travel and creative career programs. You can search their database for recreational cooking schools, golf and tennis schools and camps, high performance programs, writers' conferences, photography, film and video workshops, art and craft workshops, language vacations, and much more.

Specialty Travel

www.spectrav.com

1-888-624-4030

For those of you into walking on the wild side, this portal offers a variety of different options to connect you with vacation sites that will get your blood pumping.

VBT Deluxe Bicycle Vacations

www.vbt.com

1-800-245-3868

VBT led the way in designing bicycle tours that both invigorate and pamper. They still offer the incredible bike tours of Vermont, but you can also try everything from Hawaii to the California wine country to European destinations. For a doubly amazing journey, combine a bicycle and barge tour of Alsace-Lorraine, or explore the medieval towns near the France/Germany border.

The Wayfarers

www.thewayfarers.com

1-800-249-4620

Inspiring coastlines, world-class wine country walks, and lovely mountain vistas are all on the stress-beating menu.

Island Oases

Club Med

www.clubmed.com

1-800-248-5463

Club Med's secluded villages—in sensuous beach locales such as the Bahamas, Cancun, and Bora Bora—feature all-inclusive dining and a potpourri of beachy activities, such as snorkeling and windsurfing.

Grand Pineapple Beach

www.allegroantigua.com

1-800-858-4618

At this Antiguan resort, with its white sand beach, walk alone or hand-in-hand with a loved one through 25 acres of lush gardens and experience serene seclusion. Getaways here are all-inclusive. No stressful decisions to make.

Jakes, Jamaica

www.all-jamaica.com/hotels/jake_descr.html

Use e-mail through site

This laid-back boutique resort is set by the fishing village Treasure Beach and features 15 pastel cottages nestled into the landscape, some with decks just above the lapping sea. A music business entrepreneur partially founded the resort, and there's a comprehensive library of world music for you to dance to—or just relax to.

Palm Island

www.grenadines.net/palm/palmhomepage.htm

1-800-858-4618

Craving extreme seclusion? Situated in the island chain of St. Vincent and the Grenadines, Palm Island is its own private 135-acre island hideaway at the end of the Windward Island group of the Eastern Caribbean. Its 37 intimate guest rooms feature island motifs, custom rattan furnishings, and luxurious amenities. The vantage point from your private balcony or patio provides a sweeping panoramic view at every turn.

Sandals

www.Sandals.com

1-888-SANDALS

Sandals is a collection of twelve resorts on the Caribbean's best beaches, created exclusively for couples in love in Jamaica, St. Lucia, Antigua, and the Bahamas. Enjoy an astounding array of land and water sports.

Stress-Free Couples Getaways

Love Tripper

www.lovetripper.com

Use e-mail through site

Trip-planning ideas for first and second honeymoons and other getaways. The couple that founded this site travels the globe in search of its most romantic places. The site features an e-newsletter as well.

Romantic-Escape.com

www.romantic-escape.com

Use e-mail through site

This site includes many links to and ideas about couples who love and who love to travel.

Glossary

adaptive micro trauma   The process by which exercise wears the body down and the body then repairs and rebuilds itself in response.

altruism   From the Latin *alter*, or "other," altruism describes actions performed in a selfless manner for the benefit of another.

anabolic process   A process in which energy is used to construct complex molecules from simple ones.

body language   The communication of emotional signals through non-verbal means such as gestures, posture, and facial expression.

catharsis   An experience that serves to bring emotions to the surface and release them. The cathartic experience itself is not the primary source of the emotions—it's an outlet for them.

cortisol   A hormone produced in the adrenal glands that primes the body for activity in the face of stress by increasing the blood sugar.

counterpose   In yoga, a pose deliberately sequenced after another pose to gently stretch the body in the opposite direction.

dopamine   A chemical compound involved in the formation of adrenaline. It plays a role in the sensation of pleasure when it is released into a section of the brain that, when stimulated, creates positive sensations.

endorphins   Pain-desensitizing substances in the brain that attach to the same receptors as the drug morphine.

enlightened self-interest   Giving to or helping someone else in the knowledge that such an attitude helps the giver as well as the receiver.

essential oils   Substances that are necessary to the biological processes of the plants and trees from which they are extracted, and that also provide scent. These oils can be taken from herbs, flowers, woods, and spices.

external locus of control   An underlying belief that the outcome of events is out of one's hands, which is characteristic of a pessimistic outlook.

feng shui   An ancient Chinese discipline dealing with the design and layout of dwelling places. In its modern form, much of it focuses on arranging objects in the home so as to allow one to live in balance and harmony.

fight-or-flight response   A sequence of internal reactions that prepare an organism to do battle or to seek escape from a stimulus that it considers a threat. (The term was coined by physiologist Walter Cannon.)

glucocortoroids   A class of steroid stress hormones that the brain triggers the adrenal gland to produce after initial adrenaline is released. They affect our blood sugar levels as they back up the activity of adrenaline over the course of minutes or hours.

Glycemic Index (GI)   An index that measures the amount of quickly digestible glucose in a food. Values are from 70 to 100 are considered high. Those between 55 and 70 are considered moderate; those under 55 are considered low.

Glycemic Load (GL)   An index that measures the amount of actual carbohydrate content in a typical portion size. High GL values are over 20, moderate are 11 to 19, low are from 1 to 10.

glycogen   Also called animal starch, this is a compound stored in our muscles and liver that can easily be converted to energy in the form of glucose.

guru   From the Hindu language, this term refers to a spiritual leader, teacher, or counselor.

hatha yoga   The aspect of yoga that focuses on physical postures. The word *hatha* is sometimes translated as "willful" or "forceful." But *ha* also means "sun" and *tha* means "moon," so the word also incorporates the concept of natural balance.

hydrotherapy   Literally meaning *water healing*, this term refers to any water or liquid-based treatment, such as soaking in natural hot and cold springs. Back in the fourth century B.C.E., the Greek physician Hippocrates was among the first to prescribe hydrotherapy.

internal locus of control   An underlying belief that one can impact the outcome of events. It is characteristic of an optimistic outlook.

left prefrontal cortex   The prefrontal cortex is a region of the brain that appears to play a critical role in modulating emotions. Left prefrontal cortex (LPFC) activation appears to be associated with a cluster of positive attributes, including reduced levels of the stress hormone cortisol.

life change units (LCUs)   A point system used on the Social Readjustment Rating Scale to indicate the degree of stress associated with different kinds of change. The idea is that by tallying one's LCUs over the last year, one can measure one's current stress level and (perhaps) one's risk for stress-related problems.

management by objective (MBO)   A workplace strategy whereby managers and those whom they manage agree about goals and also about specific actions and timetables that will allow those goals to be achieved.

mantra meditation   Meditation that takes as its point of focus the repetition of a single simple sound (such as *Om*) or word (such as *peace.*)

mind-body connection   The inseparable connection between the human mind and body and the complex interactions that take place among thoughts, feelings, behaviors, and physical health.

mirror neurons   Specialized neurons that fire when we observe the behaviors of others. They are one reason human beings are so good at social imitation.

neuroplasticity   The concept that the brain is "plastic" or malleable, and that it can be reshaped by inner as well as outer events. It signifies that the brain grows and changes depending on how it is used.

om* (or *AUM)   From the Sanskrit, this word is said to be the essence of all mantras, encompassing the entire universe. A stands for creation; U stands for preservation; M stands for dissolution.

parasympathetic nervous system   The half of the autonomic nervous system that promotes calm and initiates activities that contribute to our body's maintenance, growth, and development.

play face   This primate facial expression is a relaxed, open-mouthed display. Accompanied by panting noises, it signals a primate's availability for friendly social interaction.

positive psychology   The scientific study of characteristics and attitudes that lead to optimal human functioning, especially in the face of stressful challenges.

REM (rapid eye movement) sleep   The phase of sleep in which we dream. During this phase there is a marked increase in metabolic activity of some brain regions—akin to brain aerobics. The regions that integrate visual information become exceptionally active, and the eyeballs jerk in various directions even though the eyes are closed.

seasonal affective disorder (SAD)   A mood disorder associated with depressive episodes and related to seasonal variations of light. SAD was first noted in the mid-nineteenth century, but was not officially named until the early 1980s.

social capital   A measurement of one's involvement in situations, organizations, and communities where opportunities abound for feeling like part of something greater than oneself.

social play vocalization   This refers to the uniquely human ha-ha sound that we instinctively use to get and hold a listener's attention and offer incentive to go on interacting.

spirituality   Spirituality deals with the transcendent, intangible dimension of existence. The word *spirituality* comes from the Latin root *spiritus*, meaning "breath" and referring to the breath of life.

stress hyperphagics   People who typically respond to stress by eating more.

stress hypophagics   People who typically respond to stress by eating less.

stress response   The brain and body's alarmed and alert response to a threatening situation.

stressor   Any stimulus or situation that we perceive as endangering us.

sympathetic nervous system   The half of the autonomic nervous system that is switched on during emergencies, or what we think of as emergencies. It helps us be aroused, active, mobile, and vigilant.

t'ai chi   Chinese form of exercise, martial art, and "moving meditation" characterized by slow, deliberate movements.

temperament   The biological basis of personality, consisting of inborn character traits such as the degree of sensitivity to stimuli and intensity of reaction.

tend-and-befriend response   Reacting to threats by caring for one's family and forming social alliances. (The term was coined by psychologist Shelley Taylor.)

undo effect   The power of positive emotions to counterbalance the impact of stressful negative emotions, as well as providing an added boost beyond the initial emotional starting point.

white blood cells   The collective term for lymphocytes and monocytes (*cyte* means "cell"). Lymphocytes themselves are divided into T and B cells, both of which attack infectious agents in different ways.

yoga   An Eastern discipline, the focus of which is on union—the binding of opposites, and a joining of the energies of mind, body, and spirit. The word *yoga* comes from the Sanskrit word (*yuj*) that means "to yoke or bind."

Index

F

G

M

T